'WEE JOE'

Sean McMahon is a native of Derry, where he has lived for most of his life. He has more than fifty titles to his credit as author and editor, most of them in the fields of Irish history, literature and biography. He is the author of *The Bloody North: Infamous Ulster Murder Cases*, *The Belfast Blitz: Luftwaffe Raids on Northern Ireland, 1941*, *A Brief History of Belfast* and *A Brief History of Northern Ireland* (all published by The Brehon Press), and his editorial credits include the highly praised *Derry Anthology*.

'WEE JOE'

The Life of Joseph Devlin

SEAN McMAHON

THE BREHON PRESS
BELFAST

Published by
The Brehon Press Ltd,
19 Glen Crescent
Belfast BT11 8FB
Northern Ireland
www.brehonpress.co.uk

ISBN: 978 1 905474 35 6

CONTENTS

Acknowledgements

I would like to thank those who were generous with time, advice and help: the staff of the Central Library in Derry, especially Jane Nicholas and Gerry Quinn; the staff of Magee College Library, Derry, especially Rose Norris; the staff of the Linen Hall Library of Belfast, especially Monica McErlane and the librarian John Killen; the staff of the Newspaper Library, Library Street, Belfast; Maeve Breslin; Ruairi Crilly; Frank D'Arcy; Netta Donnelly; Henry McCabe; Marie Louise McCrory of the *Irish News*; May McGurran-Crilly; Brian McMahon; Paddy O'Carolan; Jo O'Donoghue; David Parfrey and Trevor Temple.

Note: Throughout the text the word 'Nationalist' with an uppercase initial refers to the party led by Devlin after 1921; with a lowercase initial it is used generally as non-Unionist, including all supporters of Irish independence: Home Rulers, Nationalists and Sinn Féin.

Foreword

A MONG THE CAREFULLY GUARDED TREASURES OF the Linen Hall Library in Belfast are a number of decorative scrolls, including one presented to Brother Joseph Devlin from the Cork County Board of the Ancient Order of Hibernians (Board of Erin), stating that 'in honouring you we feel we are honouring ourselves'. Others were humbly offered to Mr Joseph Devlin during his tour of Australia in 1906 by staff and pupils of schools in Windsor, Penterfield and Sydney, and inscribed from 'your devoted little friends'. Of this kind of illuminated presentation, pride of place must go to a gilded address, dated February 1922, to 'Mr Joseph Devlin MP on his return from Westminster 1906–1922'. Constructed and beautifully lettered by Joseph Dempsey it was typical of the eulogies of the time but, in spite of the elaborate setting and language used, there is a genuine feeling of affection for 'Wee Joe' and a palpable sense of regret that he will no longer be the member for West Belfast.

The document, four vellum pages long and bound in leather, is kept secure by the library in a specially constructed container. It is a riot of colour with each uppercase initial (and there are many) done in rubric red, and the initial word of each paragraph surrounded in red, green and blue. Each page has appropriate illustrations: St Mary's CBS, his old school; St Peter's Pro-Cathedral, where he was baptised;

St Mary's, Belfast's oldest church; Cavehill, Glenariff and Cushendall, favourite places; and, on the final page, a representation of Ireland, the beautiful, sad maiden, complete with wolfhound and round tower. I give the text in full because it acts as a summary of the political and social achievements of the man, then forty-one years of age, and forecasts the implicit re-inventing of himself for a different role in his moral constituency.

Dear Mr Devlin

The absorption of the Electoral Constituency of West Belfast into a larger Electoral area of the City compelled your retirement from its Parliamentary Representation and for the purpose of expressing the feelings of your old constituents and your supporters in the North-East, your friends avail of the opportunity thus presented of tendering you in a formal way an expression of gratitude for and an appreciation of your record of work as Parliamentary Representative and leader of the Catholics and Nationalists of Belfast.

Endowed by nature with intellectual talents of rare excellence you responded to your country's command from your earliest years and devoted yourself to her cause. The reunion of the divided sections of the Catholics and Nationalists of Belfast and the consolidation of forces for the spiritual and temporal good of the community – a mighty task, insuperable to others – was accomplished by you and your capture of the Parliamentary Representation of West Belfast on 19th of January 1906 was the crowning achievement of your political life. In Australia, New Zealand and America as well as in Great Britain and Ireland, with matchless eloquence you pleaded your country's right to liberty and "West Belfast" became a name honoured in the Representative, who won respect and love for himself and distinction for his Constituency throughout the English speaking world.

During your political activities of twenty years, the good of your people was the dominating object of your ambition. The benefactions of charitable and religious institutions in Belfast, many of them of incalculable value, and the advantages and benefits to communities and individuals throughout the country, bestowed by, or through you, exceed in number and magnitude those of any other man of this period.

A career of surpassing public usefulness, in some respects never before equalled, was ended by the old enemy – Ireland's fateful curse – venomous dissension and factional strife. The foresight and judgment of the experienced politician, the beneficence of the peacemaker, the ever-increasing confidence and admiration of a Constituency, the resolution of faithful followers and the affection of steadfast friends availed nothing in a land whose people coerced to pitiable subjection by the cant of patriotism and the tyranny of sham politicians, became bewildered and distraught in the universal destruction of life and property wrought by an evil policy of unrestrained violence and "West Belfast" ceased to be.

Your policy, the policy of the Irish Party of Parnell, Davitt and Redmond, the policy of justice, truth and reason, remains the only flexible and efficient policy whereby the just rights and virtuous aspirations of a people can be accomplished with a hope of permanency. The Vindication and the triumph of that policy will come – perhaps we shall witness it in the near future – and when the history of this generation is written, the achievements of the Member for "West Belfast" will receive the merited distinction of manly sentiment, honourable enterprise and heroic endeavour in the noble work of patriotism.

Your acceptance of this Address is requested as a tribute from those who esteem your personal worth and recognise your public service and from those who love you for your enduring loyalty, the gentle patience, the overflowing generosity and the sweet kindness of your friendship.

The concluding pages of the tribute contain the signatures of 177 people, including twenty-five priests. A printed card in the box has a couplet from an anonymous poet scrolled on it:

Without him heaven would be hard to bear
And hell would not be hell if he is there.

The tribute, in spite of its overblown fulsomeness, is genuine in its affection but it cannot escape a sense of ending, a sort of kind *nunc dimittis* to a man whose political life is virtually over.

It is a rare document, one of few, since Devlin left instructions that his papers should be destroyed on his death, rendering the task of the biographer rather more difficult.[1] Devlin was too true to his own constitutional ideals to prosper in the political climate of the time and he remained a quixotic figure, a ideological sport, beloved at home but as spent a firebrand as his associate and party leader, John Redmond (1856–1918), who had died four years previously. He was no longer a player on the grand stage of Irish politics but the abounding energy for which he was famous was now to be channelled into work for his constituency and attempts to mitigate the miseries that were compounded for northern Catholics with the passing of the 1920 Government of Ireland Act. There was a time, though, when he was a significant figure in Irish life, one of the most significant, but for him at least the time was then out of joint.

1
Catholics in a Protestant City

B ELFAST BY THE LAST QUARTER OF the nineteenth century had almost completely redefined itself from the small liberal, largely Presbyterian, town that so happily supported the foundation of the Society of the United Irishmen in 1791 and contributed generously to the building of a second Roman Catholic 'chapel', St Patrick's in Donegall Street, twenty-four years later. By the 1870s it was one of Europe's leading industrial towns and on the brink of being declared a city, a formal recognition that was granted in 1888.

The Catholic population that had been 4,000 in 1808, when it represented 16 percent of an estimated population total of 25,000, had risen to 41,406, 34.1 percent of the total 121,602 according to the 1861 census. The next ninety years saw a considerable decrease from this proportion, the mean percentage a few points above a quarter. The reasons for this substantial rise and its subsequent fall are various.

One of the likely causes of its rise mid-century was the Great Famine of the 1840s that drew into the town hungry people of all creeds, largely from the neighbouring counties of Down and Antrim. It was known that the urban relief systems, though ungenerous, did provide sufficient food and shelter to prevent the famine deaths that so afflicted the west of the province. The effect, as in Derry (where the numbers seeking help were greater because of the misery caused by the famine in Donegal), was to increase the numbers of poor Catholics in what had been an essentially Protestant city.

In Derry they tended to cluster outside the west of the city wall, thereby creating in the generically named Bogside an enclave of the troublesome ethnic minority that would in time rob the city of its vaunted maidenhood. In Belfast they settled mainly in the Falls district, called after the trunk road that led westward out of the city. The name, like so many other Belfast place-names hiding a Gaelic past, came from *Tuagh na bhFál* ('the territory of the enclosures') that with Shankill (*Seanchill*, or 'old church') formed the County Antrim part of the settlement.

Another more significant cause of Catholic in-migration to an essentially unwelcoming society was the natural metropolitan draw of the larger town with its promise of employment. The burgeoning industrialism of Belfast, with its manufacturing of cotton, then linen, rope, tobacco, mineral waters, ships and the rest was a real generator of work. There was plenty of it for men, women and children, much more than the existing population could supply. When Catholics were employed, however, it was in the most menial of jobs. As Barney Hughes (1808–78), the Catholic baker, one of their champions, put it in biblical fashion, they were 'hewers of wood and drawers of water', while being the 'bone and sinew' of the town.

They were, however, not the only poor people in Belfast. Many Protestants lived in houses as mean and were only slightly less badly paid than their Romish brethren. This was evidenced when during the Luftwaffe raids in the spring of 1941 whole streets were 'domino-ed' by bomb blast. Some Protestants, however, had the means of improvement since *their* brethren controlled the granting of apprenticeships and could make sure of continuity in their ranks. Even outside of the closed world of trades they held advantage over Catholics: a typical example could be found among the dockers: Protestants loaded and unloaded the short-haul routes where work was regular; Catholics were assigned to the deep-sea cargoes where work was intermittent.

It was the consciousness of their second class status, reported by family relatives who had sought shelter and work in the city, that made rural Catholics more reluctant to move as the century progressed and prevented their influx from continuing at the same rate as before. Apart from endemic discrimination in the workplace, and lack of local and national representation, there was another reason for Catholics to have second thoughts.

As a number of regular recurring events were to demonstrate Belfast had ceased to be a *safe* place for them to live. The radicalism of the eighteenth and early nineteenth centuries soon evaporated largely due to growing prosperity and the efforts of such brilliant preachers as Henry Cooke (1788–1868), who strongly supported the Act of Union and had no difficulty in making odorous comparisons between the dynamic northern town and the depressed and dirty Dublin, the population of which it was fast overtaking. The mills, shipyards and heavy engineering works of Belfast made the visitor feel he was in another Glasgow, Manchester or Birmingham, though assimilation of mainly Irish Catholics in those places proved measurably less troublesome than in what was eventually known as 'Linenopolis'. The country people who sought succour and later work in their metropolis brought with them atavistic fears and convictions. Protestants with carefully nurtured folk memories of the real but exaggerated massacres of 1641 found kindred in the pullulating streets of what soon became recognised as 'Protestant' areas, and had their prejudices and genuine fears greatly reinforced there. A similar pattern of Catholic intensity became visible in smaller parts of the city, most especially in the streets on both sides of the Falls Road and in Smithfield. Other knots of 'Fenianism', as it was erroneously termed, were the New Lodge, the Markets, Short Strand, Dock and Greencastle that developed later as 'ethnic' areas. In Ardoyne, a comparatively new 'Mick' area, the complement of Catholics was increased as a direct result of serious rioting in the 1930s.

A notable feature of life in the city was the frequent recurrence of sectarian rioting. The regular and minor outbursts of civil unease usually coincided with the annual July celebration of the indecisive

Battle of the Boyne (1690) by the Orange Order. The Order, founded in 1793 as a counterblast to the Catholic Defenders, had grown, often with aristocratic patronage, to be a significant part of Ulster Protestant life throughout the nineteenth and twentieth centuries. The trouble rarely amounted to more than a few scuffles with the police, resulting in bloody heads, some broken windows, and fiery rhetoric from politicians or grandmasters, listened to with admirable patience by audiences at the various 'fields' to which the members 'walked' through often deliberately chosen Catholic areas.[1]

Polling-days and celebrations showing evidence of growing confidence in Catholic ranks could also kindle fiery demonstrations of Protestant supremacy. The years 1813, 1825, 1831, 1835 and 1841 saw flare-ups usually lasting no more than a day or two but the violence and the danger continued to escalate, as witnessed in the years 1843 and 1852. Really serious, long-lasting, bitter sectarian battles in 1857 and 1864 set a pattern of extreme uncontrollable violence with many deaths and serious injuries. The years 1872 and 1886 saw persisting civil disturbance that besmirched Belfast's reputation abroad and, even after a long, relatively quiet period that lasted until the summer and autumn of 1912, it proved simple to resurrect old hates.

The trouble in 1872 had originated on 15 August, the Catholic feast of the Assumption of the Blessed Virgin into heaven. By then the date had become the 'Mickies' Twelfth', the annual Catholic counterpoint to the Boyne celebrations on 12 July. The trouble started after a fiery speech by Joseph Gillis Biggar (1828–1890), a Protestant Nationalist who would become the ablest lieutenant of Charles Stewart Parnell (1846–1891). Hannahstown, a parish just under the Black Mountain on the outskirts of west Belfast, had during the middle years of the eighteenth century been the site of the Catholic 'chapel' nearest to Belfast and still was regarded as a 'Papish' enclave. Biggar, a stalwart of the Home Government Association, the precursor of Home Rule, begun by Isaac Butt (1813–1879), used the place and time to complain about the treatment meted out to Fenian convicts. It was a clear example of 'Taigs' getting above themselves, and the Orangemen had again to remind them of their position in the town.

There followed a nine-day siege with the Catholics of the lower Falls beset by Sandy Row Protestants to the south and mobs from the Shankill Road to the north. Hamill Street, where the eighteen-month-old Joe Devlin lived, was in the centre of the Catholic enclave known as the Pound Loney, and the street suffered broken windows, and missiles gouged from the street cobbles flew indiscriminately. Most of the aggression came from the Protestants, spurred by almost universal membership of the Orange Order, but there still existed pockets of residual Ribbonism constituted as defence mechanisms in Catholic areas.[2] It was they who manned the barricades, hastily constructed of handcarts, cabs and timber planks. It was not until Monday, 26 August that Catholic workers dared return to their essentially menial jobs in the mills and shipyards, and the refugees who had to live on the sectarian boundaries returned to the damaged houses with the precious possessions that they had taken with them piled on prams and handcarts.

Growth within the Catholic areas was commensurate with a steady birth rate and low life expectancy, though for some of these years the Protestant birth rate was in fact greater than that of Catholics. There was no reliable way to determine the religion (and from now on, the politics) of particular people by looking at their faces. Long held beliefs about different racial physiognomies were really mythical; names helped, though, and later the schools attended often gave a clue, especially since the Church eventually won the battle for educational control. Someone called Bernadette O'Connor taught by the nuns was a bit of a giveaway as was a riveter called, say, Sammy Orr from the Shankill Road.[3] The social atmosphere was intermittently like that of fifteenth-century Verona with Montagues and Capulets armed to the teeth, except that *their* champions were aristocrats who cared little for the 'curs of low degree' who tended them and that it was not always possible to distinguish individual members of one lot from the other.

Those Catholics who stayed to form a quarter to a third of the city's population as a whole instinctively began to develop a parallel inner state with its own beliefs: a very devotional Catholicism, an aesthetic that could call upon a wider, whole-Ireland culture, and a system of politics eventually based upon the Home Government Movement (1870) that seven years later became the Home Rule movement under its successful leader Parnell. They depended for leadership mainly upon the Church that, after the wide-ranging reforms of Paul Cullen (1803–78), Archbishop of Dublin since 1849 and Ireland's first cardinal (1866), had greatly increased its influence upon the political as well as the religious life of Irish people. Cullen, who had seen the effects of revolutionary violence during his years in Rome, came out strongly against anything savouring of similar social unrest at home, condemning Young Ireland and later the Fenian Brotherhood as immoral. Under his influence the Irish clergy began to play a much more intrusive role in Catholic life, leading to charges in Belfast of the not necessarily untrue cry of 'Home Rule – Rome Rule' that became the chief anti-reform mantra of Unionist politicians and their willing followers.

The equation 'Catholic = nationalist' had begun to be established when the few Catholics who actually had the franchise withdrew from a longstanding Liberal/Presbyterian alliance against the Tories. This had been encouraged by the now automatically intrusive Church leaders, especially in Belfast by the Cullenite Patrick Dorrian (1814–85), who was consecrated bishop in 1865, and to a lesser extent his successor Patrick McAllister (1826–95) until it became clear that, with the 1884 Reform Act, Catholics/nationalists had already more than a nucleus of political power.

As ever the Church waited upon political events to determine the advice (really admonitions) it would issue to its members. Not all Catholics were submerged in the hopelessness of the proletarian condition; there had arisen a minuscule middle class, consisting mainly of doctors, surgeons, lawyers, and minor merchants, whose clients were almost exclusively of their own faith and whom a future bishop would try to groom as the representative Catholic body, not only politically but even spiritually – and, of course, socially as well. Dorrian, in his report to Rome that accompanied the Catholic census of 1882, when in round numbers the breakdown was 70,000 in a total of 220,000, had written in terse Latin: *'Catholici sunt tamen pauperiores dum heretici sunt opulentissimi'*, or 'Catholics are still the poorer lot while Protestants tend to be very wealthy.'

The Catholics of the nearly-city had, however, accompanying a greater inner coherence, a sense of detachment from mainstream nationalist action. They remained a minority and had little or no say in the municipal government. Dublin, Cork and the larger towns, except Derry, had by the 1870s established their local government authority and had made it clear that some form of home rule was inevitable. There was nothing in Belfast politics to suggest that it was going to happen there. Even Belfast nationalists, though grieving at countrywide neglect, took a perverse pride in their distinctiveness. The bishops cautiously supported Parnell while he was the 'Uncrowned King' and inevitably joined in the public rejection when O'Shea ruined him. The *Irish News*, the paper that still represents the views of northern constitutional nationalism, was first issued on 15 August 1891 as a formally anti-Parnellite paper.

Belfast Catholics were on the whole too concerned with actual survival to bother themselves overmuch with the detail of politics. Their priests acted as un-ignorable canvassers at election times and any sense of coercion was stilled by the belief that what the clergy told their flocks to do in the polling booths was almost a commandment. Their primary concern was for the amelioration of the appalling social conditions and work practices that a majority had to endure. Any extra-clerical persuasion would have to come from a laity, irreproachably Catholic, but unawed by episcopal pressure. Bishops Dorrian and McAllister would certainly have preferred Catholic representation in the local council (and dreamed of it for the Westminster parliament) by 'acceptable' people such as the comparatively rich men who lived with no sense of unease in the new Protestant suburbs. They, however, had no real acquaintance with their co-religionists in the 'Catholic' ghettos and neither of the bishops made any overt political moves to woo these 'acceptable' people.

Hughes, whose bakeries had gained a populist reputation with coarse tributary verses because of his very cheap 'baps' that helped stave off hunger during the Famine years and after, died in 1878 before his full political capacity could be felt. One rhyme that persisted until the middle of the twentieth century and chanted by children who knew little, if anything, of its provenance, went:

> Barney Hughes's bread
> Sticks to your belly like lead;
> It's no wonder you fart like thunder
> Barney Hughes's bread.

There were other members of a Catholic elite: John Hamill, who owned land west of the city and whose mansion, Trench House, equalled that of any non-Catholic grandee in splendour; the mill-owner William Ross; the whiskey distiller Peter Keegan; and William Watson, who owned many housing developments in the town. Dorrian estimated that there were between seventy and ninety Catholics who could afford to donate a yearly £100 to the Church without pain; most of these were associated with the liquor trade but there was also a statistically predictable number of professional men and merchants.[4]

These Catholics, mainly economically independent, had shown a degree of lay action as soon as they had become aware of their strength. In 1859, led by Hughes and Ross, they founded a Catholic Institute that had no clerical involvement. The bishop at the time was Cornelius Denvir (1791–1866), whose tendency was to keep a low profile during his episcopate (1836–65). A brilliant scientist, his apparent weakness was disapproved of not only by Archbishop Joseph Dixon of Armagh (1806–66) but by Paul Cullen, the real power in the Church, who had moved to Dublin for political as well as ecclesiastical reasons. There was no doubt that the post-Famine Church in Ireland was in need of reform. Yet its centralist approach that strengthened the structures countrywide were not necessarily the most appropriate for Belfast, where Catholics were outnumbered at least three to one. Denvir was accused of fear of Orangeism, if not of general dysfunction as a prelate. He was only too conscious that visible evidence of the growing strength of Catholics and their insistence on control of education seemed greatly to increase hatred among more vocal Protestants and cause more violent anti-Catholic demonstrations. Perhaps his 'weakness' was simply a form of quietism that would have been seen as appropriate, even sensible, in the circumstances of the largest northern town, by churchmen more sympathetic than the pair of senior clerics that were his archiepiscopal masters.

Probably more important and to Cullen's eyes more sinister than Denvir's joining such 'mixed' agencies as the Charitable Bequests Board and the board of the National Schools (in which he followed the practice of his predecessor, Bishop Crolly) was the hint of independence from the Vatican. This was known as 'Gallicanism' from the old right of appointments of senior clergy arrogated to themselves by the kings of France and later used as a general term for the semi-independence of local churches. Its opposite was 'Ultramontanism', referring to the practice of the centralising of all ecclesiastical authority and practice with Rome, and Cullen was Ireland's leading 'ultramontane'.[5] He was a leading light in the formulation of the doctrine of papal infallibility as defined by the First Vatican Council in 1870, but ironically made every effort to rule the Irish Church more stringently than Rome would have dared. He took to referring to any suspected trace of independence in Irish prelates as 'Presbyterianism'. His influence, whether for good or not on the Church in Ireland, led to the appointment of a series of bishops in Down and Connor who were nearly as ultramontane as he.

Denvir could do little but acquiesce when Dixon (acting for Cullen) appointed Dorrian as coadjutor in 1860. Dorrian immediately assumed the powers of ordinary though he did not become the twenty-third Lord Bishop of Down and Connor until 1865 when Denvir was finally persuaded to resign. He died in 1866. The contrast between the two men was striking. Though Cullen thought little of Dorrian (he was second choice as coadjutor), considering him no more than 'a good parish priest', he proved to be the man Cullen wanted and felt he needed. He introduced many religious orders, including the Irish Christian Brothers, the Cross and Passion Fathers, and four religious sisterhoods, built three more churches, and made church attendance implicitly compulsory.

Like Cullen he insisted that the clergy, led by their bishop, should control many aspects of Catholic life. He showed his hand and his power in his attitude to the Catholic Institute, founded, as we have seen, as a lay initiative, by the handful of rich Belfast Catholics to provide facilities for education, recreation and study.[6] The truth is that, apart from the 'recreation' aspect of the Institute's aims, its members had little need of it. Most had access to other systems of study and education, and they were accepted as part of the town's 'aristocracy'.

This may have been the reason for the unsatisfactory state of its finances that showed itself after five years of existence. It did, however, give the ambitious Dorrian his opportunity. With less than full authority he demanded in 1864 that any society bearing the name 'Catholic' should be controlled in its objectives, management and daily running by the clergy – in essence, by the man soon to be bishop. The Institute lasted for two more years before making its finances and property over to the Church, indeed nominally to the new bishop, probably with a sense of relief. From then on, for at least a hundred years, any social and recreational activities in the city that involved Catholics were Church-controlled. In this they replicated the situation that existed countrywide. Some few initiatives like the Gaelic League, founded in 1893, tried autonomy and non-sectarianism but with little success. The idea of an exclusive Catholic club remained in the minds of senior clerics, notably the awkwardly named Henry Henry, who became bishop in 1895, but his involvement in a similar initiative was to mark a rare defeat for the Church.

Such was the city into which Joseph Devlin (never known as such except on official documents, in Unionist newspapers and obituaries) was born in 1871. He was baptised in St Peter's Pro-Cathedral a few hundred yards from his birthplace and remained a practising Catholic for all of his life. He understood the urgency that possessed his clergy to 'run things'. He knew that it was part of their moral duty as they saw it. To outsiders it seemed at best condescending, at worst interfering, though some divines of other faiths must have envied the acquiescence of the flock and the ease of organisation because of this. The roots of this imperative lay deep in the culture of the Counter-Reformation and the proscriptions of the Council of Trent (1545–1563); the Tridentine demands could not be applied to Ireland, though a Catholic country, while her history for three centuries was so troubled, but now, however late, there was essentially no bar to their fulfilment. The interpretation by an over-eager hierarchy that it applied to all aspects of Catholic life meant that early success was in time diminished. While it lasted, and its golden age entirely included Devlin's life, care had to be taken by social reformers like him to work entirely within the system – or seem to.

2
Duodecimo Demosthenes

HAMILL STREET IS UNUSUAL IN THAT, though set in what was one of the poorer parts of Belfast, it is a remarkably wide thoroughfare. With twenty-eight feet between houses on opposite sides of the street it was comparatively simple for the twenty-first-century city council to cut bays in the pavement to accommodate car parking. In the 1870s it was a playground for the many (Catholic) children of the street who had little to fear from passing traffic. Number ten had just been occupied by Charles and Elizabeth 'Lily' Devlin when Joseph, their fourth son (and fifth child), was born on 13 February 1871. The house fifth in on the left-hand side facing south has gone with its four neighbours to be replaced by an urban garden but the street still holds more than fifty houses.

Charles Devlin had been born in east Tyrone on the shores of Lough Neagh, no surprise to genealogists since the western shore of the lough is true Devlin country. Lily King was from Faughart, four miles north of Dundalk, believed birthplace of St Brigid, and set in a region rich and thick with both pagan and Christian mythology. The two, both illiterate, had headed for the city in the hope of settled, less arduous, work than that associated with agricultural labour. They were married on 13 December 1858 in St Malachy's Church in Alfred Street, which had been opened in 1844 as the town's third church to serve the Catholics of the Markets area. Charles was a self-employed 'jarvey' who owned his horse and trap, and had room to park it outside his house in those less officious days. The stable where he kept horse and trap was close by. He would have found a good stand outside of the Ulster Railway terminus in what would later be called Great Victoria Street, conveying the travellers from Dublin and the midlands to different parts of the growing (though not yet incorporated) city. Lily, whose surgical neatness and cleanliness she passed on to her famous son, sold bread and vegetables from what would have been the 'parlour' of the little house, and may have added some of her own cakes that later fed the members of her loquacious son's debating society. Devlin in maturity was always impeccably turned out and he could be uncharacteristically sharp with employees with grubby collars or fingernails 'in mourning'.

The street was part of a conglomerate that constituted an intensely nationalist/Catholic area of the town, known as the Pound Loney. Pound Street, called after the enclosure for straying beasts and temporary holding place for livestock whose owners awaited permission to take them to the town market, ran from the bottom of the Falls to the end of Barrack Street. The word 'loney' is probably the same as the Ulster-Scots word 'loanen', meaning a laneway through; because the Loney stream ran conveniently through the middle of the pound some have glossed it as a 'burn'. In the early part of the nineteenth century, the 'Loney' was home to a number of Protestant families while an equivalent number of Catholics lived in the Sandy Row, later the best-known Protestant area. Especially after the 1864 disturbances this tolerance changed; there was a mutual rationalisation of religion/dwelling-house occupancy. Both sects, especially those with mixed marriages, sought the safety of appropriate accommodation. This deliberate relocation tended to increase the intensity of feeling (and fear) at the yearly flammable festivals. The opening of the impressive St Peter's Pro-Cathedral in 1866, virtually in the centre of the Loney, intensified the exclusivist nature of the lower Falls Road as the heart of Belfast's Catholic/nationalist citadel though other much smaller areas could be made to fit the description.

As a child Joe was 'delicate', subject to chest complaints. He seems not to have played much in the streets and was not expected to attend school because of his chronic ill-health. This condition was diagnosed by his mother, who may have cosseted him a little. The lad showed early promise and took eagerly to the training offered by the Irish Christian Brothers in their national school in Divis Street at the foot of the Falls Road, which he attended from the age of four and a half years. When he was seven the promising pupil was transferred to the junior department of St Mary's, the Brothers' secondary school, just round the corner in Barrack Street. (Both schools were literally yards from his home.) He gave up this formal education when he was twelve since it probably never occurred to him to seek further formal learning and his parents, though ambitious, could not have afforded the fees, small as they were, for continuing grammar school education. He did sit and obtained honours in two Intermediate subjects, English and Natural Philosophy (a judicious mixture of sciences, mainly physics with some balancing chemistry), in 1883 when he was twelve. He was the only candidate entered for the latter subject. Most biographical references to him underline the fact that his formal education stopped then (with, among his adversaries, the added, deliberately pejorative, detail that he then worked as a 'potboy', serving the clientele of a public house), and also that he never married.

These two facts need to be considered within the context of the times. His lack of marital status was shared by two-fifths of the male population in his lifetime and had not then the connotation it possesses in some of today's scandal sheets. Further, no one thought it remarkable that the rising politician should have continued to live in his parents' house until he was thirty-two, in 10 Hamill Street and later in the nearby 41 Alexander Street West; both lay in the heart of his constituency and were less than five minutes walk from the town centre. The Intermediate Examination in which he had achieved passes in two important subjects required a standard much greater than that of today's GCSE. He more than compensated for his lack of further education by prodigious reading and all the other ploys of autodidacts who have notoriously hard teachers. His self-education was lifelong and it would have been a courageous university graduate who would have lightly crossed debating swords with him. He left school in 1883 equipped with a strong green-tinged romantic view of history and the skill in computation and excellent penmanship that was then part of primary education. An important part of any application for a clerical post was a formal letter rendered in the candidate's own handwriting.

Education by the Brothers, given in mostly 'southern' accents, would not have lacked a consistent and continuous affirmation of national identity, with particular emphasis on a rather simplistic view of Irish history. The textbooks could hardly avoid an Irish account of the distressful country from the time of the twelfth-century 'English' invasion right up to the 'genocide' of the Famine. The pupils were urged openly to remember the 'glories of Brian the brave' and to grieve at the Flight of the Earls, the curse of Cromwell, the Broken Treaty, the Wild Geese, 1798, and the criminal Act of Union. The romantic ballads published in *The Nation* and the pleas of Thomas Davis (1814–45) for nationality, historical pride and the preservation of the dying Irish language found an emotional response in the subtext of all these cleverly compiled manuals. Though the admission of 'Celtic' as a subject for the Leaving Certificate after 1880, and the foundation in 1893 of the most successful agency for language restoration, the Gaelic League, came too late for 'Wee Joe' to learn the language, it was not long before the *Christian Brothers Irish Grammar* was in print and stayed in print until at least 1960.

Devlin was and remained a 'Brothers boy'. It was a description that gained in significance as the nineteenth century progressed. It implied an excellent education, a career in the civil service or other good pensionable employment, and a residual intense pride in the pastoral care provided by the order and loyalty to its ideals. Not all pupils conformed to the ideal but a surprising number benefited from its rough benevolence. He remained a source of intense pride to the order and, in his worldwide travels in America north and south, Australia and New Zealand, he was an honoured guest at its schools and monasteries. The 1927 souvenir booklet published by the Brothers at Brow-of-the-Hill in Derry contained a fourteen-page profile of 'the most famous living lay ex-pupil of the Irish Christian Brothers'. It is, not unexpectedly, a near-hagiographic account but at least one sentence is the simple truth: 'That he was their pupil is a fact in which he takes pride, and to the great teaching order he has on many occasions paid tribute at once generous and deserved.'

His first job was as a clerk in a jam factory at two shillings and sixpence a week. Immediately we come up against one of the difficulties of writing the man's biography. As we have noted he ordered that all his papers be destroyed on his death and, lacking any autobiographical details, except those items recalled by others from conversations or in letters, the biographer has to become a kind of super detective building up a profile from local folklore, stray remarks, attributive stories, and firmly held, almost mythic beliefs as befits a latter-day paladin. There is only a very light sprinkling of elderly people still surviving who went on his famous summer excursions for children but many of the succeeding generation still treasure Devliniana.

In response to a story in the *Irish News* Nesta Donnelly from Lurgan sent me a photocopy of his 'In memoriam' card, carefully preserved by her aunt Mary McConville, who taught for many years in Slate Street that once nestled in the heart of Devlin territory, between Leeson Street and the Falls Road. It is likely that she was one of the voluntary stewards who helped with the scary task of supervising the kids on their annual day trips to Newcastle, Bangor and Portrush. The card, one of many printed at the time of Devlin's funeral, was typical of its period and shows a young Joe with smart wing collar and cravat, the obligatory Irish wolfhound couchant at the foot of a round tower, lit by a rising sun, with the legend 'He lived for Ireland', and on the verso side, a map of Ireland with St Patrick on the northwest, St Brigid in the southeast and the Sacred Heart in the centre.

A friend told me that a teapot given by Wee Joe to his aunt was preserved by his mother in a china cabinet and never polluted with use. The aunt was the wife of Devlin's close friend, Dan McCann. McCann was a prosperous fish and vegetable merchant with several branches about the city, and a director of the *Irish News*, and, apart from contributing continuing financial advice and support, was one of the architects of his successful election for West Belfast in 1906.

If he had been as vulnerable and self-publicising as Charles Dickens (1812–1870), another talented boy whose formal education was nicely stifled then in a blacking factory, he could have left an account that might have illuminated his true personality more clearly. He once said that he had been refused employment as a clerk in the office of a linen mill because of his religion. This not unexpected event should have left a sectarian animus but Joe's view of his working class fellows was of concern and determination to improve their social condition, whether Catholic or Protestant. He told the story later that, after the successful interview for the clerkship, he was asked which school he had attended. He was only too aware of the likely reaction to his mentioning the Christian Brothers and carefully replied St Mary's. Then, in answer to the next question, he said it was in Barrack Street. He had some residual guilt about denying the Brothers but in the circumstances it would have made no difference. The antennae of Protestant employers were notably sensitive to the presence of a 'Mickie'. The official then asked for his address and said that he would soon get a card telling him when to start. No card came but years later he met the interviewer again when he received a delegation of linen bosses to the House of Commons. He smiled his famous broad smile through the customary heavy swirl of cigar smoke and, gesturing unthreateningly with his corona, admonished the magnate that he had forgotten to send the card. He then eased the tension by taking the man by the arm and inviting the delegation to afternoon tea on the terrace, saying, 'I want to hear all about Belfast.'

While it is true that he was the most pragmatic Catholic advocate that Belfast has ever known, and an avowed enemy of Unionism in his concern for the amelioration of the conditions of the Belfast poor, he was politically colour-blind. He was also possessed of a sunny nature, a personality ever ready to bubble over into laughter and with hardly a trace of self-pity. He had none of the cold extremism that marked his adversaries, both Unionist and those of Sinn Féin, but at the height of his political power, when the strands of Irish nationalism were united finally to wrest Home Rule from Britain, his pragmatism, his non-violent constitutionalism, his respect for the feelings and awareness of the genuine fears of ordinary Protestants were undervalued. In the way of things the personality that made him so charismatic eventually caused his final disillusion and dysfunction.

He was luckier that many children of his own age whose only future consisted of menial jobs in the mills and other industries. From the age of ten the 'lucky' ones accepted by the factories were half-timers who worked from 6am to 6pm on alternate days, amounting to three days of a six-day week. Conditions of employment would have made a modern Health and Safety inspector blanch. Of all children born in industrial Belfast, 30 percent died under the age of two-and-a-half years. Even as late as 1901 the death rate of Belfast people between the ages of fifteen and twenty was twice that in Manchester. Illiteracy was greater than in Glasgow or Leeds. Even as a child Devlin was very conscious of his own perceived advantages as the son of an employed father and caring mother. Improvement in the social conditions of his constituents remained his priority, taking pride of place even over his Herculean efforts for Home Rule. His next employment was as a live-in potboy and bottle-washer in a public house on the Antrim Road. Here he was lucky enough to have an employer who encouraged further education. It was then that his career as a powerful public speaker began.

An important art of young Joe's informal training as a public speaker would have been performances of 'recitations' – the dramatic rendering of set pieces. Also known as parlour poetry these monologues were recognised items in the music halls, holding place with singers, instrumentalists, acrobats and comedians as part of the bill. One such performer, Bransby Williams (1870–1961), Joe's near coeval, continued to act out such items with titles redolent of their heroic content as 'Old Devil-May-Care' and 'The Whitest Man I Know' right up to the coming of television and the discovery of an eager new audience.

There existed a plethora of DIY manuals in that 'self-help' era that would have helped compensate for a lack of formal education. A typical one was *The Reciter's Treasury of Verse* that provided an array of many pieces arranged in alphabetical order of the versifier preceded by a long introduction on the 'art of speaking', with chapters on respiration; inflection, modulation, pitch and the change of key; articulation; gesture; and recitation. These were followed by verbal exercises and rather intimidating anatomical sketches. This 'treasury' had 848 pages plus an index and contained a plethora of poems 'suitable' for declamation, with the text of many usually shortened poems given in full. This was the sort of book that the young, intensely ambitious, teenager seized on to further an as yet vaguely perceived public career. It was a time when ability at public speaking was as valued as elegant penmanship.

In 1885, when not yet fifteen, he attended classes given by a Professor Coleman of St Malachy's College, the junior seminary of the Down and Connor diocese. (The description 'professor' was an entirely honorary title granted to the underpaid lay teachers on junior seminary staffs.) The professor held evening elocution classes in the minor hall of St Mary's, the new Catholic hall, built in 1875 behind Castle Street and since demolished. Armed with a strongly 'fraternal' approach to history he was able to argue that 'Fontenoy' by Thomas Davis was a more appropriate text for recitation by Catholic/nationalist lads than Tennyson's 'The Charge of the Light Brigade'. 'Fontenoy', a battle fought in Flanders in May 1745, between France and the allied forces of Britain, Holland and Austria in the War of the Austrian Succession, described how the Irish Brigade of 'Wild Geese' turned the tide against the allies. It makes a good party piece, if a trifle long, and ends with the triumphant sestet:

> The English strove with desperate strength, paused, rallied, staggered, fled.
> The green hillside is matted close with dying and with dead.
> Across the plain and far away passed on that hideous wrack,
> While cavalier and fantassin dash in upon their track.
> On Fontenoy, on Fontenoy, like eagles in the sun,
> With bloody plumes the Irish stand – the field is fought and won![1]

It was a remarkable stand-off between master and pupil when Joe startled the professor by his knowledge of Irish history. It was significant that because of the lad's brilliant persuasiveness, tact and forensic ability, that Coleman yielded and allowed Joe to use it as his test piece which eventually garnered him the gold medal in the verse-speaking competition. In fact Tennyson's poem is much superior to Davis's on any level and is not at all complimentary to the British establishment but that made no difference. As he explained to his teacher, *The Story of Ireland* (1867), a romantic history of the distressful country, by A M Sullivan (1830–84), was young Devlin's bible and the non-violent approach of its author to the Irish Question fitted well with Devlin's own ideas. It was also Winston Churchill's unreliable handbook for his skewed understanding of the Irish race.

Devlin was not a literary man, not a 'great reader' in the phrase current at the time, at least after he entered public life. In his younger years he had devoured poetry and biographies but his greater aesthetic pleasure lay in grand opera and the artistry of the Irish tenor John McCormack (1884–1945). He knew his *Spirit of the Nation*, the collection of the ballads and songs of the journal of Young Ireland, first published in 1845 and still in print in the 1930s. Davis was the supreme balladeer of the paper and we may assume that the rousing 'A Nation Once Again' was part of the lad's repertoire. It is not too fanciful to suggest that it was in the following lines that he found his own destiny:

> And then I prayed I yet might see
> Our fetters rent in twain
> And Ireland, long a province, be
> A Nation once again.

He was clearly conscious of his unusual verbal ability, his prodigious memory, and his capacity for rapid assimilation of knowledge. In his usual altruistic way he began to consider how these gifts might be put to the achievement of his twin goals: amelioration of the conditions of his working class neighbours and Home Rule.

The young Devlin's other dramatic party piece was 'Rienzi to the

Romans', describing the appeal made by the Italian patriot Cola di Rienzi (c.1313–54) to the citizens of Rome to rise against the tyrannical nobility. Cola became a hero again in the nineteenth century during the struggle for Italian unification. Once the subject of an ode by the contemporary Petrarch (1304–74) he was the protagonist of *Rienzi* (1840), the second opera of Richard Wagner (1813–83); and the assassination of Cola's brother formed the subject of a famous painting by Holman Hunt (1827–1910). His story so inspired Lord Byron (1788–1824) that he mentioned him in *Childe Harold's Pilgrimage* (1816):

> The friend of Petrarch – hope of Italy –
> Rienzi! last of Romans! While the tree
> Of freedom's wither'd trunk puts forth a leaf
> Even for thy tomb a garland let it be –
> The forum's champion and the people's chief –
> Her new-born Numa – with reign, alas too brief.

It was, however, the novel *Rienzi – The Last of the Roman Tribunes* (1835) by Edward Bulwer-Lytton (1803–73), the popular Victorian historical novelist, that made his story and name familiar; and it was from this that the dramatic recitation was taken. It was stirring stuff, beginning:

> Friends, I come not here to talk. Ye know too well the story of our thraldom – we are slaves. The bright sun rises to his course and lights a race of slaves. He sets and his last beam falls on a slave.

He goes on to speak of the condition of the common people of Rome ruled by a usurping baronial class and then expatiates upon the death of his brother, his junior by fifteen years:

> ...a gracious boy, full of all gentleness of calmest hope, a sweet and quiet boy; there was a look of heaven upon his face, which limners give to the beloved disciple... In one short hour the pretty harmless boy was slain. I saw the corpse – the mangled corpse – and then I cried for vengeance: Rouse ye Romans; Rouse ye slaves! Have ye brave sons? Look in the next fierce brawl and see them die. Have ye daughters fair? Look to see them live, torn from your arms, distained, dishonoured; and if ye dare call for justice be answered with the lash.

And there is what would not in those more sober days have been called a big finish:

> And once again – hear me ye walls… once again I swear the eternal city shall be free; her sons shall walk with princes.

It is the kind of speech that Devlin's contemporaries could identify with, finding equivalents to their own situation in what was their own beleaguered city.

He took these recitations very seriously but not solemnly. Even as a boy he was noted for his good humour and charisma, a word he would not have used but clearly displayed. The need to sharpen his oratorical ability was instinctive as if he already sensed that his destiny would rest in his ability to persuade, to motivate, and finally, to inspire his listeners. It never occurred to him, however, to mitigate in any way his strong Belfast accent. Among the more mellifluous accents of his southern colleagues it had its own charm, especially to southern ears. E M Forster (1879–1970), the novelist, began an essay about his friend Forrest Reid (1875–1947) with the sentence: 'Belfast, as all men of affairs know, stands no nonsense and lies at the head of Belfast Lough.' This generally held opinion that its citizens are somehow much more in touch with the 'real' world than their rather fey fellow countrymen from other provinces Devlin continued to use to advantage, but was careful to let implicit honesty seem to shine with difficulty through the rather abrasive vocal register. This became one of his trademarks, as later did the whiff of expensive cigar smoke, the carnation or orchid in his exquisitely tailored jacket, his formal wing collars, and his densely thick hair, magnificently coiffured with the parting straight and gleaming as though etched by a sculptor's knife. Even then he was a natural leader, able to persuade boys of his own age to join in discussions and debates about literature and politics, especially the turbulent politics of the time. It was a sound apprenticeship that would make him later the voice of his people and cause Tim Healy (1855–1931), his sharply witty adversary, to dub him the 'Duodecimo Demosthenes'.[2] Though not meant as such, Devlin accepted it as a compliment.

The boys met in a sweet shop at 120 Divis Street – their world was small too – owned by people called Carson, ironic in light of future confrontations, and regularly in their discussions would evidence a fixed concern for Belfast workers, both Catholic and Protestant. Inevitably their greater concern was for the Catholics who, numbering more than 60,000, formed about 27 percent of the city's population. In spite of this they had virtually no presence on the council. The conditions under which they worked were intolerable by today's standards and they had neither municipal nor parliamentary representation. In 1891, when the population of the city was 255,950, the number of infant deaths was thirty-three per thousand; ten years later, by which time the population had increased by 36 percent, the infant mortality rate was still thirty-one per thousand. This high death rate began to concern even the sluggish members of the Belfast Corporation. Edward McInnes, a member of a group appointed to consider public health, reported that the diet of tea and soda bread that the pregnant workers subsisted upon was bound to weaken the unborn children. Having seen for himself the conditions under which a majority lived he wondered how infants lived long enough to be registered.

An example he took was a mill-race that ran near Durham Street, then and later a flashpoint between the Loney and Sandy Row. It was used as a depository of effluent and could make people nauseous, especially during the summer. One of the worst places the committee had visited was Millfield Place. Dr Roger Blaney's monograph, *Belfast – 100 Years of Public Health* (1988), included excerpts from McInnes's report and showed a photograph of the cul-de-sac in Millfield of small houses with no rear exits who had to make use of a communal dry toilet. The tiny houses were let in two or three compartments to two or three different people. Those worst off were the ground floor tenants who had no plaster cover but the bare beams holding up the upper floor. The people upstairs had stuffed bags, old clothes and scraps of rags in place, through which sewage dripped down. His conclusion that the places were unfit for human habitation was given a wry postscript when McInnes remarked that there was a piggery in nearby Barrack Street Place that was more fit for human occupancy than any of the houses mentioned in the report.

Devlin did what he could to improve the conditions of all the Belfast workers but improvements came at a painfully slow rate. The year 1910 saw him making an impassioned if irrelevant speech as the member for West Belfast in the British House of Commons detailing the working conditions of women and children mill workers. He reminded the House that they worked a seventy-two hour week for five shillings: 'There are children in Belfast with wizened faces – old before they ever know what it is to be young, who go to work at six o'clock in the morning and work till six o'clock at night for three shillings a week.'

In the spring of 1941, a mere seven years after Devlin's death, the German bombs revealed a hardly improved situation when a majority of working class evacuees were seen to be undersized, suffering from malnutrition, lice-infested, tubercular, and 'unbilletable', to use the word of Dawson Bates (1876–1949), the egregious and incompetent Minister of Home Affairs:

> There is unfortunately a class that can only be described as unbilletable and which the Ministry would be very loath to billet on any householder in Northern Ireland, such people are so inhuman in their habits.

The young debaters, with a terrible thirst for reform, however light-hearted the tone of their debates, could not but be aware of industrial health risks. The conditions are detailed in Jonathan Bardon's excellent *Belfast – An Illustrated History* (1982). Every aspect of the linen trade was fraught with hazards to health. The flax was first retted in the dams and the fibre dried before being taken to the mills for processing. The earliest operation was known as 'roughing', combing the fibres into lengths. The 'machine boys' further combed the material, separating 'tow' from the long strips that was used for the finest finished material. Throughout the whole process flax particles filled the air in the mills and caused the 'roughers' chronic bronchitis, and the 'machine boys' (of the second stage) a condition known then as 'pouce', caused by flax dust. The 'roughing' was described by Dr

John Moore in 1867 as 'drawing the fibres of the flax across a coarse iron comb. The atmosphere in which they work is certainly not one of the purest, the dust and fine particles of the flax load the air, and consequently a good deal of bronchial irritation results.'

The 'pouce' in the machine shops produced an even more alarming effect. C D Purdon, a surgeon who dealt with the resulting pathology, wrote the following report about the progress:

> The first symptom is a sensation of dryness in the throat. Thence into the lungs, soon bringing on the attacks of cough and dysnoea, which seize them, especially in the morning and at night. In severe and well-marked attacks, the paroxysm of cough and dysnoea lasts for a considerable time, and does not pass off until the contents of the stomach are rejected, and often blood is spat up. During this period the worker seizes any article that may be near, in order to enable him to get over the attack more easily. In case of the machine boy suffering from a severe paroxysm whilst at work, the table at which he is engaged is caught with both hands, and when thus observed by his companions he is said to be poucey.

Purdon added that recruiting sergeants were warned by army surgeons never to allow 'hacklers', as the male workers were known, to enlist. They became prematurely aged with a life expectancy of less than forty-five years.

The women who generally worked on the later stages of the manufacture were equally at risk. The more refined the fibre, the more insidiously dangerous the effects. Those who worked in the spinning room in temperatures ranging from 32° to 50°C were subject to oedema as well as bronchitis. Many of these had become whiskey drinkers while still in their teens to ease the pain these conditions caused. Purdon reported that 'they suffer in the same manner as the males but in a far more aggravated degree'. Often pregnant or nursing mothers, they had to rise at five o'clock in the morning to be at the mill for six. They suffered from an even more deleterious form of pulmonary disease known then as 'phthisis', a form of rapidly acting tuberculosis. Devlin and his band of young reforming Turks knew that, uniquely in heavy industry, the larger part of linen-making was done by women. There were several different tasks approximating to the future line-assembly devised by Henry Ford (1863–1947) for the rapid assembly of his automobiles.

'Rovers' removed the yarn-covered bobbins from the spindles and took them to the 'spinning rooms' where the air was heavy with steam, staphylococci and tubercle bacilli. There the 'doffers' replaced the bobbins that in turn were carried off by the 'pickers'. Here the workers were subject to the usual pulmonary complaints with the extra scourge of fallen arches and 'onychia', a painful fungal disease of the toenails caused by the workers standing barefoot in water impregnated with metallic particles which, in the primitive treatment practice of the time, required the wrenching out of the nails. The whole operation from flax to fabric had not a single aspect that would not have resulted today in criminal prosecution of the factory owners.

Devlin, as president, named his talking-shop the Sexton Debating Society, after Thomas Sexton (1848–1932), a Waterford journalist who was the first Nationalist to hold West Belfast (1886–92) until his defeat by a Unionist. Sexton was another Brothers boy, a past pupil of Mount Sion CBS, Waterford, the original Christian Brothers' school opened by Edmund Ignatius Rice (1762–1844), the founder of the order, on 7 June 1803. Like Devlin, Sexton plunged early into Home Rule activity, using the same relentless system of continuing education as his Ulster neophyte. His was one of the most eloquent voices in the House of Commons when William Ewart Gladstone (1809–98) introduced his First Home Rule Bill in 1886, and he was paid the ultimate compliment by the 'Grand Old Man' as he crossed the floor of the House to congratulate him. The society was, in Devlin's words, 'founded for the purpose of creating a national taste for Irish literature among the youth of the city of Belfast and for the fostering of a healthy spirit of educated criticism amongst its members'. It deliberately used the same kind of language that had characterised the first numbers of The Nation (1842–4), founded by Thomas Davis. They even chose as a motto one of Davis's slogans: 'Educate that you may be free.'

The programme for the spring session of the Sexton Debating Society, Belfast, had thirteen weekly events held each Monday from

5 January until 29 March. There were seven lectures on such subjects as Young Ireland, Thomas Moore, John Philpot Curran, and Home Rule. The lecture on Thomas Francis Meagher (1823–67), the Young Irelander who had found fame in the American Civil War, was given by the fourteen-year-old Devlin. Debates were held once a month, on 12 January and 9 February, with a prophetic 'Parliamentary Debate' on 1 March. The sessions on 19 January and 23 February were 'concerts' with songs and readings given by the members, including, of course, young Devlin, who loved both singing and declamation. The whole showed a remarkable degree of organisation on the part of the society's founder; organisation was to be his outstanding characteristic. Also associated with the society were a football team, a dramatic society and a library for the members' use.

The concerts were extremely popular. They attracted crowds to the house in Mill Street where the Sexton Society held their sessions when the number of members grew too large for the original meeting place in Divis Street. The evenings of music, song and readings were a kind of relief from the earnestness of the debates and the seriousness of the lectures. Devlin loved music and song. He was a fine parlour performer himself and could assemble a worthy programme of instrumentalists, Irish tenors and even comedians. A regular was Cathal O'Byrne (1875–1957), the Belfast antiquary, author of *As I Roved Out* (1947), a collection of sketches of old Belfast.[3] The audience had often to bring their own chairs but though known for gaiety and what was not then called 'crack', they were still educational events since much of the material was Irish, and all of it prime stuff.

Sexton made his first attempt to win West Belfast that November. He had the useful honour of being imprisoned with Parnell in Kilmainham four years before, in October 1881. He knew already that policies were irrelevant; Catholics, if they got to the polls, would vote for the 'southerner' while Protestants would be equally party-aligned. Devlin, the stocky young lad, as tall then as he was ever going to be, learned the first rule of electioneering in Irish elections: 'Get them out.' He knew his constituency well and already showed that flair for organisation that, after his eloquence, was to be his great practical quality. He soon had a team of lads like himself whom he sent round the overcrowded houses delivering leaflets, reminding the newly enfranchised voters of their moral duty and urging them to turn out to vote for Sexton. The result of his efforts, and similar canvassing on the other side, produced the unheard-of, before or since, turnout out of 93 percent. As it was, Sexton lost by only thirty-seven votes.

It was a time of an intense political baptism for the slightly undersized, enthusiastic, unvenal ward-heeler. He was personally proud when the following year Sexton was able to win the West by 106 votes. His assistance was admitted by the successful candidate himself, who had readily responded to an invitation to address the Sexton Debating Society after his election. Devlin was master of ceremonies by virtue of his office and, at the end of Sexton's address, the Waterford man praised Devlin's speech with the ultimate compliment:

> I have listened to many speeches in my time... but I have never listened to one, which gave me more pleasure than the one in which your chairman addressed me. I regret the rule, which obliges all members of the House of Commons to be at least twenty-one years of age. For otherwise I think the chairman of this meeting would be amongst us.

Such a compliment may have assuaged slightly his father's recurring embarrassment. Not long before he had come home from work and complained to his wife: 'You must do something about that fellow Joe spouting all over the town. I'm ashamed and disgraced before my mates on the car-stand.'

At the time of this fierce spate of electioneering 'that fellow Joe' was working in a wholesale/retail spirit shop, known then as Kelly's Store, in Bank Street, off Royal Avenue in the city centre; it is now called Kelly's Cellars. It was one of the oldest liquor stores in the city, built in 1720, and used as a meeting place for the United Irishmen in the years leading up to the rebellion of 1798. When Sexton got to hear of this he asked him to come to his hotel and suggested that he could find him a more appropriate position, in a government office or the like, but the very mature youngster refused politely: 'I'm grateful for your suggestion but I will never accept any position until I have obtained Home Rule.' The answer was a remarkable mixture of innocence and bravado, not without some arrogance. It seemed either to ignore or discount the work done by Parnell and other members of the Irish Party outside of tight little Belfast. As in the best or worst fairy stories the boast almost came true. Certainly the years preceding Sexton's election and during his period as MP were a thorough grounding in Irish politics. It gave Devlin a career and a crusade, and all his energies were given to his ultimate goal.

It was inevitable, considering the Barrack Street education in Irish history, that he would become exhilarated by the land agitation, led mainly by Michael Davitt (1846–1906), and the energising of the Home Rule movement under its coldly efficient new leader Charles Stewart Parnell. During his active impressionable teens Devlin had found in Home Rule politics a purpose, a worthy ambition and a means of personal success after years of depressed acquiescence. His self-imposed regimen in 'elocution' was probably necessary but it was built on great courage and selfless patriotism. Money then and afterwards seemed to have no interest for him. His people in West Belfast served as a microcosm for the country as a whole. He had seen how Sexton during his period as MP had managed to achieve some amelioration of ward boundaries in favour of the nationalist population.[4] Nationalism was the means of achieving the ambition of all Catholic/nationalist figures since the passing of the Act of Union: self-determination. With Parnell the vanquished ambitions of Emmet, the Young Irelanders and the Fenians might just be realised. Devlin would have had little in common with any of these movements in their methods, though he undoubtedly approved of their aims.

The brilliant Rev Henry Cooke (1788–1868), the Presbyterian leader who had banished Belfast's original radicalism and laid its foundation as the unrelenting citadel of Orangeism and unionism, had made the position clear in a speech at Hillsborough on 3 October 1832: 'Repeal [of the Union] is just a discreet word for Romish ascendancy and Protestant extermination.' He virtually expelled

Daniel O'Connell (1775–1847) when he visited the city in 1841, escorted by the city police and local militia 'for his own protection'. O'Connell's Catholic supporters, however, had no protection and the occasion led to an attack on Catholics by militant Orangemen, aided by the urban police. As the century continued there was no lack of fiery mob orators to carry on with less subtlety the anti-Catholic rhetoric. To a lad with antennae as sensitive as Devlin's the *realpolitik* of city life was assimilated early. He had, like thousands of his fellow townsmen, been called a 'Fenian bastard' and worse many times, running the gauntlet through non-existent peace lines.

Yet, probably because of his awareness of the social conditions of what later could judiciously be called his 'kingdom', his vision was a non-sectarian one. He was aware that, though Catholics were and would continue to be the underclass, poverty was also a large part of the lives of the Protestant majority. He fought for social justice for all and, realising how long and weary a fight it was going to be, he kept in shape, so to speak. Cathal O'Byrne, his near contemporary, once described a typical encounter. Devlin was then the very young manager of Kelly's Cellars, indulged in his political career and self-improvement by the owner, Samuel Young. O'Byrne found him in his 'office', not engaged in checking supplies or other managerial activities, but declaiming a set piece of speech for a competition. Until O'Byrne arrived he had only the bare four walls for response but 'then and there he pressed me into service, and audience of one, made me sit in judgement on his efforts'. Cathal, four years younger, was, of course, a member of the Sexton Society and it was his pleasure a few days later, in the company of the other members, to witness the success of Devlin's efforts: 'Our society was present as one man and had the pleasure of hearing and seeing our president win and carry off the gold medal for his rendering of the selected item.'

One notable change in the political situation in his youth was the active part now played by the Church. The leading figure in the compact little Catholic enclave was Bishop Dorrian. He, like many of his episcopal colleagues, had come to power in a surge of Catholic reform and increased devotional practice. It was reported that in his first month as bishop, during a special mission, 20,000 people had gone to confession, a figure that represented nearly half the Catholic population from the age of ten years. This remarkable figure was doubled in 1877 when, in six churches, a band of missionary fathers from the Order of Mary Immaculate (OMI) held a month-long mission during which 40,000 Belfast Catholics renewed their baptismal vows. Dorrian's episcopate saw, as Denvir had dreaded, a growth in sectarian bitterness and greater violence than before. This was partly explained by the politics affecting the rest of the country. Home Rule had become not only a possibility but, from the Unionist viewpoint, a serious threat to the Union that was their badge of superiority.

The hope of accommodation between the now warring tribes flickered and died. Retrenchment and self-sufficiency characterised the embattled minority and, even in peaceful times, they were wary and distrustful of the opposition. At the time there were nearly fifty newspapers in Belfast and it was a natural development that the bishop should either found or take over a paper that would represent the 'agreed' Catholic viewpoint. That view was subject to subtle change in the larger politics of the country as a whole. Though the media in those years had not reached the alarming levels of influence of the twentieth and twenty-first centuries they were beginning to feel their power. Dorrian was sufficiently astute to grasp the need to influence Catholic opinion and, realising the remarkable effect that *The Nation* had in the 1840s, soon became involved in a Catholic press.

A paper called the *Belfast Morning News* had been founded in 1854 as a Catholic daily when Denvir was bishop but it proved too 'Whiggish' for the later clergy. By this they meant too like the old Liberal alliance and not sufficiently directed at the new Nationalism. Two years into his coadjutorship Dorrian founded in opposition the *Ulster Observer*. Its editor, Andrew McKenna, proved to be too much of a loose cannon, echoing in his editorials some sentiments that reeked of Fenianism, and its independence could have been interpreted as anti-clerical. The 'bishop's paper' lasted five years, until 1867. McKenna began a new periodical, the *Northern Star,* its title harking back to the days of the United Irishmen, while the new 'episcopal' journal was named the *Ulster Examiner*. Considering Dorrian's workload it was a remarkable extra burden to be taken on. McKenna, who was by now Dorrian's adversary, and whose talent if not his politics Dorrian admired, died in 1872, and the *Northern Star* was taken over by the *Ulster Examiner*.

The merged paper had more copy of a religious nature and bore more obvious signs of clerical control. It proved to be too much of a financial burden for Dorrian in 1877 and he allowed it to be bought by Charles J Dempsey, another of the 'rich' Catholics of Belfast, whose Home Rule credentials were impeccable. He also took over the *Belfast Morning News* and used that name for the composite paper. It followed a strong Home Rule agenda and was the chief Parnellite organ in Ulster.

Dorrian died in 1885 while Parnell's star was happily in the ascendant. His successor, Patrick McAllister, continued where Dorrian left off, building four new churches: St Paul's in the Falls Road, Sacred Heart in the Old Park Road, Holy Family in Newington, just off the Antrim Road, and St Brigid's in Derryvolgie Avenue, off the Malone Road. Like his predecessor, McAllister was a Parnellite until the scandal of the 'Uncrowned King's' divorce. Up to this point he gave Parnell a guarded support, mainly because of his popularity with his flock, though the Home Rule Bill of 1886 generated the worst civic unrest and anti-Catholic violence in the town's history till then. The rioting was believed to have been a direct result of the Conservatives' 'playing of the Orange Card' but many nationalists in Belfast were annoyed when Parnell, warned of Orange reaction, had shrugged off the danger with the ignorant dismissal of the threat: '1,000 men of the Royal Irish Constabulary will be amply sufficient to cope with all of the rowdies that the Orangemen of the North can produce.' This was murderous innocence indeed and the fifty people who died in Belfast that summer showed how wrong he was.

3
'Put Up the Gossoon!'

WHEN CAPTAIN WILLIAM O'SHEA DIVORCED his wife Katharine, naming Parnell as co-respondent, and their ten-year affair became public knowledge, McAllister like the other bishops publicly disowned him and he went the further step of ordering that the sacraments be refused to any residual supporters. It was not made clear just how rank-and-file supporters could be identified, unless they chose to reveal the fact themselves. At the time it was the ultimate episcopal threat, a more than hefty smack with the crosier. The scandal was to a majority of Belfast nationalists a crippling blow and many were greatly offended by the extra blow of effective excommunication. This ruling that echoed others in dioceses countrywide was expressed by McAllister in 1891 in his Lenten pastoral as follows:

> We have in Belfast what is called a 'Parnell Leaderships Committee', the ostensible object of which appears to be to honour a man who by his persistent and impudent attempts to force himself on the attention of the country, defiled as he was with the leprosy of his loathsome crime, continues to outrage the public sense of morality and decency, and tries to subject to his dictation the independence of our country and Church. The Catholic members of this committee by enrolling their names have proclaimed their disregard of Christian decency and their contempt for the instructions which the bishops of Ireland considered their duty to impart to their people.
> They have thus become the propagators of public scandal and have by

their own acts placed themselves in the category of those to whom it is unlawful for priests to administer the Sacraments of the Church...

Even allowing for the fact that the bishops were the moral guardians of Irish Catholics and could not possibly countenance such flagrant immorality as Parnell's flaunting of his English mistress there is a sense of relief as well as a barely concealed delight that the austere Protestant from Wicklow, who had never courted the Irish prelates, would no longer have emotional control over Catholic laymen.

Gladstone had to distance himself from Parnell since he relied on the votes of British non-conformists who had reacted to Parnell's 'leprosy' with even greater fervour than the Irish clergy. His rejection of him was not so much a question of morality as of political acumen. He certainly took no pleasure in the downfall of 'the Chief' and might have helped him back into power after a timely divorce.

Adultery was not unknown in Victorian Britain – or even Ireland – but there were acceptable procedures that Parnell was too ill and too arrogant to follow. In the long history of Ireland's missed chances none seemed more painful than the collapse of yet another charismatic leader. At other times, earlier and later, the faithful followers would have ignored the ham-fisted wielding of the crosiers but at that time (and for at least seventy more years) respect for ecclesiastical authority among Irish Catholics was supreme. Apart from these pulpit precepts, McAllister, aware of the effect of the press, decided to sponsor a new anti-Parnell daily. The *Irish News* was already on the streets by the end of the summer in 1891 and has remained the chief supporting organ for such constitutional parties as the Anti-Partitionist, Nationalist, and the Social Democratic and Labour Party (SDLP).

Devlin was three months short of his twentieth birthday when the bombshell hit. He had been active in local politics, almost by instinct, from an early age. A lad of his temperament and sensitivity could not help becoming aware of the conditions of the Catholics of his neighbourhood. He had learned to ignore the mournful factory sirens that called the often barefoot 'shawlies' to work at 6am at the beginning of a long laborious day, and at the mercy of the fine water mist in the mill laundries and the even more deadly 'dry' rooms filled with invisible lethal fibres that worked like asbestos on the lungs. He was conscious that poor as his family was they had been able to give him a tolerable education and that he had been blessed with a 'gift of the gab', as his bewildered father might have put it. This blarney, as many outside Ulster would have called it, was uttered in a strong Belfast accent, unmitigated throughout a long career.

While still a teenager he shared a platform with the Chief at a rally at Kells in County Meath, and was one of the preliminary speakers, a kind of warm-up act before the star attraction. It was probably Sexton who arranged for him to attend and, once the nervous fear that he invariably experienced before any public speaking was overcome, he soared. When Parnell came forward to speak the crowd roared, 'Put up the gossoon; we want wee Joe. Put up the gossoon.' The Chief's reaction is not recorded but some years later, when the news of the scandal burst upon a startled and disappointed party, Devlin became a noted anti-Parnellite. In this he reflected the general nationalist opinion in the city where the lost leader had fewest supporters.

The exhausted Parnell came to speak in the Ulster Hall in Bedford Street on 29 May 1891, less than five months before his death. His speech was oddly at variance with his earlier dismissal of Orange resistance to the 1886 Home Rule Bill. He said: '…until the religious prejudices of the minority [Unionists in this context], whether reasonable or unreasonable, are conciliated… Ireland can never enjoy perfect freedom. Ireland can never be united.' During the parade that followed Devlin was said (with what justice, it is impossible to say) to have jumped on to the running board of the Parnell carriage, shouting, 'Kitty O'Shea! Kitty O'Shea!' If that unverifiable story was true it must be seen as a measure of Devlin's passionate disappointment at the time and shows a lack of the equanimity that characterised his later political career.

He was now twenty and poised on the brink of a public life that would have dismayed a lesser man. Though many of his political mentors, especially John Dillon (1851–1927), who, after the fall of Parnell, was the austere conscience of the Irish Parliamentary Party (IPP), urged him to become an MP, he refused out of a mixture of pride and practicality. MPs were not paid until 1911 and all of Devlin's money went on his own limited needs, his contributions to charities and unofficial handouts. Dillon, the son of John Blake Dillon (1814–66), the Young Irelander, was, after Parnell, the leading Nationalist politician in Ireland. He relinquished the leadership of the IPP to John Redmond in a necessary move to achieve party unity after the Parnell debacle.

Devlin had invited him in 1891 to address a kind of development of the Sexton Debating Society, known as the Belfast Young Ireland Society, the 'young' as much representative of the members' ages as a tribute to Dillon's father, Charles Gavan Duffy (1816–1903), and Thomas Davis, the original founders of the Young Ireland movement. Devlin and Dillon were notably dissimilar, the one university educated, diffident, depressive, humourless, insecure, intensely private; the other energetic, self-educated, ebullient, witty, impatient – and twenty years his junior. Dillon had no gift for intimacy and did not make friends easily. Relations between him and his protégé were formal for many years but there was no doubt in the older man's mind that the stocky lad with the strong Belfast accent was unusually gifted and had distinct leadership qualities.

One remark of Dillon about universal suffrage illustrates graphically their different approach to politics – and to women. In 1912, when addressing a group of women suffragists, he said: 'Women's suffrage will, I believe, be the ruin of our western civilisation. It will destroy the home, challenge the headship of man, laid down by God. It may come in your time, I hope not in mine.' Devlin could not have been even provoked to make so injudicious a comment but it was typical of Dillon's austere and unbending 'Victorian' attitude about social morality and his utter unawareness of how damaging a policy statement it was. Devlin, even had he shared Dillon's condescension towards women as voters (and there is no evidence of that), was too much aware of public reaction to blind prejudice. Later, at a National Volunteers' event in Derry, on 18 October 1914, when he was approached by a party of 'suffragettes' (as they were nicknamed) about his views on 'votes for women', he replied honestly that he had voted for the motion but that was a personal view and that he could not speak for his party as a whole.

Dillon had arranged for him to attend the inaugural meeting of the anti-Parnellite Irish National Federation (INFed) in 1892. A story associated with that first meeting, frequently recalled by Dan McCann, one of Devlin's lifelong friends, was that Devlin came slightly late and knocked at the door of the committee room. It was opened by one of the IPP MPs with the words, 'Well, boy, and what is it you want?'

'I am the Belfast delegate.'

'And is it possible that Belfast has no better representative than a mere boy? Come in.'

In spite of this deflating introduction he greatly impressed the other delegates in spite of his youth and 'that accent'.

In the months after Parnell's death, on 6 October 1891, the coherence of the IPP began to crumble. As long as the Chief was at the helm such personalities as Dillon, Tim Healy and William O'Brien (1852–1928), the latter both from County Cork, were held in check. Healy had acted as Parnell's secretary and when, on 6 December 1890, he delivered his savage retort that made the split visible, there was a patent sense of betrayal. When Redmond had said with uncharacteristic irony that Gladstone was the 'master of the party', Healy retorted furiously, 'Who is to be *mistress* of the party?' Now their fissionable personalities tended to prevent the re-establishment of the united centralised system that had made the IPP so potent a force.

Each of these lesser but commanding figures felt that he now had leave to advance his own ideas. Healy's personal animus had been in evidence long before his savage wit had helped bring down Parnell and now his political emphasis was on widening the base of control. It was he who referred to Parnell's mistress Katharine as 'O'Shea who must be obeyed', a reference to Ayesha, the chief character in *She* (1887), the popular romance by H Rider Haggard (1856–1925). He was also believed to have been the first to refer to his Phoenix Park residence (later Áras an Uachtaráin) when he was governor-general

(1922–8) as 'Uncle Tim's cabin'. He did not actually say that politics was too serious a business to be left to politicians but he a wanted much greater input from what would now be called the grass roots. He knew, of course, that meant an increasing influence by the lower ranks of the Catholic clergy, whose pulpit admonishments amounted to moral direction. He had the support of most of the naturally conservative senior clerics, whose care about Catholic education was stronger even than Home Rule considerations.

Among these were most of the Ulster bishops, Michael Logue (1840–1924), Archbishop of Armagh and Primate of All-Ireland, Charles McHugh (1856–1926), Bishop of Derry, Patrick McAllister, Bishop of Down and Connor, and his successor, Henry Henry. They were a formidable phalanx with flocks possibly more obedient than in any other part of Ireland because of their beleaguered position in the 'wee North'. The only northern bishop who was friendly with Dillon was the more sophisticated, even liberal, Patrick O'Donnell (1856–1927) of Raphoe. He became a friend of Devlin as well and helped lift ecclesiastical disapproval from the body with which he was most strongly identified, the Ancient Order of Hibernians (AOH).

Irish bishops as a class had never felt the need to be other than direct in their pastoral instructions to their flock. They had the truth and any temporising was, in fact, an unnecessary waste of time. During the Parnell era they had found it judicious generally to follow his political leadership providing there were no moral objections. Now after his moral collapse they became increasingly involved personally in public affairs, fearing a rise of secularism and a perceived diminishment of their social as well as ecclesiastical power.

The third party, William O'Brien, had been like Dillon a loyal Parnellite, and showed the same reluctance in disowning the Chief as Dillon, regretting the necessity but feeling the need to remove him for the ultimate good of the party and the nationalist people of Ireland. O'Brien took little part in IPP politics in the years immediately after 1891, concerning himself once more with the land question in his adopted County Mayo where famine conditions had again recurred. His agitation for redistribution of large tracts of grassland among the subsistence tenants in the west occupied all his energies until his founding of the United Irish League (UIL) in 1898 introduced a new element into Irish politics. It became an excellent constituency organisation and its growth in popularity and membership threatened the friable IPP. The final effect of its existence was the eventual re-uniting of nationalism under Redmond, who, though not in the front echelon of the party in Parnell's time, had remained faithful to his leader and his principles. Redmond's own generous if politically naive temperament hastened the healing. By 1900 the IPP was whole again and its only enemy within was Healy.

Devlin's background, his social origins and his urban upbringing were in notable contrast to those of these three survivors of the age of Parnell. He was younger by twenty years, by their standards undereducated, and a biological sport as a 'wee lad from backstreet Belfast'. He was a young man of sharp political acumen and must have realised that, in spite of the maelstrom of nationalist politics, he could find a way ahead. His genius for organisation had already been witnessed and now he was ready to represent his own people of Belfast in a uniquely appropriate way. Certain problems remained; he was still required to work for a living and had little regard for the accumulation of personal wealth. One of his Nationalist godfathers, T P O'Connor, known universally as 'Tay-Pay' (1848–1929), the only member of the IPP with a constituency in Britain – Scotland Road, Liverpool – once said that you couldn't make a rich man of him. He had a part-time job as a journalist with the *Irish News* and then, through Dillon's influence, moved to take charge of the Belfast office of the Dublin-based *Freeman's Journal*.

As secretary of INFed he was active in the 1892 general election when, due to the demolishing of some houses in the Catholic Falls Road and the building of more in the Protestant Shankill, Sexton's West Belfast seat was again made marginal. He organised bands of canvassers, whose purpose was not to explain finer points of policy but to get the nationalist vote out. He arranged for Michael Davitt, the one-armed victim of a Lancashire cotton mill and hero of the Land War, to appeal to the few Protestant voters who were more concerned with factory conditions than the Battle of the Boyne. Devlin's efforts were in vain; Sexton was defeated by the Unionist candidate H O Arnold-Foster (1853–1901) by 839 votes. In spite of this setback Devlin's work was appreciated at home. A dinner was held in his honour at the Linen Hall hotel in the spring of 1893 and at the presentation he was praised as 'the guiding spirit' of INFed in the city. It was quite an honour for a twenty-two-year-old but his response could justly have been the Belfast equivalent of Al Jolson's famous 'Yuh ain't seen nuttin' yet!'

His first brush with the internal opposition was at a rally at Sheepbridge, near Newry, County Down, in 1894. He had given up his work with the *Freeman's Journal* and was back in the liquor trade, employed as assistant manager in Kelly's Cellars. The money was probably better and his employer, Samuel Young, regarded him as a young man with a political future who deserved encouragement. Young had entered the House of Commons for the first time at the age of seventy as an anti-Parnellite MP for East Cavan in 1892. One of few Protestant Nationalists he frequently boasted that his father had been 'out' in Antrim during the rising of 1798. He was generous with leave when Devlin had to be about his political business but he discouraged him from standing in South Armagh in the general election of 1895. He let it be known that he thought Devlin 'young enough' — an Ulsterism that means 'too young' — to fight his first election, suggesting that there was political work still to done at home in Belfast, and there was always the glittering prize of West Belfast, now in Unionist hands. Devlin was quite prepared to wait. When Dillon offered him the safe seat of South Louth, he wrote to him, saying, 'I believe that within the sphere of my own influence here I can do infinitely more good and render far more service than I could hope to perform at any time in the House of Commons.' This included travelling frequently throughout East Ulster as the northern leader of INFed, making speeches in favour of Home Rule, breaking new ground and reassuring the nationalist population that, though the King was dead, a new leader of a united party would eventually be found.

It was while doing constituency work for Young in 1894 that Devlin heard of the death of some children in Raglan Street in Belfast.[1] Throughout his whole life he responded to the needs of the children in his constituency, and to that of their parents, mothers taking precedence. At a Christmas party in the second floor of Raglan Street School with nearly 400 children in attendance, someone for a prank doused the gaslight and the terrified children rushed for the stairs. Four were killed in the crush and many were injured. Devlin hastened back by train from Cavan to comfort the bereaved parents and set up a relief fund. Funerals were an important part of family pride and they were expensive. In spite of his practical approach the disaster left him emotionally drained to the point of wanting to give up politics. Injuries and deaths of children bore very hard on him, particularly in light of his belief that his own childhood had been especially happy. When the early months of 1895 proved to be unseasonably harsh he and his mates presented themselves, at his urging, as volunteers at a relief centre also set up in Raglan Street. There bread, soup and coffee were served to thousands of destitute men from the Shankill as well as the Falls. It was an important part of the political education of the vest-pocket paladin for whom the social conditions of the working class of his city, of whatever persuasion, had possibly a greater claim on his energies and talents than Home Rule. Indeed, he believed that the second would eventually heal the first.

Already his reputation as a stirring and persuasive orator was province-wide and he was frequently in demand as a speaker on nationalist platforms. He was at Sheepbridge at the invitation of Michael McCartan, the local MP, and had made sure to have a number of INFed supporters in the crowd. Three hundred came from Lurgan while Fr Frank O'Hare, one of Devlin's earliest supporters and lifelong friend, had brought a contingent from Hilltown, a few miles away, to prevent if necessary 'division' at the meeting. The invitation of Healy to a strongly Dillonite rally had been a matter of formal politeness and his actual speech was unexceptional but he was still howled down. Afterwards he approached his rival, who was his junior by sixteen years, with the words 'Your name is Devlin and I see you have your men well placed.' It was typical of Healy's edge that he seemed to introduce a personal spleen in what could have been a gentleman's agreement to differ. He seemed intent on preserving a kind of maverick independence in spite of his ecclesiastical support and of having as patron William Martin Murphy (1844–1919), the transport chief and main thrust of the Dublin lock-out of 1913.

On 12 July that same year, in a speech in Liverpool, Healy strongly attacked the early moves by Dillon and Redmond in forming a united nationalist party (not achieved until 1900) and continued his reckless independent stance for the next ten years. The attempt to control Healy by having him on the inside rather than a deliberate enemy outside worked for some time but he was eventually expelled from both branches of INFed, from the British league on 7 November 1895, and from the executive in Ireland six days later. He remained deeply suspicious of the Liberal Party and was at ease with such Conservatives as Gerald Balfour (1853–1945) and George Wyndham (1863–1913), both of whom played a significant part in the final settling of the Irish land question. He had always resented Parnell's metaphorical 'whipping-in' of the IPP and worked assiduously to prevent the same kind of central political control being vested in Redmond with Dillon as *éminence grise*.

Since Devlin's commitment to Dillon was absolute, enmity with Healy was unavoidable but in other circumstances they would have been uneasy bedfellows. Both were brilliant speakers, with Devlin lacking Healy's mordant savagery; both eventually enjoyed clerical approval; and both had talents that were wonderfully complementary if they could have been persuaded to be allies. Healy's final dismissal from the IPP in December 1900 was inevitable after his founding and flaunting of his People's Rights Association in 1897. In this initiative he was supported financially by Murphy and clergy from all over Ireland. He left the UIL with a typical Healy flourish: 'The honourable member for Cork [O'Brien] has created two united Irish parties – of which I am one.'

4
Beating the Bishop

A POSSIBLE SOURCE OF HEALY'S IMPATIENCE with Devlin was the latter's apparent preoccupation with unimportant or at least irrelevant matters like working conditions in Belfast factories and the lack of Catholic representation on the city council. Only three Catholics had ever served, two Liberals and one Conservative, and none were nationalist. This general lack of representation was reflected in employment opportunities. Of corporation employees only two were Catholic, and local boards with a membership of 143 Protestants and thirteen Catholics employed 335 Protestants while the twenty-seven Catholics who worked for them had the most menial jobs.

Since Dorrian's time as bishop Belfast Catholics were no longer content to acquiesce in quietism. Bishop McAllister had continued his predecessor's policy of active if guarded political advance. Parnellism had meant that Belfast nationalists were no longer cut off from mainstream politics and, though the man was vigorously condemned, especially by the senior clergy, his campaign and his methods were still valid. McAllister was ill for most of 1894 and it became clear that a replacement would soon have to be found. His own choice would have been Daniel McCashin, his vicar-general, but in the rather murky world of ecclesiastical politics nothing was quite straightforward. The other candidate, one that had greater Vatican influence, was the finally successful Henry Henry, president of St Malachy's College, the diocesan junior seminary, and he was ordained bishop in St Patrick's Church, Donegall Street on 22 September 1895.

He had joined the staff of St Malachy's immediately upon ordination in 1870 and had been appointed president in 1876 when he was thirty. This fast-track 'promotion' was not uncharacteristic of diocesan practice throughout Ireland and continued to occur for as long as the seminaries were clerically run. These men were efficient and conscientious, though some might have preferred a pastoral rather than an academic career. Those who were later made parish priests, or in Henry's case bishop, had had little experience of ordinary parish work. This might have been problematic in the ordinary running of the diocese, though episcopal shortcomings were compensated by the parish clergy, but when the bishop took over the politics of nationalist Belfast, his lack of knowledge of the real life of his flock became quite patent.

He had the same concern about the lack of representation of Catholics in the council as Devlin but disagreed about who those representatives should be. He took his responsibility as a spiritual leader, stretched to the widest sense of that word, very seriously, confiding in his friend Michael Kelly (1850–1940), the Rector of the Irish College in Rome and afterwards Archbishop of Sydney, that he was 'deeply impressed by the *onus* imposed upon me in this heretical see'. What soon became clear was that his model was Bishop Dorrian, whose active supporter he was when, as president of St Malachy's, he was active in the campaign against the Christian Brothers.

Henry's political career began when the city fathers asked parliament for a redistribution of the city wards. It was clear that, in spite of the obvious injustice, the significant minority of Catholics (84,992 out of a total population of 349,180, according to the 1901 census) would have virtually no representation. The Catholic fraction of the total population, at just under 25 percent, would change little over the next seventy years, varying by no more than a few points and highest at 27.5 percent in 1961. INFed, anxious to be involved in any campaign for better representation, had appointed Devlin to a

Catholic Committee. In response Henry called a meeting in the twenty-year-old St Mary's Hall in Bank Place, ostensibly to discuss tactics but really to announce the tactics that he had already determined. Devlin and other representatives of the INFed were not formally invited but were part of the attendance of at least seven hundred people.

The mere 'politicians' were not welcome since Henry's aim was not political in the wider sense of nationalism, but rather municipal and concerned with local Catholic civil rights. He caused to be formed a Catholic Representation Association (CRA) out of which he fashioned a committee of forty members, thirteen of whom were Down and Connor priests. Devlin (and Dillon) assumed that, once some positive discrimination would allow a modicum of Catholic representation, the Federation, as the only true representative of the majority of Catholics in the city, would pick the candidates and run the elections. Henry, however, had no intention of allowing interference from the people's choice. His troops were going to be Catholics of substance, as became clear in later contests.

The nationalist wished-for ideal of a change in the voting system, a kind of PR with a single transferable vote, then known as 'cumulative voting', was not going to be granted. The House was adamant about the efficacy of the 'first past the post' and still held to it for another 120 years. The same system was regarded as perfectly appropriate for municipal elections as well. The other means of permitting a little representation for the Catholic minority was to have the extended city territory divided into twenty-five small wards with boundaries so drawn that Catholics would control five of them. It was short of their notional entitlement of one quarter but it would have represented a marked improvement on the older system.

These arrangements were fought for at a sitting of a select committee established by Gerald Balfour after representation by Vesey Knox MP, who, though Protestant, was a member of the IPP. The committee heard from twenty-eight witnesses and asked many questions but Devlin was excluded from Henry's list of suitable people. Devlin afterwards told Dillon that the bishop did not want politicians and he admitted that he was 'too much of a politician'. It is hard to see the logic in Henry's attitude unless he rather snobbishly thought that a better class of delegate might be able to make a better case. And if the word 'political' had any meaning in the bishop's lexicon his own stance was political without the implication of finesse that the word should possess.

In fact neither of the options was accepted. The parliamentary committee decided that fifteen wards was sufficient for a city the size of Belfast but offered as a kind of palliative that two wards, Falls and Smithfield, would be Catholic-controlled. The cumulative voting system would have been preferable from a nationalist point of view since there were pockets of Catholic residents in other parts of the city, in the Markets, in Short Strand, Dock, Ballymacarrett, Shore Road, and Ardoyne, who would have no representation. The kind of delegates approved by Henry would later be selected as candidates in the municipal elections. Only one lived in west Belfast; the others – two surgeons, two prosperous estate agents, an architect grown rich on commissions from the Church, three solicitors, a brewer, and a publican – lived comfortably with their Protestant neighbours in the suburbs north and south of the city centre.

Against this Devlin's group had only one doctor (with a dispensary on the Falls Road), a solicitor who lived above his parents' pub, while the rest were 'in trade': a publican, a bookie, an eating-house proprietor, and a butcher who sold his wares from a basket as he walked the streets. As Fr Henry Laverty, who had succeeded Henry as president of St Malachy's College, was to say during a later electoral campaign, 'We do not want on the public boards of Belfast men without education, men without manners, men who would be a disgrace to the Catholic body.'

Vesey Knox, with assistance from Healy, had won a small victory and the bishop was pleased, convinced that it was the calibre of the witnesses (all members of his Catholic Committee) that had impressed the select committee of the House of Commons. He called a meeting in St Mary's Hall when the bill became law as a kind of victory rally. Knox and Healy were given a vote of thanks achieved by a margin of only three votes, but an amendment by Devlin praising the IPP and John Dillon was lost. It was the beginning of a schism that over the next twelve years was to debilitate nationalist politics in Belfast.

Henry proposed a Belfast Catholic Association (BCA), with himself as president *ex officio* and most of the key positions held by clergy, and the rest by successful middle-class lay Catholics of the sort described above. The blueprint for this 'Healyite' body was published at a meeting in the usual venue on 25 October 1896. To Devlin it was as crude a disenfranchisement as anything perpetrated by the Unionist council. He knew that it was the INFed that was the true voice of the greater part of Catholic/nationalist Belfast and immediately proposed that the intended association had no place in municipal or national politics. Henry as chairman declared the amendment 'out of order', causing the normally imperturbable Devlin to leave the hall shouting, 'We will fight it at the November elections.' The BCA and other avatars of the bishop's political cohort had in common the aim of 'the religious, moral, social and educational benefit of the District'. Members had to take a near-Masonic pledge of personal loyalty to Henry and were expected to 'do all that may be required when called upon by the President'.

The split still had Parnellite echoes. The *Irish News*, that had been originally founded to counter Parnellism and as such had the blessing of Bishop McAllister, remained the voice of the INFed but instinctively tried to keep on the right side of the vengeful crosier. Their London correspondent was the same ultra-Healyite Vesey Knox who deliberately ignored INFed activities; such emphasis led Devlin to the belief that the paper had sold out to Henry. As he should have realised, and would have admitted if chided privately, the paper had to tiptoe through the minefield of current politics. As the non-specific voice of Catholic Belfast (indeed of nationalist Ulster) it had to cover all aspects of the political situation. It could not afford to alienate a bishop; the shareholders were all practising Catholics and were used to accepting episcopal 'diktats' as gospel. Its working policy was to reflect the *national* struggle in supporting the IPP while seeking to find in the bishop's BCA a legitimate and effective means for the amelioration of the condition of its readers. By a subtle semantic shift, what was formerly the CRA became known as the BCA, suggesting a wider constituency. In spite of the reasonableness of the *Irish News*'s stance Devlin, who had once worked on the editorial staff and held shares in the company, felt sufficiently betrayed to start a rival newspaper. As he rather intemperately put it, the paper 'had gone over body and soul to Bishop Henry, and we may shortly look for a dose of Healyism'.

It is significant that from Devlin's first meeting with Healy, enmity was inevitable. To the Belfastman, Healy was the enemy because his maverick independence, called 'factionalism' by Devlin, seemed to him to weaken the unity and strength of the nationalist cause. In the same way, when William O'Brien later urged a policy of 'conference and conciliation and consent' with southern Unionists, Devlin moved against him too as a 'factionalist', not because of personal animus nor of any personal distaste of the opposition, but because Devlin believed that the structure and cohesion so carefully built up by Parnell must not be weakened. In that sense he remained a Parnellite and welcomed the reunification of the party, even admitting that Redmond, whom he probably regarded as too soft, was a better candidate for leadership that the austere flinty Dillon.

He willingly became Redmond's man in Ulster but did it because of Dillon's instructions, and he continued to rely upon the older man's advice and follow his directions. In fact neither Dillon nor Redmond was in a position to advise him in his struggle with the BCA and its master. It was really because of Devlin's insistence that they concerned themselves with northeast Ulster at all. The battle, they erroneously believed, would be fought in Dublin and Westminster. The northern Unionists objected vocally to the blatant ward-rigging that would allow three Catholic councillors and one alderman to take their Corporation seats but, allowing for their instinctive near-paranoiac eternal vigilance, there was nothing in the situation then to cause them any disquiet. That would come later.

Since the *Irish News* directors had come out publicly in support of the BCA, Devlin, though he had relied on the paper's support until then, at least temporarily regarded the publication as having gone over to the enemy. He called his new paper, to be published weekly, with a certain amount of deliberate mischievousness, the *Northern Star*. This had been the name of the organ of the United Irishmen (1792–7), founded by Samuel Neilson (1761–1803), and was very popular until it ceased publication after its offices were wrecked by the Monaghan militia. As such it fitted neatly with the coming centenary of the 1798 rising. It was also the name of the paper set up in 1867 by Andrew McKenna – the Fenian sympathiser who had been called a 'clever but troublesome and dangerous man' by Dorrian – in opposition to the bishop's own *Ulster Examiner*. Thus, the new paper's nationalist and mildly anti-episcopal credentials were made clear and one can be sure that it gave the new owner a certain gleeful satisfaction on that account. As a weekly it would have a less immediate impact than the daily *Irish News* but it could afford a more leisurely and thoughtful approach to the political situation. The publication heralded itself as 'A National Democratic Weekly' and its stated aims were

> ... strenuously to advocate the rights of the working classes to all that is claimed for them by their trade organizations, and while strongly maintaining the rights of the Catholics of Belfast and Ulster to their fair proportion of representation on all boards and bodies, care will be taken to avoid encouraging any attempt to stir into activity the spirit of religious bigotry.

The nod towards non-sectarianism was not just public piety but a genuinely held view by Devlin who was conscious of the Protestants living in west Belfast, many of whom were no better off than their Catholic neighbours. His main adversary, however, was the BCA, who seemed to have usurped the right to represent those whom Devlin regarded as his own. The BCA members, he believed, knew nothing of the true condition of the ordinary people of the city. As an instinctive politician at the beginning of the campaign, he made an electoral pact with the residual Parnellites, adding two of these to the six of his own INFed. These were, as we have seen, mainly lower middle class, shopkeepers, bookmakers, small publicans. The election literature reflected the needs of the candidates and of the people they hoped to represent. They wanted 'better houses, cheaper gas, better-lit streets and cheaper tram fares for the toilers of neglected west Belfast' but also cared for 'the over-rated and overtaxed shopkeepers'.

Devlin was not himself a candidate but he was the organiser of the campaign and as such came in for most of the attacks from the *Irish News*. His manifesto stated that their sole aim was the upholding of a broadminded nationality and the safeguarding and promotion of Catholic interests. It should have been the *Irish News*'s own position but Devlin was briefly their target; he was twenty-six and, in the eyes of Bishop Henry's men, lacked the *gravitas* necessary for his position as the leader of northern nationalists. A certain amount of the leading Catholic newspaper's attitude would have been conditioned by the fact that the bishop was deeply involved in the campaign. In the ecclesiastical atmosphere of the time its editorial staff, and board of directors, could no more have opposed the bishop than *L'Osservatore Romano* criticise the pope.[1]

One of the BCA candidates called Devlin a 'youthful potentate' and 'manager of Sam Young's Punch and Judy show'. The bishop essentially owned St Mary's Hall and was able to forbid its use to the Joint Committee, as the ad hoc alliance called itself for their meetings. They responded with open-air meetings in Dunville Park, where the tone of the speeches was distinctly socialist – 'the old fight of capital against labour'. Even when, at Devlin's request, Davitt arrived for an eve-of-poll rally, St Mary's was not available. Instead a dramatic procession with many torches lit up the Falls Road when 20,000 people marched from the centre of the city.

In the municipal elections held in November 1897, the BCA won all eight seats, with 62 percent of the votes in Falls and 60 percent in Smithfield. The Church party led by Henry had won decisively, and Devlin had the lesson taught him again that in Catholic Belfast at least the influence of the clergy militant was too strong for a lay organisation to combat. The bludgeoning style of Dorrian had re-emerged in Henry, and McAllister's attempt at involving the laity in consultation seemed a temporary aberration.

The personal enmity between Henry and Devlin continued. Some time later Henry denounced him for 'encouraging a handful of Catholics in a vain attempt to disassociate Irish nationalist politics from the hallowing influence of religion'. Henry had won the battle but not the war; that would last until his inept handling of publicity and his loss of control of his own clergy diminished him as bishop as well as leader of Belfast's Catholics.

The struggle with the bishop was intermittent but it continued for Henry's whole term of office. There were years of attrition punctuated by sharp encounters at election times. Not all of Devlin's energies were expended in confrontation with the bishop. Some was concerned with sheer personal economics. He still lived in the family home, now at 41 Alexander Street West, not far from Hamill Street, but closer to St Peter's, the citadel of the lower Falls. He began to think that it was perhaps time for him to leave the city and he sought help from his friends in Ireland and Britain to find him an equivalent position in a bar in Dublin or London.

'A time of quietude here may do no harm and perhaps my severance from Belfast may tend to the good.' He added, 'For over six years I have been spending all I could earn.'

In spite of this belief he was persuaded to stay in Belfast, still refusing financial help and the offer of more appropriate employment than that of under-manager of a liquor store. He was soon fired with new energy and the organising ability that, apart from his eloquence, was his outstanding gift, spurred him on to success in two significant events in 1898: the centenary of the rising of 1798 and the acceptance of the northern leadership of the United Irish League, the ancillary body of the IPP, founded by William O'Brien that year.

Most of the years 1902 and 1903 were spent travelling in America, Canada, Australia and New Zealand but he still found it possible to become the unopposed member for Kilkenny. During that first decade of the twentieth century he also resuscitated the Ancient Order of Hibernians, and successfully stood for his native West Belfast, while continuing to run and enlarge the northern branch of the UIL.

The enmity with Henry could at times be tedious and was certainly wasteful of time and talent. The BCA still held the municipal seats but continued to provide prima facie evidence that they were Church-controlled and that Home Rule would see the same situation obtained in other northern dioceses. Devlin's undoubted charm and wit hid a steely loathing of what he called 'factionalism'. Henry's elite BCA was, in Devlin's eyes, deleterious to the final cause of independence; they were well-meaning, as far as they had the right to think for themselves, but even they must have realised that as rich Catholics they were totally unrepresentative of the majority of their fellow nationalists. Henry either could not see this or did not much care. A typical move was the founding in April 1897 of St Peter's Catholic Club (later known as the Central Catholic Club and, later still, colloquially and permanently, as the 'Three Cs') at 123 Royal Avenue in what had been a hotel. This he felt necessary because of the existence of many grander gentlemen's clubs frequented by members 'of the other side of the house', to use the contemporary euphemism.

Its desirable clients were 'young men engaged in business', and there would be both social and educational opportunities for those who wished to avail of them. Phrases like 'a source of enlightenment' and 'a means of innocent amusement' were bandied about. In his inauguration speech Henry 'dwelt on the benefits, moral, mental and social, which it will be the means of conferring on its members', as reported in the *Irish News*, then almost a diocesan journal, so closely did it follow the episcopal line; but these gestures were seen by Devlin as polite meaningless words, imperatives at the time, as were the *obbligato* references to the 'terribly unhealthy lives lived by many thousands of operatives, particularly in the mills that are a matter of worldwide notoriety'. The number of members rapidly grew to 537 in the first six months but not many took the bishop at his word, as reported in the *Irish News,* that 'the humblest working-man will be as welcome in its halls as his wealthiest brother'. The paper's reporter observed that 'all classes may not receive equal benefits, for all will not feel the same keen want of such a club'.

It was something of an understatement; such an institution was by definition elitist and catered for those who had countless opportunities for entertainment and enlightenment elsewhere. Its members lived at ease in leafy suburbs and regarded the 'Three Cs' as another perquisite. The bishop was president and the committee was dominated by senior clergy and stalwarts of the BCA. For the people who mattered it provided convenient access to each other at times of decision-making and it was a less obvious venue for top-level Catholic planning than the nearby St Mary's Hall. Unfortunately it was seen as evidence of Catholics on the rise, embodying the threat from the Vatican against Protestantism, that bulwark against popery and the protector of the 'ould cause /That gave us our freedom, religion and laws', as the comic song 'The Ould Orange Flute' put it.

As the years passed the CCC lost its glitter; it no longer was a palatial resort for the Catholic rich but it remained a convenience for after-hours and Sabbath drinking still extant in the 1950s, where snooker and table tennis might pass a wet Sunday afternoon before a session in the bar. One of the legends associated with the 'Three Cs' oddly enough makes reference to Devlin. Members – all male Catholics – could introduce occasional guests and, after a successful game of snooker, one member with his Protestant friend repaired to the bar. It was the stranger's first visit and he studied three large portraits that adorned the wall. They showed three iconic figures from Catholic/Irish history: Devlin, Pope Pius XII and Daniel O'Connell, the Emancipist. The Catholic member noticed his preoccupation and prompted him to speak. 'Well,' said the friend pointing, 'that's Wee Joe and thon's the pope but who's the third "C"?'

In its heyday, however, it remained an affront to Devlin for its exclusiveness, its evidence of factionalism and its sectarianism. He found it a mockery of all he stood for. Three years later, in Berry Street, just a furlong away on the opposite side of Royal Avenue, he opened the National Club that soon had as many members as the Central Catholic Club. It was not as grand as the bishop's but served its purpose better. Devlin was delighted to report to Davitt that 'Nationalists will have a club and hall second to none in Belfast.' It too far outlasted its founder, finally disappearing in the welter of re-development, some intended and some imposed by the Ulster Troubles.

The IPP had rediscovered unity under Redmond by January 1900 but in Belfast – and essentially in east Ulster – the schism continued. In March, Devlin, ever the peacemaker for practical as well as emotional reasons, made another attempt at reconciliation which would have been graciously granted – on certain terms. Henry added condescension to his native arrogance. All he required was that the local UIL, in the persons of Devlin and his friend John Rooney, who had been derided by members of the BCA during the 1897 municipal election campaign as 'the proprietor of an oyster room', should satisfy certain conditions.[2] Devlin informed Dillon in one of the many letters written to his mentor over a period of nearly forty years that all that was required was that they express 'humble contrition for… past conduct… and profound regret', coupled with 'an appeal by us to his Lordship to allow us to conduct the national affairs of Belfast with cooperation of the Catholic Association and subject to, and under his Lordship's guidance'. Devlin's response that such a move would make it 'impossible for self-respecting men to take any part in the public affairs of their own city' was mild considering the rage and the disappointment that he must have felt personally at Henry's recalcitrance, and tactically at the continuing damage that such public dissension was doing to the cause. Support for the UIL in Belfast had begun to erode and nationalism there was written off as a bad bargain by the rest of the country.

Henry persisted in his obdurate, and to the majority, damaging stance. In October 1903, H O Arnold-Foster, the sitting member for West Belfast since he defeated Sexton in 1892, was appointed Secretary of State for War by Arthur James Balfour (1848–1930), Conservative Prime Minister (1902–5), and according to the parliamentary rules of the time had to resign his seat and stand for re-election. Devlin, MP for Kilkenny since 1902, was living in London but felt that the time had come for another attempt at winning the seat back. John Rooney and Thomas Maguire, a local solicitor, who were Devlin's men on the spot, thought that according to their figures they were only 280 votes short of a majority. The BCA, having claimed the right to organise the register of voters, held an updated list, an essential for getting the voters out since there were no considerations of things as irrelevant as policies. Nationalists would vote for the nationalist candidate and if enough of them could be delivered to the booths, there might be a change of member.

Immediately the rivalry with the BCA became a paramount issue and the need for wooing the bishop, however distasteful, was accepted. Devlin asked him to supervise a meeting to choose an agreed candidate, adding that Redmond would attend. Henry refused to accept without an assurance 'from you and from Mr Redmond that you would put an end at once to this foolish opposition to the Catholic Association and to me. I would then feel justified in entertaining the request contained in your letter.' There was no time for diplomacy. Even before the bishop's letter arrived a 'unity' candidate was found in Patrick Dempsey, the proprietor of the Linen Hall hotel, who in happier times had organised a dinner in honour of the then twenty-two-year-old Devlin. He had the same social status as any member of the BCA; his brothers, Alexander, a senior hospital consultant, and James, an alderman in the city corporation, were members of the bishop's association while another brother, William, was a parish priest in the diocese. Dempsey's credentials were impeccable, with obvious appeal to both sides of the divide but he was not the bishop's choice. His papers were handed in only three days before polling day but Devlin's band of active electioneers were out in force. Arnold-Foster, with mild distaste, did not engage in electioneering at all, staying in London and claiming, it was felt falsely, that he was ill.

The BCA refused to make available the updated register that would have been Dempsey's best hope while William Martin Murphy, Healy's sponsor and later organiser of the notorious Dublin lock-out in 1913, attacked him. In his widely read *Irish Independent* he claimed that 'the only possible result of the insane policy of the local leaders of the UIL, approved as it is by Mr John Redmond, will be the infliction of a damaging defeat on the home rule cause'. The fragmentary nature of Redmond's 'united' party was clearly demonstrated to both Healy's and Henry's satisfaction. Yet Murphy was Healy's patron – they shared the same strong clericalist views – and his People's Rights Party was a greater source of division than even the BCA. The result was another Unionist victory by 241 votes.

The bishop's action, even to his supporters, seemed quixotic; he and his senior clerics did not vote and there were immediately accusations that he had made a secret deal with Arnold-Foster by which he would withhold support for Dempsey in exchange for a bill on university education consonant with the hierarchy's requirements. It was another example of Catholic Church priorities, where doctrinal matters took precedence over matters merely national.

Devlin fought on, forming a strong new political machine consisting of the UIL combined with a body known as the National Registration Union (NRU). It was able to deliver the crushing blow that effectively meant the beginning of the end of Henry's political power and even his credibility. In spite of mounting criticism, often from his own clergy, he set his BCA against the UIL/NRU complex in the municipal elections in January 1904, and again many of the Catholic voters were bullied in a kind of spiritual blackmail into voting for Henry's men. The UIL got only 42 percent of the votes in the safe Catholic ghettos of Falls and Smithfield, but even the conservative *Catholic Herald* in London had to report that many complaints had been made to Rome by Henry's own clergy and large numbers of the laity: 'The Bishop of Down and Connor may be a very saintly and holy man but as a bishop he has brought disorder, chaos and the most violent animosities.'

Henry's Miltonic response was to dub his UIL opponents as 'rebels of Lucifer'. The blurring in his mind between his spiritual and his political authority was made obvious by another public outburst when appointments were being made for the city's water board. As Thomas Maguire stated in his memorandum to Cardinal Gotti in the Vatican: 'The board is not concerned in any possible way with questions affecting Religion but the occasion was nevertheless availed of by Dr Henry to publicly denounce, in churches, halls and also in the public streets Catholic citizens who dared to question the exclusive privilege of his lordship to the absolute nomination of candidates.' His extreme political ineptitude, to put it no more strongly, was made obvious again when, in 1905, the clerically approved support of the IPP engendered countrywide collections for its funds. Henry gave the task of collecting the diocese's contribution to the BCA. Their contribution to the general fund was immediately returned on Redmond's specific instructions.

In spite of all the appalling publicity Henry's conscience was clear; devotional practice in his city and diocese was never more sincere nor expressed with such public fervour. His venture into publishing with the Belfast Catholic Truth Society was extremely successful. Booklets and pamphlets about Catholic doctrine, church history, and saints' lives were made available in stalls at the rear of churches for a few pence and the success of the scheme caused it to evolve into a Catholic Truth Society for the whole of Ireland, with headquarters in Dublin. Early in his episcopate he had made peace with the Passionists, whose church in Ardoyne catered for an outlying pocket of Catholics in the north of the city. The dispute about the right to collect alms in other churches besides their own was settled only after a face-to-face meeting with Mathias Raus, the superior general. He encouraged the Redemptorist Fathers to set up a monastery at Clonard between the warring Falls Road and Shankill, and established a college of education in the Upper Falls Road.

Even as late as 1907, the year before his death, the Catholic Defence Association (CDA), as the BCA became after its petulant dissolution by Henry in 1906, had a picture of him in full canonicals seated on the episcopal throne as centrepiece. Its main proponent was P J Magee, Henry's strongest supporter, who remained a bitter opponent of Devlin, trying to unseat him in the 1910 general election. The only items of panoply missing were the mitre and the often-wielded crosier. The face is grim, arrogant and politically inappropriate. The left-hand panel called on Belfast Catholics to 'Rally round your reverend bishop.' Underneath a shortened CV was given: 'The Most Rev. H. Henry, D.D., Bishop of Down and Connor. Consecrated 22nd Sept. 1895, Emancipated Belfast Catholics 1896. Persecuted by irreconcilable factionists and denied the right to direct and guide

Catholic Organization.' On the right side of the poster were posed a number of questions:

> Answer:-
> Do you approve of organized rebellion against Ecclesiastical authority?
> Do you approve of the alleged free "democracy" – politics divorced from religion?
> Do you approve of yielding to the forces of secularism?
> Do you approve of the Berry Street War Cry – "Less of the Bishop"?
> If you do not – and we know you do not – Vote for…

Underneath were the names of the CDA candidates for Smithfield and Falls, O'Connell and Savage, and Magee and McDonnell. The last words were the unexceptionable 'God Save Ireland' – except for 'from Anticlericalism', written in small print underneath.

It was quite a performance but really a last hurrah. The united UIL/NRU reversed the trend of the previous ten years when the 'safe' nationalist wards of Falls and Smithfield had been created, obtaining 59 percent of the vote. Devlin was no longer 'potboy' in Samuel Young's Kelly's Cellars but a Westminster MP who, elected on a majority of sixteen in 1906, held the seat until 1922.

Henry had used his episcopal authority to punish any of the Down and Connor clergy who did not give full assent to his political manoeuvring. He ignored a diocesan tradition that parish priests had tenure and could not be moved without their consent. Any who went against the BCA could find themselves transferred to distant parishes and for that reason few risked revealing their true political views. It was, of course, strictly within his powers to move his clergy as he thought appropriate. In this he was supported by Cardinal Michael Logue, who remarked that 'things are coming to a pretty pass in Ireland when a bishop cannot change his curates without leave of the newspapers'. Logue was, of course, no friend of Devlin, largely because of the latter's control of the AOH, an organisation execrated by him as 'a pest, a cruel tyranny, and an organised system of blackguardism', an outburst not unworthy of Henry himself.

By the spring of 1908 the bishop was a spent force politically and showed signs even of pastoral disarray. His attempts at control were ineffectual and savoured of mean-spiritedness. His appointing of Henry Laverty, his close ally and successor as president of St Malachy's College, to the rich parish of St Matthew's in east Belfast was unexceptionable – seminary presidents usually got plums. His refusal to promote Fr McCashin, who could so easily have been his bishop – in the *terna*, the straw poll taken among parish priests when the appointment of a new bishop is imminent, he had had the same number of votes as Henry – away from the small and poor parish of St Malachy's that included the Catholic Markets, was clearly vindictive. One priest, Fr John Nolan, had disobeyed Henry's instruction not to support the UIL/Parnellite alliance and Henry had initiated formal proceedings against him. Nolan took his case personally to Rome and was received sympathetically. Henry's standing there and at home was further eroded when nearly a score of diocesan priests complained to the Vatican of the bishop's unfair treatment of his clerical charges.

The Holy See was already worried at the number of 'reservations and censures' instituted by Henry. These were technical terms, the first requiring that certain nominated sins be confessed personally to the bishop while 'censures' involved personal humiliation from pulpits through the diocese because of public scandals. Prelates were given such powers to deal with heinous offences against faith and morals but Henry added the doubtful extra sins of not voting for BCA candidates and supporting Devlin's UIL. Logue hastened to defend him, writing to Archbishop William Walsh (1841–1921), then and later a strong nationalist, that 'Poor Dr Henry was harassed almost beyond endurance. A number of his priests have got completely out of his hands and he can do nothing with them.' Their refusal to obey Henry was strictly in the field of temporal affairs. He made no distinction between his respected authority as ecclesiastical superior and the assumed one as political leader of the diocese and the city of Belfast in particular.

Henry's death was sudden. Chastened by the admonitions delivered by Cardinal Gotti in Rome, he took no further part in politics, concentrating on purely spiritual duties. On Sunday, 8 March 1908 he had a full schedule, administering the sacrament of Confirmation in two city churches and chairing a meeting of the St Vincent de Paul Society in St Mary's Hall before having an evening meal in the presbytery in Chapel Lane. He was due to attend a sacred concert in the hall that evening and found it convenient to eat in the presbytery rather than travel to his home in Chichester Park, off the Antrim Road. As he climbed the stairs to the main hall he complained of a slight weakness but took his seat. Almost immediately he collapsed. No fewer than five doctors in the audience attended him but there was nothing they could do except confirm his death as 'resulting from cardiac failure'.

The funeral crowds were large, as appropriate for a religious and community leader, and newspaper reports approached the hagiographic, dwelling on his charities and pastoral care. The *Belfast News Letter* of 9 March skated lightly over his political career: 'He was a keen politician and as founder and president of the Catholic Association he paid close attention to electoral and municipal matters.' This clever non-committal summary may reflect a lack of awareness of the internecine turmoil that convulsed Catholic Belfast for a dozen years. The *Derry Standard*, in its short report of his death on 9 March, observed that his political stance had split those under his pastoral care into two regularly opposed camps.

The *Irish News* marked the occasion by surrounding its coverage with black. It deemed any discussion about Henry's political career and the BCA as inappropriate and preferred a near-hagiographic tone. Its coverage of the removal of his body to St Patrick's Church in Donegall Street on Tuesday, 10 March was as elaborate as one might expect in what had been the diocesan organ. It described the crowds outside the church where the Requiem Mass was to be held and at Chichester Park, where the faithful waited in the cold and wet to accompany the cortège. In the custom of the time, and in common with other Catholic papers, it listed all the priests of the diocese as 'among those present or represented'. The list included the clerical staff of St Malachy's College, one of whom, the twenty-five-year-old Rev Daniel Mageean, would be Bishop of Down and Connor by

1929. The body 'was enclosed in a suite of coffins' – one of lead – and at about three o'clock it began its slow journey down the Antrim Road to the church where it would lie in state until the following day; then, at 1pm, it was taken to Milltown Cemetery via Donegall Street, Royal Avenue, Castle Street, Divis Street and the Falls Road. Henry was the first bishop to be buried in those burial grounds first acquired by his predecessor and exemplar, Patrick Dorrian, in 1866. Among hundreds of tributes sent by bishops, priests and 'prominent Catholic Belfastmen', many from outside the diocese, was one which the *Irish News* editor had decided deserved its own headed paragraph. It read: 'Deeply shocked and grieved by the Bishop's death. Please accept respectful sympathy.' It was signed: 'Joseph Devlin.'

When one considers the cordial relations that Devlin managed with other bishops, especially Patrick O'Donnell of Raphoe, one wonders if some working system could not have been managed between these two leaders of Catholic Belfast. The bishop's temperament was against it; he was arrogant, even snobbish, and almost pathologically anxious to have at least some Catholics thought well of by the Protestant middle class of the city. He seems genuinely to have believed that such acceptance would have been to the advantage of working class people. Though he would have been unlikely to admit it, his wish for if not actual ingratiation with the majority then a workable if stilted amity, marked him as more like Denvir than Dorrian. When Queen Victoria celebrated her golden jubilee in April 1897 he wrote to the lord mayor of Belfast saying that he had 'great pleasure in authorising you to place my name in the list of subscribers to the proposed Victoria hospital for £100'.

Devlin, as a traditional Catholic, would have understood and sympathised with the exacting nature of Henry's pastoral conscience. Yet his upbringing, education, and academic pre-episcopal career isolated him from the greater part of his flock. Historical speculation is, of all parlour games, the most pointless, yet a situation that might have occurred, an alliance of two bright dedicated men, even if a generation apart in age, might have resulted in a more accelerated amelioration of conditions in their city. Even had such an alliance existed, and had Henry survived to continue in it, they would surely have come up against twin (and probably insuperable) obstacles: the recalcitrance of Unionism and the growing rebellious fervour of the resuscitated Irish Revolutionary Brotherhood (IRB). In full flow Henry's rhetoric would have added strength and certainty to the Unionist belief that 'Home Rule was Rome Rule' and his response to Eoin MacNeill's Irish Volunteers, Arthur Griffith's Sinn Féin and James Connolly's (1868–1916) Citizen Army would surely have been the same as that of the prelates who condemned Fenianism, the lineal descendants of which these movements were.

There would be one last call on the bishop's name. In the general election held in January 1910, P J Magee, Henry's greatest supporter, stood against Devlin in West Belfast as an Independent Nationalist. His election handbill harangued the constituents, as it turned out, unsuccessfully, with an appeal from an episcopal ghost:

> Catholics of West Belfast a voice from a lonely and unadorned grave in Milltown Cemetery, deserted except by the prayers of the Faithful and True, calls upon you to remember the falsehoods and calumnies of the past twelve years, to revere the bishop's memory and thus free the sacred soil of West Belfast from all connection with this puerile and vulgar little leader of an ecclesiastical rebellion.

The 'puerile and vulgar little leader' held the seat, beating both Magee, who received only seventy-five votes, and his Unionist opponent by a margin of 587. A second election had to be held, straddling December 1910 and January 1911, because of the struggle with the House of Lords and this time, in a straight battle of Unionist and nationalist, Devlin won by 463 votes. The lonely grave in Milltown remained unadorned.

5
'Who Fears to Speak...?'

DEVLIN'S TEMPERAMENT WAS SUCH, AT LEAST in his younger years, that occasional bouts of depression were successfully banished by new social or political challenges. In the last couple of years of the nineteenth century it was his work for the UIL and plans for the celebration of the centenary of the United Irishmen's rising that gave him new energy and purpose, and reassured him that his place was in Belfast.

Though Belfast had played no actual part in the rebellion, being too closely guarded by the militia and with the authorities kept well abreast of the rebels' intentions by informers, Antrim and Ballynahinch, the two Ulster battles, were near enough to allow the involvement of some of its young men. Word of the centenary had generated a number of commemorative ballads to add to the many published in *The Nation* in April 1843. Possibly the best known of the later ones was 'Boolavogue' by P J McCall (1861–1919), written specially for the Dublin centenary celebrations, but 'The Memory of the Dead' by John Kells Ingram (1823–1907) got a new lease of life. A noted Trinity academic and stern anti-Home Ruler, Ingram wrote it when he was nineteen. Its opening verse figured widely fifty-five years after its first appearance:

Who fears to speak of Ninety-eight?

Who blushes at the name?
When cowards mock the patriot's fate,
Who hangs his head for shame?
He's all a knave or half a slave
Who slights his country thus;
But a true man, like you, man,
Will fill your glass with us.

The reaction in non-nationalist Belfast was a mixture of the fear and blushing as anticipated by Ingram. The coverage by the *Belfast News Letter,* the chief Unionist organ, combined condescension and mild mockery. The reporting of the event was conditioned by a sense of the imminent violence that caused the Riot Act formally to be read in the Shankill Road on the night of 6–7 June 1898.

Devlin was asked by Dillon in the summer of 1897 to become president of the Belfast and Ulster United Centenary Association, effectively making him the grandmaster of the celebrations. There was a certain irony in the nationalists of Ireland, famous for their constitutional non-violent approach to the Irish question, wishing to celebrate an event that in its violence and bloodshed was formally anathema to all the INFed stood for. Dillon and the rest shrugged off the inconsistency by suggesting that things and attitudes had altered greatly in the hundred years since the event. Devlin must have felt some dissonance and was anxious to avoid any confrontation with the Orange Order, knowing how easily one side's celebration could become a source of offence to the other. He was able to organise a parade involving 30,000 people that passed off peacefully. There was trouble later but it was insignificant and opportunistic, and not associated with the parade or the pageant.

Dillon's intervention in the proceedings was entirely political; his organisation through Devlin of an INFed committee for the centenary commemorations was to prevent Redmond's Parnellites from benefiting from the Irish Republican Brotherhood's (IRB) much more vigorous programme elsewhere. The Dublin 1798 Centenary Committee was chaired by John O'Leary (1830–1907), the old Fenian, and included Maud Gonne (1865–1953) and W B Yeats

(1865–1939). Belfast's best known republicans were Alice Milligan (1866–1943) and Anna Johnston ('Ethna Carbery') (1867–1911), whose poem 'Roddy McCorley', about a County Antrim United Irishman, was published in the *Shan Van Vocht* (1896–9) magazine of which they were joint editors. They urged non-collaboration with Devlin's committee but after much typical wrangling a compromise was reached. The official laying of the foundation stone of a Dublin statue of Wolfe Tone (1763–98) by O'Leary had a platform party of the widest possible spectrum, shared by Gonne, Redmond, Dillon and Devlin, on 15 August 1898. Two thousand of Devlin's men had travelled with him to the event.

Devlin's own parade had taken place on 6 June to Hannahstown. Thirty thousand had marched the eight miles in atrocious weather with twenty bands playing 'The Boys of Wexford', the popular ballad by R D Joyce (1830–83) who had died after a long exile some years before, and other suitable airs. On the way up the Falls Road, they passed, according to the *News Letter*'s sardonic reporter, 'Old women, wrinkled, toothless and gaunt, grew hysterical in their cries of greeting and baby hands waved branches and flags, the lives of many tiny infants being imperilled by the wild enthusiasm of their parents.'[1] They came to be addressed by Dillon and two other Nationalist MPs, Margaret Pender (1865–?), the author of a popular novel about Ulster in 1798 called *The Green Cockade*, and the 'Duodecimo Demosthenes' himself. According to the admittedly prejudiced *News Letter* reporter:

> Mr John Dillon MP, wearing an expression of fixed gloom, which was quite warranted by the surroundings, and carrying a bouquet of peonies and laburnum, conducted a sort of official inspection of the forces. He was observed to handle one of the formidable pikes… and to test with his finger the sharpness of its point and edge. Some of the processionists went further than this, using their weapons with great destruction among the frogs and field-mice which had ventured abroad to ascertain the cause of the hubbub.

The meeting, which commenced at about 2pm, was held in a field 'on rising ground overlooking McCance's Glen and facing Colin

Hill', and began with Devlin's taking the chair on a motion of his friend J T Donovan. His speech cheered the crowds up in spite of the rain and the mud. He congratulated those assembled on the 'magnificent outburst of national feeling' and said with less than total sincerity that 'they were rebels still at heart'. He was never prouder, he said, of being a Belfastman than on that day when he saw such a magnificent outburst of national enthusiasm. He went on to accuse the 'government of adopting today a more refined system of torture towards the people of Ireland than in 1798'. In light of the use made of such items as the pitch-cap and the walking hangman, that last remark may be forgiven as rhetorical exaggeration. Dillon's much longer speech was given in full and his assertion that 'on the day that Ireland forgot Wolfe Tone and the United Irishmen, her name would be blotted out from among the nations' got the loudest cheer.

The journey down from Hannahstown was virtually incident free. A large stone was thrown over the wall at a part of the Whiterock Road, known as the Giant's Foot, but it fell harmlessly between an open carriage and some of the marchers coming behind. Later some enthusiast discharged six revolver shots but even the *News Letter* admitted that they were an expression of 'exuberance of spirits' as 'in the Wild West'. The report concluded with the slightly dismissive sentence: 'Smithfield was reached at 6.30 and about half an hour later the processionists, who had met with a cordial reception on their way thither, dispersed.' Devlin had kept his nerve and found to his satisfaction that he had gathered quite an army of controllable supporters.

Things were different a few hundred yards to the north in the Protestant Shankill. There, the sense of 'Mickies' on the move caused temperatures to rise rapidly and what better target that the RIC's finest, especially the ones from the deep south drafted in, as was the custom, for special events like the '98 celebrations. With those accents they couldn't be decent Protestants and so were appropriate targets for the Orange hotheads, especially since their numbers were considerably fewer that the 30,000 soaked but elated Fenians on their return journey. They first gathered on the link roads of Dover and

Percy Streets, engaged in shouts of defiance at the returning crowds, who responded with equal noise and much waving of banners, flags and greenery, making them look like Birnam Wood on its way to Dunsinane. The serious business between the police and the rioters began after the Hannahstown tumult had dispersed. At each corner of the warren of little streets the constabulary were assailed by a hail of stones, from broken paving flags. By eight o'clock it was decided to call out the troops. A squadron of Inniskilling Dragoons led by Major O'Connor arrived, later supported by a company of infantry under Major Hawtrey. Major Hamnett, a 'military magistrate', was ordered at 8.30 to read the Riot Act and the RIC members were withdrawn. The soldiers made a wide sweep down the lower Shankill but met with no opposition. Instead the rioters actually cheered them as they ran or rode towards the city centre. Yet, even with the military on the streets, the rioting continued for a second full day.

Devlin, judiciously enough, made little comment on the trouble, even when over the next few days the usual number of Catholics were intimidated out of their jobs from the shipyards and other factories. He announced that his 'supporters absolutely refused to be drawn into a quarrel either with the Orangemen or the police'. He did mock Arnold-Foster when he suggested that it was Devlin's Hannahstown speech – 'an incendiary statement and an incitement to future rebellion' – that caused the rioting. Devlin insisted that 'our people' behaved splendidly, and that no arrests were made, in contrast to the violence and 'numerous arrests' the *News Letter* reported on the Shankill. He added with characteristic irony 'the police and the Shankill Road men can be safely allowed to deal with each other'. Devlin also drew attention to the fact that none of the Protestant shopkeepers in Catholic areas had been interfered with, unlike the attacks made on Catholic public houses and property in the Shankill. His colleague, Michael McCartan MP, who had been with him at Hannahstown, wrote to Dillon to report that 'King Mob had full sway and exercised it with a vengeance.'

If not a mighty victory it undoubtedly gave the twenty-eight-year-old Devlin a degree of satisfaction. He had commemorated the rising as efficiently as his sponsors expected him to do, and he had managed to stimulate a renewed interest in national politics in Belfast and generated a kind of unity. The old Parnellites and the '98 clubs seemed to meld well for the celebrations and their combined strength as members of the UIL bolstered the move to a re-united nationalism. It was slightly bizarre that a movement primarily begun for the redistribution of grasslands in Mayo, the watchword of which was 'The land for the people', should have found a healthy second home in industrial Belfast. Its blanket title was unexceptionable and, as its membership increased throughout the country, it effectively provided universal support for the IPP. Its success in Belfast was largely due to Devlin's genius for organisation. It essentially superseded the ailing INFed and reassured Redmond that he had an able lieutenant in the young Belfastman.

The success of the June celebrations was all the more remarkable in that a fortnight before, on Monday, 23 May, Devlin was subject to a public humiliation that would have dismayed a lesser man. He was invited to address a rally in Strabane, to be held on the precise centenary of the first day of the '98 rising, a fact to which many of the speakers adverted. It was a grand affair with fourteen marching bands with banners in green and gold. After a march through the predominantly nationalist town the public meeting was held in a field beside the Great Northern Railway track. At the time the battle with the bishop was at its most intense and the priests in the Derry diocese were strongly for Henry.

Devlin's speech was continually interrupted by hecklers and the crowds had frequently to be admonished by the chairman. One priest sharing the platform had damned him as 'more of a priest-hunter than a nationalist' and some sections of the gathering took that as an invitation to give him a rough ride. On several occasions an unidentified fife and drum band tried to drown out his words. Time and again he felt it better to sit down rather than withstand the minority barracking. In his last – successful – attempt he claimed he had the confidence of the majority of the meeting and he had the confidence of his fellow citizens in Belfast. He had come that day to give his voice to help the men of Strabane in celebrating the centenary of '98. He had never, and would never, be put down by a few interruptions. There was much more in this vein with plenty of references to Tone, McCracken, Jimmy Hope, and other '98 heroes, and an inevitable quotation from Ingram's most famous of all ballads about the rising:

> They rose in dark and evil days
> To right their native land
> …
> But true men, like you men,
> Are plenty here today.

One of the platform party at Strabane was Margaret Pender and it gave Devlin the opportunity to invite her to take part in the June centenary celebration at Hannahstown.

He was encouraged to travel beyond the city by Dillon and Redmond to find new members for the UIL in Britain. He went to Glasgow and then to Manchester, places with a preponderance of Irish immigrants. It was while he was speaking in Manchester in 1900 that he came under the notice of John Dulanty (1883–1953), the Irish diplomat, then a young man of seventeen. In a broadcast on Radio Éireann in January 1940 Dulanty remembered the effect Devlin had on him:

> A young man from Belfast whose name I had never heard swept us off our feet. He was small of stature and thickset, presenting an almost boyish figure. He had a big head, a mass of coal-black hair and a clean-shaven face. He was strong and resolute in expression, with subtle intonations that helped drive home the full meaning of every word. One was struck by the humorous look in his deep-set eyes… his love of Ireland was free from all hates.

Another characteristic, apart from an elaborate dress collar, the ubiquitous orchid or carnation in the jacket (often a morning coat), and the permanent haze of cigar smoke, was the hair parting, mathematically straight and white, cutting right of centre through the thick mane of hair that rarely even in later life showed a trace of grey.

Though never as completely his man as Dillon's, Redmond knew his worth and frequently praised him, dwelling on his 'superb debating power, dauntless courage, combined with a cautious mind and cool judgement, transparent honesty and integrity, all combined with an absolute and untiring industry – and a most loveable disposition'.

Devlin was now on the threshold of greatness in the nationalist cause, though born twenty years after Dillon and fifteen after Redmond. His success at recruitment for the UIL in Britain made him the obvious delegate to sow the seed worldwide. Redmond, with the reluctant approval of Dillon, who hated 'huckstering', asked him to accompany his brother Willie.

6
Going West – and Down Under

DEVLIN AND WILLIE REDMOND LEFT FOR New York early in 1902. They were sent on their fund-raising way with dinners in Belfast, Dublin and London. Banquet tributes were a significant part of the political culture of the time and Devlin had to endure many of them, leading to the threat of alcoholism that from time to time he attempted to stay by periods of total abstention. The dinners at which he was expected to speak, and never disappointed, were also informal fund-gathering events, more elaborate versions of Phil the Fluther's practice:

> And when writin' out he was careful to suggest to them,
> That if they found a hat of his convanient to the dure,
> The more they put in whenever he requested them
> The better would the music be for battherin' the flure.

His leaving of the security of west Belfast for the wider world of national politics was a significant moment in his political career and in his life in general. He was no longer a potboy, part-time journalist or manager of a liquor store. He was an accredited representative of Irish nationalism, a politician on expenses and a specific honorarium. His response to Redmond's suggestion was the understated, almost submissive, 'I shall be happy to go to America if you think I can serve the movement there.'

It would have been impossible to find anyone better equipped for the job. The contrast between the boyish, sturdy appearance and the brilliance of his rhetoric was marked. And there was ever the rich, rough native accent that sounded so different to the gentler 'southern' accents of Dillon, Redmond, Healy and O'Brien. It was regarded either as hopelessly discordant or freshly charming by worldwide audiences but was impossible to ignore. During one of his visits to Australia in 1906, a local journalist wrote: 'Mr Devlin's accent would secure his immediate admission to any Orange Lodge.'

By the year 1900 the number of people who called themselves 'Irish-American' had reached 3.5 million. Immigration between 1846 and 1851 had increased their numbers by 1.5 million; these were mainly Catholic and refugees from the disease and hunger associated with the Great Famine. The inflow of Irish immigrants continued steadily, though with a gradual lessening from 1900. Based mainly in cities on the eastern seaboard the Catholics were a cohesive, not to say familial, entity since their coming to the new world was a 'chain migration' not only of relatives, neighbours and colleagues but even of whole parishes.

They had suffered at the hands of Nativist activists who claimed that their true allegiance was not to America but to a 'foreign prince' (the current pope) and they and their clergy had been pilloried unmercifully by such brilliant caricaturists as the German-born Thomas Nast (1840–1902). He was the artist who gave the world its version of Santa Claus, jolly, red-coated, white-bearded and benevolent, but his cartoons were searing. Bishops in mitres were turned by him into crocodiles, a simian Paddy was portrayed climbing a ladder with an overloaded hod of bricks and captioned 'I'm risin' in the world' and a slatterny, near-cretinous chambermaid announced, 'I'm stayin' in the Grand Hotel.' Nast's chief targets were the Tammany 'bosses', notably William Tweed (1823–78), whom he showed as a tiger rampant in a Coliseum, strewn with bloody corpses.[1]

The notable performance of Catholics in the War between the States and their growing bourgeois respectability, plus their significant role in state and national politics, had changed attitudes at least overtly.

The emotional links with the 'old country', cemented by a new kind of Irish-American sentimental ballad and refurbished by a stream of new arrivals, had kept these offspring of older immigrants in touch, at least emotionally, with political events in Ireland. Their attitudes varied from a vague romantic attachment nourished on the gentler aspects of Irish life to extreme revolutionary views.

In many ways the only effective Fenians were Americans and the IRB, partly rebranded as Clan Na Gael (imperfect Irish for 'The Irish Race'), was rather more active there than in Ireland. Clan Na Gael had played its part in the land agitation and would re-emerge as a player in 1916 and later. Devlin and Redmond did not expect to influence such leaders as John Devoy (1842–1928) but expected that many of its members would attend their UIL rallies. Devlin was very interested in a less obviously radical group, the Ancient Order of Hibernians, that had a long, convoluted history at home in Ireland but, since its beginnings in America in 1835 as the Friendly Sons of St Patrick, a fraternal society, was concerned to succour newly arrived immigrants and improve their economic and social standing.

In Ireland the word 'ancient' was deliberately chosen for the title to emphasise, or rather claim, remote ancestry. The society looked back to the Defenders of the late eighteenth century, who were an unwitting and certainly unintended stimulus to the founding of the Orange Order in 1795, and which, in its use of ceremonial dress, banners and panoply, it was accused of aping. By the time that the more vigorous American AOH had become the chief benevolent association for Irish Catholics and a specific defence force against the violence and destructiveness of the Nativists and their 'Know-Nothing' mobs, the home version remained low-key with fewer members and less influence than even the Irish National Foresters that was social rather than political in its activities. The 'Know-Nothings' were so-called because of their curt response to questions as to what happened at secret meetings of their Order of the Star-Spangled Banner. In June 1854 the *Cleveland Plain Dealer* wrote:

When one Know-Nothing wishes to recognize another one, he closes one eye, makes an O with his thumb and forefinger and places his nose through it – which interpreted reads 'eye-nose-O', I knows nothing.

A man like Devlin, whose organising ability was even greater than his oratory, could not fail to notice that the AOH reintroduced to Ireland and organised by him would become a prodigious force in Irish politics. One of his first tasks on arriving home was to effect a reconciliation between the Irish and American orders, establishing a Board of Erin as a unifying executive, of which he became president in 1905, remaining in that office for the rest of his life. These considerations were kept in mind during his first American tour but marked for future deliberation.

He and Redmond landed at New York on 10 February 1902 and at once he felt something of the heady energy that struck visitors to the New World. It was three days before his thirty-first birthday and he needed all his young man's strength and reserves of energy for the exhausting amount of travelling he would be engaged in during the succeeding fifteen months. He was given a psychological boost by his return unopposed as member for Kilkenny at the end of the month. It also helped his billing at the various rallies and meetings at which he spoke.

They received a general welcome in east coast cities and towns from all shades of US greenery except from the more extreme members of Clan Na Gael and the old IRB. He was subject to not very subtle insinuations that he had said that 'the only way of achieving Irish freedom was by the sword'. It had been the mantra of such activists as John Mitchel (1815-75), who had fought for the Confederacy during the Civil War, and it had become the soubriquet of Thomas Francis Meagher (1823–67), another Civil War hero, though on the side of the northern forces, who did not long survive it. He gloried in the title 'Meagher of the Sword' imposed on him by W M Thackeray (1811–63).

Devlin chose to ignore these attempts at subversion. His purpose was not to engage in polemical debates with die-hards on whom argument would have little effect. He and Redmond were there to sow the seed of support for the UIL and that was the burden of all their addresses. Their welcome was general – as guests of Cardinal

James Gibbons (1834–1921) of Baltimore, who more than anyone else had set the Catholic Church in America on firm foundations, and of President Theodore Roosevelt (1858–1919) at the White House – and they were joined on platforms by public men of all creeds. Nast's caricatures were aberrations from ancient history. Devlin became acutely conscious that a significant number of Irish-Americans were rich and, while retaining folk memories of the famine and evictions that had driven their seniors to 'Amerikay', were no longer a subject people. They were generally positive to the brand of constitutional nationalism that he was advocating.

He worked hard, speaking at meetings often twice a day to boost membership of the United Irish League of America. They found that in spite of the prodigious energy that would make 'the worker in New York think he had a holiday if he got a job in my native city', as Devlin wrote in one of his regular letters from America for O'Brien's *Irish People*, the UIL branches were all but moribund. In that same report, perhaps advised not to paint too aureate a picture of the land of opportunity, he finished with a warning that while many Irish emigrants did well – just how well he was beginning to realise – without 'intelligence, enterprise and ceaseless industry' they would 'go to the wall'. A significant number of Irish ended on Skid Row.

There was no doubt about the 'intelligence, enterprise and ceaseless industry' of these Irish envoys. By the time that this first four-month foray had finished they had addressed 160 meetings, established 184 active branches, and had garnered in excess of £3,000 for the cause. (That amount should be multiplied by a factor of eighty to find its equivalent buying power today.) When he returned home on 22 July to take his seat in the House of Commons as member for Kilkenny he had visibly matured as a statesman. Willie Redmond generously and correctly ascribed their success to Devlin's indefatigable energy, his oratorical flair and organisational genius.

That year of 1902 saw the weakening if not the breaking of the bonds that linked him to west Belfast. He had moved emotionally into a larger sphere of politics. The question that continues to concern the biographer is: which was for him the cause of greater priority, the social welfare of his constituents or the wider mission of Irish independence? He strove in his parliamentary years to give equal weight to both causes but until the latter's only partial achievement in 1921 – and not for the people he regarded as his own – his instinctive socialism seems on occasion to have been relegated to second place.

It was as if an effective amelioration of conditions might have to wait until the time when the economic future of Ireland should be firmly in the hands at last of the Irish people. That greater task would require his frequent presence in London, with regular trips to Glasgow, Manchester, and other centres of the diaspora. His worldwide travel was mainly concentrated in the years 1902–6 but until the full effects of the partitioning of the country would become known in the early 1920s, he was relentless in his work for independence. He was, however, conscious that the IPP had no specific industrial policy. Its chief source of support was rural or small-town Ireland. Belfast was for many Irish politicians a kind of conundrum. They had no sense of the nature of industrial life, nor the needs of its operatives. In this respect Devlin was of extreme use to them, over and above his personal capacity.

In October 1902 the newly formed United Irish League of America held its first annual convention in New York and later in Boston, and John Redmond, Davitt, Dillon and T P O'Connor were guests of honour. Almost immediately they realised that they had left their best card at home and cabled for Devlin to come and join them. They intended that he would be the apostle of the UIL throughout the whole of the United States and even Canada where the Irish population was generally Protestant and of earlier arrival to the New World than the Famine refugees south of the Forty-ninth Parallel.

In the early autumn he had been an honoured guest at an IPP dinner in Dublin given for Sir Wilfred Laurier, the Canadian prime minister. He would later reassure his Canadian audiences in Ottawa in 1903 that his party would become 'a willing partner with Great Britain within the Empire to accept any compromise which preserved the unity of Ireland'. In a sense he was preaching to the converted when he added that devolution 'would strengthen the Empire'. It was the kind of remark that enraged the Clan Na Gael advocates of physical force, another challenge to their position like his admonition in New York the previous July to the branch of the UIL that was composed mainly of emigrants from Belfast and East Ulster. He reminded them that they had not risen 'into the foremost position in this great free republic by insane methods or lack of logical appreciation of events', and requested of them merely that they would use the same commonsense in approaching the Irish question at home. He had already clashed with the IRB over the '98 centenary celebrations, and perhaps guessed in his instinctive way that their uncompromising stance would eventually lead to a confrontation with Ulster Unionists and inevitable partition.

He was to stay in North America for eight months, working first through New England and then Toronto, Montreal and Ottawa, facing the Canadian winter but buoyed up by success. By the end of February 1903 a total of $30,000 dollars had been raised. He was given expenses plus a stipend of £20 a month from funds. This was the grant made by the IPP to MPs who had no other sources of income. It was not ungenerous by contemporary standards but he earned every penny.

He was continually in demand as a speaker and realised that his own distinctive accent in its no-nonsense drawl was not all that different from that of his Canadian listeners. Meetings varied from grand open-air rallies in stadiums to smaller 'club' events, the latter often more financially advantageous. He stayed in Chicago in March, using it as a centre to address fifteen meetings throughout the state of Illinois. In April he had travelled as far west as Salt Lake City and then north to Butte, Montana, the centre of the copper-mining industry, finally reaching Spokane in the North Pacific Washington State. He went 'wherever green is worn', finding the territories west of the Mississippi more apathetic than the Atlantic cites and those of the Middle West. The further west the emigrants moved the more isolated they became from communities of their fellow countrymen and the less the situation in Ireland preoccupied them. In these western towns he had to do most work.

Butte was a unique case since many miners with experience of copper deposits in West Cork had settled there, even though it was more than 2,500 miles from New York. Out of a population of 30,000, 8,000 were of Irish extraction and provided $4,000 dollars for the cause. Successful meetings were held in the other Montana mining towns of Helena and Anaconda. The city of Omaha, Nebraska, gave $1,000, a tribute perhaps to the number of Irish-born priests ministering there but the Irish of Denver, Colorado on the whole stayed away. The 1,182 miles from Butte back to Minneapolis were done in a single train journey, after being 'practically living in trains for the last three weeks'.

In spite of advice by US members of the UIL, particularly Col Finnerty, the head of the American organisation, who did not think the southern states worth the effort, Devlin arrived at New Orleans and then swept back up through Birmingham, Montgomery and Georgia, as if replicating the infamous Civil War 'marching through Georgia' of General W T Sherman (1820–91) but in the opposite direction. The visit to the Deep South, in spite of the counselling of northern politicians, was successful; he was pleased with the efficiency of the local branches of the UIL, who contributed $4,000 to the funds. The tour ended with a whirlwind return to New England during which he addressed eighteen meetings in twenty days and attended a mass rally in Quebec. He landed at Queenstown on 18 June 1903 having spent nearly eight months criss-crossing the two countries and earning a total of $70,000 for the cause.

What may have surprised and also delighted him was the number of offers made to him of positions in the commercial as well as the political life of the country. He was gratified but gave the usual answer that his one purpose in life was to serve the interests of the working people in his native land and to that purpose alone would he devote himself. In the appreciation included in a 1927 Christian Brothers' souvenir booklet, one of his companions on the tour, his identity indicated only by the initials FIOH (perhaps Fr Frank O'Hare), described his departure:

Many of the prominent figures in the American United Irish League of those days are gone: some have changed allegiance and not a few have ceased to take any further interest in Ireland or her affairs; but amongst those whom Mr Devlin met during his visits to the United States one thing survives all change and vicissitudes of time.

The respect and admiration, which he won from all; the deep and abiding friendship which bound him in closest intimacy with a few; the sincere regard which his earnestness and sincerity evoked – these have remained unchanged and are today as fresh and active as on that morning in New York when the White Star Pier was filled with friends who stood and waved farewell till the big liner that was bearing him home had passed from sight in the far waters of the outer harbour.

The language is the kind of adulatory prose usual in such tributes but friends and adversaries alike tended always to the superlative when they talked of 'Wee Joe'.

There was no doubt about the success of the American mission and the fifty-five-year-old T P O'Connor was delighted to have a young and vigorous adjutant who could withstand the buffets of much travelling. It was he who established Devlin as secretary of the UIL of Great Britain in July 1903, remarking, 'The more I see of Devlin, the more confidence I have in his intelligence.' By the following September he was made overall general secretary with permanent offices at 39 Upper O'Connell Street in Dublin. There was no doubt about his enthusiasm and willingness to go to extremes of fatigue to please the men who were now his colleagues. It is probable that they asked too much of him. To require him to begin a year-long tour of Australia and New Zealand two months after his prodigious success in wresting West Belfast from the Unionists in 1906 seems excessive. He beat his opponent Capt J R Smiley by 4,138 votes to 4,122 but only because some 153 Unionist votes were lost to Alexander Carlisle, who, standing as an independent Liberal Unionist, split the Protestant vote. In a straight fight it could have been Smiley in by 137 votes.

The actual result was declared, in the leisurely practice of the time, on 27 January, fourteen days after polling began. It is possible that Devlin was right in believing that some of his 4,138 votes were cast by Protestants, disaffected by Orangeism and the Unionist lack of social policy. In his valedictory address prior to his departure for Oceania, faithfully reported by the *Irish News*, he returned to that theme:

> We have built a bridge, so to speak, over the Boyne, and across that bridge, Protestant and Catholic, who perceive it to be their highest duty to work together in the cause of common humanity, are now prepared to shake hands in the belief and conviction that they have been too long kept asunder by men who used a lever to prevent democracy joining them together for their own ends... We will use our position to brighten the lives of the toiling masses whether they are Protestant or Catholic. We will remember that under the blue sky of heaven in Ireland there is room enough for all good men and good citizens.

And then, as for so many of his fellow countrymen, though in rather more comfortable travelling conditions, it was off to Botany Bay.

Non-penal Irish emigration to Australia during the nineteenth century was only about 5 percent of the total of those who left Ireland, though these Irish immigrants accounted for a quarter of the total arriving to seek a better life. A number of them received some assistance for their passage by companies looking to increase their workforces. There were few, if any, who left because of the Great Famine, but many caught the gold fever of the 1850s. A significant feature of the Catholic arrivals was their being members of teaching and nursing religious orders, especially the Sisters of Mercy and the Irish Christian Brothers. Devlin knew that he would be welcome at any of the latter's many schools. The greatest numbers of Irish in Australia were concentrated in the southeast provinces of New South Wales and Victoria but only because that was where a majority of all Australians lived. The Irish as a whole, however, were much more generally distributed, geographically and socially, than in America and were to be found not only in Sydney, Melbourne and Adelaide but also in the cities of Western Australia, Perth, Fremantle, Coolgardie and Kalgoorlie that had to be included in his itinerary.

Devlin and his friend and colleague John T Donovan left Belfast and travelled overland to Naples to catch the liner to Perth. While in Italy, a country Devlin grew to love, they sought and were granted an audience with Pope St Pius X on 21 March 1906. There is no record of their conversation but it is probable that the Bishop Henry case was discussed, since he had already been delated to Rome by some of his senior clergy and snubbed by William J Walsh (1841–1921), the Archbishop of Dublin. More intriguing is the possibility that the coming *Ne Temere* (1908) decree about mixed marriages might have been considered. Devlin's advice on the handling of its promulgation would have been invaluable in what later proved to be an item that gave much propaganda material to Ulster Protestants. The voyage from Naples to Perth took a little more than three weeks and they spent the next virtually fruitless four weeks visiting the mining towns of Western Australia, Boulder, Leonora, Menzies and Kookyril. One bright spot in a fairly pointless operation was a visit to the Christian Brothers secondary school in Perth, where they were made to feel very much at home.

As winter turned to spring, the weather deteriorated. The schedule of journeys and meetings arranged by local, sometimes ad hoc, committees was punishing. Devlin was the star attraction and the organisers at the various venues were no more interested in hearing Donovan than fans at a rock concert being fobbed off with a support band. Devlin's throat was giving him a lot of concern and the infection had spread to his ears, causing him severe pain. In September, in one of his regular letters to Redmond, he begged to be relieved of a proposed American tour on grounds of health – his chest was also affected – and fatigue. It is hard for us in the age of antibiotics and rapid healing properly to understand the debility that such a condition could cause. Devlin's complaints were partly psychosomatic; though a bewitching speaker he went through agonies of stage fright before a public address. T P O'Connor, in an article for the journal *Review of Reviews* in March 1911, described him as 'gentle, shy and almost morbidly sensitive' in private and in mental turmoil before speaking in public:

> Unconscious of his powers he shivers before a speech; cannot sleep, cannot eat; if he could he would run away; has almost to be forced to his feet by friends who realise his gifts more than he does himself. Even then, he begins with trembling voice and trembling hands.

As he grew older the frequency of his sloughs of depression increased, his hypochondria grew greater, and his struggle with alcoholism more intense. At thirty-five he could still find the energy to continue. He was probably slightly bipolar and periods of elation were often followed by deflation and clinical depression. In spite of these bouts the mere act of speaking, however dreaded in anticipation, usually restored his ebullience. Photographs taken in Australia show him sporting a rather grand cravat, fastened with a jewelled pin, high collar, fancy waistcoat, cutaway jacket and the ubiquitous orchid in the left lapel.

Devlin and Donovan fared better in South Australia, spending a total of seventeen days in Adelaide and the other boroughs, though they had to make difficult journeys along flooded roads eerily lit by severe electric storms. Devlin was delighted when the premier of South Australia caused a resolution to be passed in the local parliament in favour of Home Rule. This and Devlin's claim that a new spirit of amity was beginning to be discernible in Belfast caused some local Orangemen to cable home for evidence to disprove such a development. Though not as large as equivalent contributions in America, 'everyone at our meeting contributes something'.

Devlin was unlucky in that he was unable to attend the funerals of both his parents because he was many thousands of miles away from home when they died. His mother Lily had died in 1902 when he was in America; he was conscious that she had been responsible by example for his obsessive neatness and hygiene; and he was clearly her favourite in the family. Charles Devlin, as we have seen, was at times overwhelmed and 'disgraced' among his fellow jarveys by his son's volubility but he too must have been pleased and surprised at his success and public reputation. Devlin heard of his death not long after he reached Perth just before a meeting at Port Pirie. Another blow was the death of Michael Davitt, the great victor of the Land War, in Dublin on 31 May 1906. Devlin mentioned the event during a speech in Melbourne but broke down in tears and could not continue for some time.

It was during Devlin's tour of South Australia that V de P Gillen, a local journalist, wrote a fulsome pen picture for the Adelaide *Mercury*. (With forenames Vincent de Paul and an Irish surname the writer could hardly conceal his own politics.) The piece covered forty-five square inches of broadsheet and was reprinted in full by the *Irish News*. It began: 'Did you hear Joseph Devlin speak during his sojourn in Adelaide? If you did not, then you failed to listen to the one of the finest orators in the Empire.' Devlin would not have twitched at the word 'Empire'. One effect of his visit to Oceania was to confirm a satisfaction with the way the various dominions were being run. He would have accepted an Australian or Canadian model for a devolved Ireland. 'He came to us from the home of orators – the great country of Ireland – with a great reputation and with the splendid force of being able to speak "with the lips of an angel".' There was much more in this vein: 'Mr Devlin has a heart of fire but his head is cool and his brain works as if packed in ice.' After praising 'his rich and sweet voice... filled with music of miraculous charm and spell', and the 'slight brogue [that] adds honey to his words', Gillen adds many more words of praise, finishing with a description of the man in action:

> Mr Devlin is a natty, well-built little man with gracious and charming manner and is somewhat of a shy, retiring nature – unlike many of his countrymen. But when he rises to deliver a speech the metamorphosis of his personality is remarkable. The warmth of his delivery arouses the latent strength and pugnacity, and I heard several say, what I myself certainly thought, that he gave them the impression of a bulldog in an encounter with the enemy. He has the oratorical temperament and his greatest utterances are given with the help of the scantiest notes. Of course he must prepare his speeches with considerable care but he certainly leaves to the inspiration of the moment the language with which to clothe his words.

On 3 August in Sydney they met the redoubtable Patrick Francis Moran (1830–1911), the first Australian cardinal and a strong advocate of Australian federation and Irish home rule, as part of their visit to New South Wales. They spoke at nineteen meetings in appalling winter weather. Devlin reported that to these meetings came 'old men and women who emigrated in 1850, 1860, travelled up to 100 miles to hear them'. September saw the wayfarers in Queensland but they were back in Sydney in the second week of October, remaining there until mid-November, when it was time to head for Tasmania. It had been called Van Diemen's Land when, like Botany Bay, south of Sydney, it had been a penal colony during the years of transportation and had seen the importation of many Irish 'felons', including William Smith O'Brien (1803–64), the self-called 'middle-aged' Young Irelander and John Mitchel. It would have been injudicious of them to miss such an emotionally charged destination even if they did not share exactly the same political attitudes as the old 'felons', as the law described them.

By now the travellers, though weary, pushed on to New Zealand without any great enthusiasm, having already travelled the 1,800 miles from Hobart. They found, as many visitors then and since discovered, that New Zealand was not Australia but if anything rather more interesting in spite of its reputation for bourgeois dullness. Since the year 1870 there had been a yearly influx of 2,000 Irish immigrants, three-quarters of whom were Catholics and instinctively in favour of Home Rule. Devlin was surprised and pleased with the level of contributions and glad to lend support to a long-running Catholic campaign for state-supported independent religious schools.

On Christmas Day in Wellington the mayor took the chair at their keynote meeting. Donovan was by now used to his position as support act and the reporter of the *Freelance*, writing on St Stephen's Day, had eyes only for 'the round, chubby-faced Parliamentary Celt with his black tie riding high at the back of his collar'. It was an odd description for the cut-away collar and grand cravat that was Devlin's usual 'morning' dress, one of his few vanities that, like the orchid or lily, were his badge of distinction. The journalist continued:

> [He] orated in a manner that cannot be heard in a New Zealand parliament. It appears to us as if this Irishman who doesn't speak the brogue but has a perfectly distinct accent of his own doesn't know exactly what he is going to say when he starts... The remarkable thing... is that unlike any public speaker in New Zealand he doesn't repeat himself. He gets intense strained attention, he waxes more powerful as he advances and he perorates with power. He isn't violent and he is more sorry than angry with the passive

enemies of Ireland. He impresses with his earnestness, his honesty, his mentality, and his arguments for Irish nationality are biting, conclusive, irrefutable. He is a credit to the foresight of the Party that sent him as its envoy.

New Zealand proved to be one of the successes of the tour and more generous proportionately than Australia. They left from Auckland for San Francisco on 7 February 1907, having raised £22,000, the equivalent of £1.75 million of today's purchasing power. They did not delay in America, though a third visit had been intended in their original itinerary, crossing rapidly from west coast to east and reaching Queenstown in March, a year after leaving home. Devlin was still in indifferent health and he felt in need of a rest, besides word from Belfast suggested that his presence was needed. The struggle with Bishop Henry and the BCA was coming to a climax and there was intelligence that a serious industrial strike was about to convulse the city.

Before he left New Zealand he was invited to a soirée in Invercargill, a town on the south coast of South Island. Part of the evening's entertainment was a recital by a young lady called Hannah Sweeney. She said later that she was dazzled by his charm and courtliness, impressed by his 'deep resonant voice, his blue eyes, his immaculate dress'. Later she came to England to continue her musical studies and made frequent visits to Ireland. One day in 1910, while she was having lunch with Bishop O'Donnell in his house in Letterkenny, County Donegal, the meal was interrupted by the arrival of Devlin and a close friend, Matt Keating. It was a case of instant attraction for Matt and Hannah were married three years later and the stocky Cupid became a regular visitor at their London home. He and Matt remained close friends, though their politics were different. Matt, born in Wales of Irish parents, was a keen supporter of the Gaelic League, an Irish-speaker and a member of Sinn Féin. As Hannah remarked in an interview with F J Whitford, Devlin's first biographer: 'My husband's friends were his friends and together they enjoyed the theatre, good music and bridge.'

7

'Catholic Orangemen'

THE JOURNEYS DEVLIN HAD TO MAKE criss-crossing North America and even more exhaustingly in the 'outback' had long periods of sheer coverage of distance and these off-duty periods gave Devlin opportunities for reviewing his career so far and considering his political future.

He sensed that Henry's race was about run; it was clear that he had lost the support of his own clergy and, indeed, of the wider Church. Henry had been strongly supported by Cardinal Michael Logue, but that originated in their shared vision of lay/clerical relationships, in Logue's instinctive tendency to close ecclesiastic ranks against expected attack, and not in any real political nous they may have possessed. Devlin had no wish to be at odds with the Church and was pleased to have Patrick O'Donnell, Bishop of Raphoe, in his corner. He had missed the extremely useful support of the *Irish News* and would not have established the *Northern Star* if the former had not found it necessary to become the bishop's voice. That particular dilemma would soon resolve itself, especially now that he was the member for West Belfast. He knew the value of the UIL as a general support group for the parliamentary party but could not help envying the political capacity of the Orange Order, with lodges in most towns and villages throughout the North, for control of its members and dissemination of information and where necessary tactical instructions.

His experience of the AOH in America led him to consider the advantageous possibility of establishing an organisation of approximate power and influence at home. He was particularly impressed by the large membership, the wealth at its disposal, and its capacity for fraternal benevolence. Such an organisation would have all the grassroots support systems of the UIL with the extra panoply of marches, rallies, banners, sashes and other regalia. In time this decorative aspect of the society would lead to such dismissals as the 'Ancient Order of Catholic Orangemen', that gibe made by many, including Jim Larkin (1876–1947), the labour leader, who distrusted Devlin. Even O'Brien, who became much less influential politically as its power increased, referred to it as having debased 'the National Ideal… to the level of a Catholic Orangeism in green paint'. Sharply critical as these descriptions were, they were in essence paying the AOH quite a compliment, however oblique or unintended. Even in its heyday, in the decades before and during the Great War, it had only a fraction of the membership of the Orange Order and nothing of its political influence. Neither of these comments was made about the AOH in America that continued to care for its members and tended officially, at least, to eschew involvement in Irish affairs.

As far as ceremonial went the resemblances between the Orange Order and the Board of Erin brotherhood were striking, except that green replaced orange, its spectral near-neighbour, on sashes, banners and flags. The iconic picture of King Billy crossing the Boyne on a white horse (incidentally not the correct colour – his steed was precisely named Sorrel) was replaced by an imagined depiction of the sixteenth-century Rory O'More, who was taken to be the original remote founder of the order, and the Union flags ousted by ones showing the green-robed Erin and her wild harp. The twelfth of July that celebrated each year the anniversary of the Battle of the Boyne had its Hibernian counterpart in the fifteenth of August, the feast of the Assumption of Our Lady bodily into heaven, thereby indicating that the AOH was not exactly open to all applicants.

The Catholics of Belfast, aware of their second class citizenship, needed a little of the glamour that membership would afford. Apart from the elements of fraternal solidarity with other nationalists that belonging ensured, and was evidenced in the public occasions like the 15 August marches and rallies, and when necessary electioneering processions, the social aspects of the AOH eventually meant that most fair-sized towns, especially in Tyrone and Fermanagh, had halls that provided recreational facilities for cards, snooker, concerts, dances and any other social occasions. The 'friendly-society' aspects of branches meant that they could help members in times of need and hardship. The establishment of national insurance with unemployment payment and old-age pensions was not finally in place until 1911 and membership of an organisation that could provide welfare services in the age of voluntary provision was advisable if not actually essential.

Also attractive to Devlin about the AOH was that it was Catholic but not clerically controlled. One of Logue's objections to it was its habit of holding dances and whist drives independently and without consultation with the local parish priest. The long attrition with Bishop Henry had shown Devlin the advantages of such an arrangement. He was reported in the *Northern Star* in January 1908 as desiring to see 'a public hall in every parish in Ireland'; these would radiate 'life and light and warmth'. They would be centres where the members could avail of the education that would reveal to them the past and prepare them for the future. 'They would become acquainted with the language and music of Ireland; there they could hold their dances and merry meetings.' The speech was remarkably similar to one his more successful rival Eamon de Valera (1882–1975) would make thirty-five years later on St Patrick's Day, 1943, when he talked of

> ...a land whose countryside would be bright with cosy homesteads, whose fields and villages would be joyous with the sounds of industry, with the romping of sturdy children, the contests of athletic youths and the laughter of comely maidens, whose firesides would be forums for the wisdom of serene old age.

Another point of resemblance was that neither of these dreams was fulfilled, both aspirations too far. The AOH proved stronger than the UIL that it was intended to supplement. It was far more appropriate to industrial Belfast than O'Brien's league, which, as we have seen, had been founded as an agrarian movement in Mayo with 'The land for the people' as its war cry. It had become a kind of supportive organisation for the IPP, a local ancillary almost by default.

Cardinal Logue continued to view the AOH with suspicion, suggesting that it was an oath-taking secret society, which it was not. Most of Logue's animus was rooted in its separate 'layness'. Though he, like a majority of Irish people, desired Home Rule, as head of the Church in Ireland he believed that he had greater priorities than that of political freedom. The Church, ever since the Council of Trent, aspired to, and when possible demanded, control of education. In a sermon during the ordination of Charles McHugh as Bishop of Derry on Sunday, 29 September 1907, he expressed his views on the whole question of devolution in what was as close to the Irish Church's official line as it was ever likely to be stated:

> I have very strong views on the matter and a very ardent desire that the boon may be granted to our people. I think they would make good use of it. I think those who imagine we would make use of it as a lever to separate ourselves from the rest of the Empire are simply deceiving the people. All we want is what they have in Canada and Australia and South Africa, to have full control of our own affairs and the spending of our own money, which is at present shamefully wasted without producing much good in the country.
> ... it is a very ominous thing that we find the politicians of this country entering an alliance with socialism and secularism under the pretence of securing Home Rule for Ireland... Its policy is to banish God from the schools and from the hearts of the people.

It was a fairly obvious swipe at James Connolly, co-founder of the Citizen Army, and Jim Larkin, who had made their presences felt that summer in Belfast, and was exactly the line that Devlin had taken when addressing the Canadian parliament at Ottawa four years previously. Logue, with judicious restraint, did not mention Devlin in the 'political' parts of his address, being mainly concerned with the sacrament of ordination of the new bishop and his presentation to his diocesan flock. Yet he cannot have been far from the cardinal's thoughts.

The previous Friday, Devlin had assembled 15,000 Hibernians near to Ara Coeli, the archiepiscopal palace in Armagh city. Relations with the clergy were, to put it no more strongly, uneasy. A majority of the episcopate were suspicious of the AOH's independence, its supposed historic links with the eighteenth-century Defenders, and its still persistent image as a quasi-secret society though no oath was required of its members. In fact, it actually had a number of members who were priests. Its national chaplain was Fr J J McKinley, a Down and Connor priest, who was denied promotion by Henry, was moved vigorously about the diocese and was forbidden to attend many AOH events at which he should have officiated. The most senior supporter was Patrick O'Donnell, Logue's successor both in Raphoe and Armagh, who saw Devlin's sanitised Board of Erin as 'an organisation with Irish Catholic principles', having made members of many men 'pulled... out of secret societies'.

In 1907 the Scottish hierarchy renewed an earlier ban first imposed in 1882 but the Vatican rescinded it two years later. There was never a blanket ban in Ireland; individual bishops viewed it with greater or lesser disapproval, which gradually diminished as Devlin's position became more unassailable. O'Donnell managed to have any formal hierarchical disapproval of the Order revoked but he was its only wholehearted supporter among the episcopacy.

Things were different across the Atlantic; the Order was large, rich and pervasive in Irish America. It did have extreme elements among its members, notably IRB and the more vocal Clan Na Gael, but the majority were non-violent constitutional nationalists though they would not have used those terms. The history of the AOH in America had been one of protection not only of fellow Irish-Americans and new immigrants but also of the Catholic Church. In 1850 their members had prevented the burning of Old St Patrick's Cathedral by the Know-Nothings after Archbishop John Joseph Hughes (1797–1864) threatened to make New York 'a second Moscow', a reference to the French invasion of 1812. Its acceptance as necessary in the prevailing culture, plus its respectability (and prosperity), gave Devlin sufficient confidence to develop it and make it respectable in Ireland.

The Board of Erin Hibernians (so called to distinguish them from the American source) were shaped into use by Devlin as a personal political machine, his rivals claimed, and his close association with it did not always work to his advantage or reputation. Yet as a pragmatic politician with few independent resources he could not ignore the advantages that such a body could supply. One of the murkier episodes associated with the AOH in America was its support of the Molly Maguires, the secret society involved in the turmoil in the Pennsylvania coalmines in the 1870s. The original Mollies were an agrarian secret society in the Ireland of the 1830s, so named because of their practice of dressing up in women's clothing on their raids. With the characteristic long memories of the Irish, the cisatlantic AOH soon came to be nicknamed 'Mollies' as well. Like most such jibes it was a tribute to the Order's strength and success. It had existed in Ireland as a friendly society rather like the much larger Irish National Foresters and largely confined to Ulster. Devlin claimed that he had been a member since his youth. One Belfast division had taken part in the '98 centenary celebrations and a delegation attended a convention organised by the recently founded branch of the UIL in the city that was chaired by Devlin. Even then it was vaguely regarded as a useful if peripheral nationalist association.

In spite of 'Molly' gibes and the lawless implication of the soubriquet, Devlin applied his organisational skills to increasing membership with resounding success. He accepted the post of national president at the annual convention held in Dublin on 21 July 1905 and continued in office until his death in 1934. Its numbers rose from 10,000 in 1905 to 60,000 in 1909, with membership strongest in Belfast and County Tyrone but fairly evenly spread about Ulster and with 2,000 in Dublin, where its perceived support of William Martin Murphy and the other employers in the 1913 lock-out effectively finished it in the capital.

It provided a wide-based support system for the parliamentary party, one much more active in its organisation than the visibly deteriorating UIL. The National Insurance Bill passed by David Lloyd George (1863–1945) in 1911 gave it great respectability and significance when it was accepted as an 'approved society' under the terms of the act. Its membership continued to increase because of its broad appeal. It was Irish, it was Catholic, it was for Home Rule, and it was virtually classless, appealing to the growing numbers of successful Catholic businessmen for its exclusivist trappings – freemasonry without its sinister associations. It was a benevolent society in Belfast where Catholic workmen were socially the 'lowest of the low' and women below that again. Lastly, perhaps most importantly, with the colourful regalia, the sense of solidarity, and the occasional holiday, it was a supplier of what would now be called 'crack', a commodity not freely available in the Ulster of the time. By 1915 it had 1,800 branches throughout Ireland with 100,000 active members and twice that number registered with it as policyholders in its insurance schemes.

For so large a body it was remarkably disciplined and, with only occasional lapses, effective for its purpose. Mainstream nationalism, especially in the south, took its time to accept it and its leader; its majority of urban members with 'that accent' and the same unmitigated vocal register from its leader made it seem alien. There was also the instinctive, if unexpressed, fear that while Home Rule, however limited, was inexorable in a majority of counties, the north-eastern bloc was a wild card. The AOH's strength had not had its equivalent since the zenith of Parnell's power. Dillon, Redmond and T P O'Connor were perfectly happy as long as it was Devlin's private possession, but even so friendly a commentator as the Protestant Nationalist MP, Stephen Gwynn (1864–1950), Redmond's biographer, thought that 'while Mollies are excellent people with Devlin at their head', he worried about their perhaps uncontrolled future.

Though they were intended to march shoulder-to-shoulder with the UIL their leaders gradually drifted apart. Devlin, aware of the volatile nature of a party long in opposition, dreaded factionalism above all. He identified Healyism, with its wide, grassroots appeal and distrust of centralism, as such a divisive movement and moved vigorously and successfully against it. When, in 1902, O'Brien began to float a policy he described vaguely as involving 'conference and conciliation and consent' with southern Unionists, Devlin refused to support him, fearing a dilution of what the Liberals might offer as Home Rule. H H Asquith (1852–1928) was not against the idea of devolution in principle, though he hadn't the messianic intensity of Gladstone in his attempts to pass the First and Second Home Rule Bills in 1886 and 1893. His main preoccupations were with curtailing the power of the House of Lords and the social legislation that culminated in the passing of the National Insurance Act of 1911. Because of the fine balance of Conservative and Liberal seats he relied on the support of the IPP and accepted that Home Rule for Ireland was the price he would have to pay for it.

When we consider that O'Brien's UIL had originated as a rural movement its success in Belfast was remarkable. In fact with Devlin at its head it became an unspecific support group for the IPP in its campaign for Home Rule. The first serious clash with O'Brien came about with the latter's support of the Land Act of 1903. Called after George Wyndham, the chief secretary, it was regarded as being too favourable to the landlords by Devlin and Dillon. O'Brien had been a leading member of the Land Conference (1902) that had generated the act and had been pleased that many of his recommendations had been incorporated into the bill. In spite of many public pious statements of mutual support, relations had gradually deteriorated and, when O'Brien urged that the same 'conference and conciliation and consent' approach might be used for the greater prize of Home Rule, the policy was rejected. As far as Devlin was concerned the UIL had fulfilled its purpose and now should acquiesce in the AOH's supremacy. To twenty-first century ears O'Brien's approach seems not only reasonable but the wisest but at the time placating southern Unionists was almost irrelevant. It was the northern Unionists who would be calling the devolution tune. It is unlikely that any measure of conciliation and conference would have led to consent with them; it did not work then nor since.

The ostensible cause of the breach was the introduction by Augustine Birrell (1850–1933), the new chief secretary, of a further land bill in 1908. This was the direct result of IPP pressure on Asquith's government and was intended to reduce the amount of money available for land purchase because it was an intolerable burden on the British treasury and the Irish ratepayers. It also intended to introduce powers of compulsory purchase that O'Brien and his southern landlord friends regarded as a betrayal. O'Brien believed that it would slow down the workings of a scheme that, in his view, had proved to be the best solution of the perennial Irish land question. He insisted that the whole question should be discussed at a convention to be held in the spring. From the mainstream nationalist point of view the land war was already won, barring some small print details. What alarmed them was O'Brien's 'weakness' with regard to their main ambition, finally to give up membership of the House of Commons. It is not impossible that their attack on the 1903 Land Act was deliberate, its main purpose being to make it impossible for O'Brien to remain after such a public slight.

On 9 February 1909, 3,000 delegates packed the Round Room of the Mansion House in Dawson Street, Dublin, for the start of a turbulent two-day assembly, later described by O'Brien as the 'Baton Conference'. Two years earlier the 1907 convention had been disrupted when 250 Sinn Féin activists tried to force their way in. Redmond and Devlin decided that stewards should be hired to keep order. This anticipation of trouble became a self-fulfilling prophecy. Some of the 100 'minders' were volunteers but some were 'professionals' like today's bouncers and it was mainly the latter who were issued with wooden clubs, with the usual pious imprecise instructions to use them only in extreme circumstances. It promised to be a fairly controversial meeting and by the time Devlin arrived with 500 AOH delegates tension was high and the possibility of physical violence real. In fact the first day passed without much incident. Redmond as chairman had a table on a special small dais on the main platform with Devlin by his side, as appropriate to his office as General Secretary of the UIL. The platform party consisted of MPs and other senior officials of the IPP.

Among the various delegations in the Round Room were members of the Young Ireland Branch (YIB) led by Cruise O'Brien (1885–1927) and Francis Sheehy-Skeffington (1878–1916). As appropriate to young Turks they wished to show their impatience with the sluggish Liberals and, while supporting Birrell's bill, called for strenuous opposition to the government. It was not quite the party line, especially as Devlin had insisted that the Liberals' view on Irish Home Rule had been 'clearly ascertained and fully defined'. He reiterated the IPP's position and with uncharacteristic spleen crushed 'these eminent statesmen' and advised them that the Irish Party did not require advice from them and would not take dictation. It was fairly wounding, considering that the YIB had been largely Devlin's own creation. They did manage the following morning to have their motion making Irish a compulsory matriculation subject for entry into the new National University passed with three quarters of the votes. One of the few chinks in Devlin's nationalism was his lack of capacity, or real interest, in the national language. That success did nothing to allay the steadily increasing tension.

O'Brien spoke for an hour on his amendment to Redmond's call for support for the bill. The room was full of supporters of the party, including many farmers and, of course, Devlin's 'Mollies', who joined in the general barracking so that the speaker could scarcely be heard. It was obvious to the audience that he should stop speaking until Redmond and the stewards could restore order. Finally, Eugene Crean MP, William O'Brien's closest ally, left his platform seat and moved across to the chairman's table, intending to advise O'Brien to let the rowdies calm down and persuade him to return to his platform seat. He was not able to get near O'Brien because several of the stewards intercepted him. The sense of being physically restrained increased his rage and anxiety. He now approached the dais from behind and gripped the back of Redmond's chair as much to steady himself as to gain his attention. A scuffle involving the MPs and stewards broke out on the platform while in the main body delegates rose to their feet and shouted. Redmond, giving evidence in a subsequent court case, said that his chair was being violently shaken by an ashen-faced Crean. The stewards then seized Crean and hustled him off the platform while Devlin, it was claimed, cried, 'Throw the fellow out!'

O'Brien afterwards claimed that anyone with a Cork accent was prevented from approaching the platform by club-carrying Devlinites and prosperous Midland farmers with hazel switches. Redmond had been unable to assert his authority as chairman, so great was the uproar in the Round Room. It was not one of Devlin's finest hours; he was involved in the physical tussle on the platform and his 500 'Mollies' prevented, it was claimed, supporters of O'Brien from entering the room. Sheehy-Skeffington dismissed Devlin as a 'brainless bludgeoner' and the YIB stalwarts began to turn more and more towards the more radical policies of Sinn Féin and even the IRB. (Sheehy-Skeffington himself was murdered after his arrest during Easter Week, 1916, though he had taken no part in the Rising.) When some kind of order was restored Devlin began to speak. His offering was described by the *Freeman's Journal* reporter as impressive:

> The member for West Belfast steadily converted them the further he got with his argument, in a voice that silenced all opposition and resounded like a bell all around the great circle of the Round Room.

For Devlin the party line was going to be adhered to and if his 'men' were intimidating, their opponents were not exactly silent. When Redmond's motion was put to the meeting it was passed with an overwhelming majority and O'Brien left to form a new party known as the All-for-Ireland League, that would be based upon his 'conference and conciliation and consent' approach as the only way of achieving Unionist agreement to Home Rule. D P Moran (1869–1936), the trenchant near-scurrilous editor of the Dublin journal, the *Leader*, immediately re-christened it the 'All-for-William' League.[1]

One ironical aspect of the underlying tenor of the convention was that O'Brien's perhaps naïve belief in the efficacy of conciliation was not all that far away from Redmond's own views. Unfortunately Cork was not just 250 miles from Belfast; it was politically on a different planet. Devlin was not a deep political philosopher but the pragmatic man on the spot. His work was executive rather than theoretical and he had the advantage over Dillon, Redmond and O'Brien in that he understood, even if he did not approve of, northern Unionists. Only T P O'Connor, who lived in the intermittently sectarian city of Liverpool, had any conception of Protestant fears. As far as the convention was concerned Devlin had a job to do – support his party seniors in a vital vote of confidence – and he did it with his usual efficiency that adversaries claimed was really ruthlessness. He and his Mollies were traduced, and apart from a few scuffles, the inevitable result of heightened feelings when Irishmen engage in history or politics, batons (and hurling sticks and hazel switches) were sparingly used.

Crean, badly shaken more from emotion than actual physical injury, brought an action against Devlin and Denis Johnston, the UIL assistant secretary, charging them with acting in a disorderly manner, intending to frustrate the business of the meeting, that they incited others in this intention, and that Devlin 'had procured the commission of an assault upon the complainant'. With what seemed like pointed irony Crean retained Healy for the prosecution, even though he and O'Brien had been rivals in the past. Healy's own animus against Devlin and, by extension, troublesome Ulster, in the end weakened his prosecution case. He spoke at length and, of course, wittily with the sharp irony that made him feared. His repetition of the word 'Belfast' turned it, to the ears of those present in the Dublin police court, into a term with the same connotation as 'Tammany' or 'Mafia'. He feigned bewilderment as to why so many Belfast men were so interested in agrarian legislation: Why should these 'sturdy agriculturists of the Falls Road, who probably would not know how to tell a plough from a poleaxe' be so interested in the price Irish tenants were paying for their holdings? They were, he insisted, rather the source of the interruptions during O'Brien's proposal speech, deliberately imported by Devlin for the purpose. He also accused him of 'usurping the copyright' of the AOH in America, 'a noble and honourable institution' that had no connection with Ireland. One of the prosecution witnesses raised something of a smile when, in a strong Cork accent, he complained that the sole source of disruption were men with Northern accents who used 'filthy expressions'.

Redmond in his evidence denied that Devlin, who was seated beside him, had cried, 'Throw the fellow out!', and Crean could not deny that O'Brien had called Devlin 'a little bag of venom' at a soirée on the first evening of the conference. Serjeant Moriarty, Devlin's leader, was soon able to prove that only twenty-four of the stewards came from Belfast, that of these only seven were paid for the two days' work and only two had been on duty in the hall on the day of the trouble. He went on to show that the Belfast delegation, amounting to no more than fifty-five, consisted of twenty-five UIL members, twenty-four AOH, and six Nationalist councillors on Belfast Corporation.

Even with his case visibly unreeling Healy could not resist another anti-Belfast, anti-Devlin slur, claiming that the conference could have been finished on the first day 'because the sturdy agriculturalists of the Falls Road were anxious to get home to their bullocks and turnips', perfectly aware that many of the Belfast delegation were doctors, lawyers, publicans and shopkeepers. The case was thrown out and Crean ordered to pay costs of £250 (again multiply by eighty for today's buying power) or face two months' imprisonment. Costs would have been much greater outside of a magistrate's court. The All-for-Ireland League survived with Healy as an active member until 1916 when O'Brien's call for support for the war effort effectively ended its existence.

The net effect of the 'Baton Convention' was exoneration of Devlin and a lingering north-south potential fault-line in nationalism that continued to threaten until the post-war success of Sinn Féin and its militant wing, the Irish Republican Army (IRA), made it an entirely academic question.

As an organisation the AOH was generally well-disciplined, largely because of the integrity of its officers and its sense of Catholic respectability encouraged by increasing approval by the Church. From 1904, when Bishop O'Donnell had any official clerical disapproval rescinded, it persisted as a Catholic defence and social society, strongly associated with the Nationalist Party after the partitioning of Ireland. Since the advent of the Northern Ireland troubles its membership has sharply diminished and it takes no overt part in politics. In spite of accusations of 'Molly-ism' it remained a non-belligerent friendly society and any deviation from good behaviour, as perhaps in Castledawson in 1912, was quickly addressed by Devlin.

The AOH, though strongest in the North, soon had members throughout Ireland. The order was still viewed by some from both sides of the political spectrum with deep suspicion. For example, Cardinal Logue was not mollified. His objections could no longer be moral after the Vatican approval, and their politics were not notably different from his. Like all senior churchmen of the time he suspected any free-floating Catholic lay society not run by the Church. He frowned upon such independence but, though approved of by the bishops after the victory over Henry, Devlin still defended the need for and the value of a nationalist organisation that could not be dubbed by its enemies as clerical – or priest-ridden, as they would have put it.

Larkinites distrusted its essential bourgeois character, with its preponderance of vintners, bookmakers, 'warm' farmers, Catholic doctors, lawyers, chemists and small businessmen.[2] This disapproval became violent during the Dublin strikes and lock-out of the autumn and winter of 1913 when the AOH appeared to be strike-breakers and were vigorous in the prevention of the starving children of the Dublin poor from being taken by 'proselytisers' to Liverpool. Devlin, who might have cleared the air and established some kind of commonsense, was not in evidence. It is believed that the seeming dereliction by a man famous for his speeches and agitation on behalf of his hard-pressed West Belfast constituents was due to his almost pathological sense of loyalty to the new chief. He knew that Redmond could not abide Larkin and so, though it went against the grain, Devlin took no part. There may also have been a precise sense of territory implied in his absence from the scene. His people were the workers of the Falls, Smithfield, the Markets and Ardoyne. He may have felt that he had no business involving himself in Dublin equivalents. The decision was not one of his wiser moves and over the next decade there would be others even more damning to his reputation, not only with his adversaries but also with some historians blessed with the gift of hindsight. One result was a sharp decrease in membership of the AOH in the city.

8
'Puerile and Vulgar Little Leader'

A PROBLEM THAT CONFRONTS THE BIOGRAPHER of 'Wee Joe', apart from the absence of personal papers destroyed at his specific command, is the depiction of the many strands of his political career: social reformer, officer of the INFed, secretary of the UIL, worldwide fundraiser, Home Ruler, Redmond's trusted second-in-command, bishop battler, member for West Belfast, head of opposition in the Northern Ireland parliament and working class paladin. Such virtually simultaneous activities make a strictly chronological account of his life unsatisfactory. As a parliamentarian from 1902 until his death in 1934 his career was not so much interrupted as maintained exhaustingly while he fulfilled all these other roles, like an especially dexterous juggler. He was the man that in an ideal world was destined to represent the people of the Catholic/nationalist Falls Road and environs and this, as in all good fairytales, came true in 1906.

As member for North Kilkenny, he admitted that on his first visit to his constituency he was an absolute stranger there but that he was keenly aware of the need for close attention to local interests. In fact, and no one expected anything else, his main parliamentary business concerned Belfast affairs, and he was glad to be able to point out that there were internal dissensions even among Unionists, drawing the House's attention to the fracas that had recently occurred between rival Protestant groups on the Custom House steps, the oratorical Belfast equivalent of Hyde Park Corner. It was to his own future electioneering advantage to demonstrate that Orangeism was not seamless but he used the opportunity to remind the House of the unequal treatment in the eyes of the law between Catholics and Protestants: 'If a nationalist looked sourly at land grabbers, he was hauled before two resident magistrates and condemned to a plank bed, while an Orangeman might say with impunity that he would make mincemeat of one of the highest judicial functionaries in Ireland.'

Twenty years later, after the massacre of five members of the McMahon family by men in B-Special uniforms at the height of the Ulster Volunteer Force (UVF) pogrom, he had again to remind the House just what the partitioning of Ireland meant for Catholics in the North: 'If Catholics have no revolvers to protect themselves they are murdered. If they have revolvers they are flogged and sentenced to death.'

He also was able to prove that the publicity given to the so-called Anderson case was another vain attempt to prove the country priest-ridden. In December 1903 a Protestant policeman by the name of Anderson had been found guilty of misconduct towards his erstwhile Catholic fiancée and been dismissed. The Unionist MPs insisted that he was the victim of a conspiracy organised by the girl's priest. Devlin raised the matter nine times between June 1904 and May 1905, the first of many crusades that he led in parliament, usually without satisfaction, but in this case, he, the public enemy of Bishop Henry, was able to demonstrate that he too was a Catholic champion.

An even more scandalous affair was the McCann case that erupted during his first session as MP for West Belfast. The story began not surprisingly, as with much in Ulster history, at the sixteenth-century Council of Trent, the great Counter-Reformation definer of modern Catholic belief and practice. The rule about Catholic marriage was that both partners should be believers and their children brought up in that faith. Like many ecclesiastical strictures it was a bit short on practicalities. It actively discouraged 'mixed' marriages, required that a special papal dispensation should be obtained and solemn promises made by both parents that the children of these 'misalliances' should be given a Catholic rearing.

For historical reasons many of the Tridentine admonitions could not be implemented in Ireland, but in the post-Famine church, with a people still suffering trauma and amenable to change, Paul Cullen had it established as one of the *Acta et Decreta* of the synod of Thurles in 1850. The old practice of having the sons brought up in the father's religion and the daughters in the mother's continued but Thurles, with its resolution to discourage mixed marriages, had anticipated Pope St Pius X's *Ne Temere* decree by nearly sixty years. The decree, called, as usual, after the first two words – *Ne Temere* being Latin for 'Lest rashly...' – was applied to the universal church on 19 April 1908, at the worst possible time for Ulster nationalists. It presented what to Unionists was prima facie evidence that Rome rule was depriving Protestants of their spiritual rights and, by its active disapproval of mixed marriages, encouraging a kind of ethnic separateness.

In October 1910 Alexander McCann, the Catholic partner of a failed marriage, involving domestic violence, left his wife, taking his children with him. He claimed that his parish priest had urged him to do so as his moral duty, and immediately it became a *cause célèbre*. Mrs McCann claimed that Alexander's priest had said that, because the marriage had taken place before a Presbyterian minister in Ballymena, County Antrim, in May 1908, he had not been really married in the first instance. It was a dodgy enough claim canonically and had no validity at all in civil law, and indeed if there had been no marriage, the wife's promises were not binding. She refused to remarry in a Catholic church.

The case was a godsend to the right-wing, backwoods Orangemen; a rattled Devlin told the House of Commons on 7 February 1911 that Mrs McCann was the greatest Tory asset since William III and she spoke her lines rather well in public: 'I bore it all, hoping his old love for me would show him his error. But the power of the priests is supreme.' Sir Edward Carson (1854–1935), the new leader of the

Ulster Unionist Party, with great rhetorical skill, if little real emotion, described Mrs McCann's treatment as 'a grave public scandal'. Her story had elements of self-contradiction, as if to give sensational newspapers a good story. It was not clear whether the husband or the unnamed priest had taken the children nor how accurate was the report that when Alexander had arranged for the second child to be christened in St Paul's church on the Falls Road, his wife tried to disrupt the ceremony and both were ejected by the sacristan.

Devlin obtained statements from three priests in St Paul's, the only ones who might have been involved, that they had not made any comment to Mrs McCann as to the integrity of her marriage. These he read out in the House of Commons in a brilliant rebuttal, showing how for Unionist electoral advantage private details of an unhappy marriage were cynically used. Mrs McCann's press release had occurred five days before the West Belfast election. Winston Churchill (1874–1965), then Home Secretary, in his daily report to George V, wrote:

> Mr Devlin, who is the one new figure of distinction in the Irish Party, made a powerful reply and showed that the whole case, which was an ordinary tale of a private quarrel, had been used deliberately on the eve of the Belfast election as a means of exciting partisanship.

The readiness of the Unionists, especially Carson, from whom one would have expected greater *gravitas*, to use anything that seemed to be proof of Rome Rule was ominous. The sectarian clock was being carefully wound up so that when it struck it would do most damage. Devlin's handling of the affair was sterling but it marked the beginning of his final frustration and essential defeat.

He was able to settle the incident because of his membership of parliament, from 1906, as MP for West Belfast. The general election of 1906 (13–27 January) was a landslide for the Liberals, led by Sir Henry Campbell-Bannerman (1836–1908). In West Belfast the sitting Unionist, H O Arnold-Foster, fled to a safe English seat and the IPP thought that the prize was again almost within reach. Though the constituency held the greater part of the Catholic population of the city there was still a small majority of Protestants since the electoral boundaries contained parts of the Shankill Road. The chosen candidate would have to do battle with a possible 4,168 Catholic votes against a likely 4,704 Protestant.

Devlin's electoral blooding had occurred during the campaign of Thomas Sexton, the IPP treasurer, in 1886, when as a very mature fifteen-year-old he had helped 'get the voters out'. That time Sexton was elected with a majority of 103 votes, having been defeated the previous year by thirty-seven. In 1892, after an increase in the Protestant population, Sexton lost again to Arnold-Foster by 839 votes. A chance presented itself again in 1903 when Arnold-Foster was appointed Secretary of State in the cabinet and had, under the current parliamentary regulations, to resign his seat and stand for re-election. It was at the height of the acrimonious struggle with Bishop Henry's BCA, which had compiled the most up-to-date register. Patrick Dempsey, the UIL candidate, was not given access to that revised list and lost by 241 votes.

Devlin, though still member for North Kilkenny, was the obvious candidate and was nominated at a convention on 7 January 1906. He had stated, with rather obvious *faux-naïveté* at a rally in the Ulster Hall on 13 December, that in spite of his absence from Belfast, 'I think I could nearly know the face of every man and woman in this hall.' His opponents were Captain J R Smiley and – to most people's surprise and Devlin's delight – Alexander Carlisle, managing director of Harland and Wolff, the great shipyard. It was assumed that Carlisle's deliberately wrecking intervention was to show disapproval of the way William James Pirrie (1847–1924), his chairman and brother-in-law, had been slighted by the Unionist establishment by being passed over for the Unionist nomination in South Belfast in 1902, and now West Belfast. That establishment continued to remain somewhat suspicious of Pirrie's mildly liberal stance. It was his 153 votes that split the Protestant vote and allowed Devlin to win by a margin of sixteen, 4,138 to 4,122.

In a straight fight Smiley would have been in with a margin of 137 votes. Some of the 4,138 votes – up to 200, Devlin claimed – must have been cast by Protestants, those sufficiently independent to vote for personality and not party, or who felt that Devlin's concern for the social evils of the constituency was more relevant than a vote for a virtual absentee officer of the North of Ireland Imperial Yeomanry. Either way such 'rotten' Protestants, as they were called by the others, played some part in the 'little corporal's' victory. As reported in his own *Northern Star*, it was, in the words of the victor, 'the nearest run thing you ever saw in your life'.

It was as a triumphal event that the result declared on 10 January was celebrated. In *Wee Joe: A Radio Portrait*, written and compiled by J J Campbell (1910–79), and broadcast on 24 November 1959 on BBC Northern Ireland, one of the contributors told how her husband got so excited while counting the votes in the Crumlin Road courthouse that his nose began to bleed. Someone else took over but soon the husband was able to 'put his arms round Joe's neck and cry, "You're in – you're in!"' The effect of such an embrace in the physical stand-off culture of the time was tremendous. Men did not hug other men – certainly not in the Falls Road. It was not the result that the Orange crowd – complete with drums, bands and banners – had expected and they demonstrated their disappointment in their usual vociferous way. As Devlin emerged from the courthouse surrounded by some friends the RIC inspector on duty advised him not to proceed. He drew himself up to his full, not very considerable, height but with lightning in those memorable eyes, exclaimed: 'I am not going to sneak out by the back way.'

His personal courage was noted later by Seán MacEntee (1889–1984), the son of one of his closest supporters, afterwards a senior Fianna Fáil politician. Devlin had been a character witness for him on 9 October 1916 at a court-martial in Richmond Barracks in Dublin, insisting that 'he has always been upright and honourable in his character'. Later, at the height of the War of Independence, they found themselves caught in crossfire in Dublin: 'We took cover while the bullets hopped all around the street and I must say that, though it was probably his first experience of the kind, Devlin was as cool as could be.' They maintained that friendship though they were not close politically, a loyalty that MacEntee's boss, de Valera, never understood. On that day of his triumph the new member for the West continued down the courthouse steps, seemingly oblivious of his reception party. As he reached the gates one of the constables, moved by his courage, cried, 'Fair play for Mr Devlin!'

The *Radio Portrait*, lovingly produced by Sam Hanna Bell (1909–90), the doyen of writer-producers in the golden age of radio, had many contributions from personal friends of its subject. One coming from an unlikely source was Tommy Henderson MP (1877–1970), the independent Unionist, who slightly younger than Devlin, regarded him as an enemy until they met – and then became a close friend. He admitted to stoning the victory procession and of regularly burning effigies of Devlin on the incendiary 'eleventh' nights.

There was no lack of volunteers to help with canvassing, making sure that the franchise was exercised fully – and sometimes repeatedly, as the mantra common to both sides advised, 'Vote early and often!' Women workers were even more persistent than their men-folk, even though the female vote in parliamentary elections was not granted until 1918, and then only for women over thirty.[1] They repaid his solicitude for his women constituents by voting solidly for him in 1918, reversing the universal trend towards Sinn Féin, and defeating de Valera, 8,488 to 3,245. In 1906 the women joined enthusiastically in the celebrations. The Falls Road was full of black shawls, burning torches, bonfires, and the hero in a horse-drawn carriage. Several enthusiasts attempted to decouple the horse and draw it themselves in true triumphal style. The crowds – the road was black with supporters – sang as they walked along a verse improvised to the tune of 'A Nation Once Again':

> Joe Devlin won the West;
> Joe Devlin won the West.
> Sure it's true, it's true.
> The whistle blew
> Joe Devlin won the West!

That night the West was truly awake and stayed so until the wintry dawn as men, women and children danced the night away.

Joe never lost the West again. Though it is impossible to quantify the actual Protestant vote there must have been some support for him from that quarter. There were two elections in 1910 – the second reaching into January 1911 – brought about by the Liberals' struggles with the Lords. In the first there was a hint of the danger of a split nationalist vote because, as we have seen, P J Magee, Bishop Henry's most loyal acolyte, insisted upon opposing the 'puerile and vulgar little leader of an ecclesiastical rebellion'. In fact Magee got seventy-five votes, presumably from diehard residual members of the old BCA, while Devlin's 4,651 saw his Unionist rival, Boyd-Carpenter, defeated by 587 votes.

In the end-of-year polls Devlin's majority in a straight fight with his 1906 rival Smiley had shrunk to only 463. During and after the campaign he was accused of that perennial ploy of all Ulster elections, before and since: votes 'from beyond the grave'. Through fair days and foul, as he became politically more marginalised, his care of his constituents grew more intense. His post-electoral mission statement included a determination 'to keep social problems of Ireland and Belfast especially before the Commons' and 'help to win and hold the workers of West Belfast for Home Rule'. These remained his twin priorities but it is difficult to determine which had the greater claim for his attention.

Two hostile postcards by the same (unattributed) caricaturist were published after Devlin's success in 1910 by a Shankill Road firm called the Ulster Publishing Company. The standard of workmanship is not very high though the first, showing 'Joe Gabriel', suggested that 'Devlin's reserve voters' depôt' was Milltown cemetery. Devlin, hatted and nattily dressed as ever in a fine suit and bow-tie, holds a fashionable walking-cane in his left hand while he blows a trumpet with his right as the latter-day archangel, uttering the command, 'Rise to vote', while a dozen complaining corpses cry to be left in peace. Some of the complaints are quite funny: 'Joe, go to h—l; I am tired.'; 'I wish I was dead.' One positive death's head boasts, 'By gob, sir. I have voted three times.' Round the edges are primitive drawings of skulls, spades, and coffins, one labelled 'A voter's villa.'

The second caricature, labelled 'Our Artist's Dreams of West Belfast Sub-tenancy', deals with multiple voting for municipal elections based on house tenancy and with women allowed to vote since 1887. The standard of drawing is not any better though the message is even more pungent. It shows Devlin and Redmond viewing a disease-ridden slum called Microbe Row with many, many inhabitants all claiming the residential vote. The unsubtle caption reads:

> Redmond: 'By gobs, Joe, your division around here smells somewhat high.
> Devlin: 'Whist, hould yer gab or the microbes'll hear ye!'

It is hard to tell from the inferior drawing which of the two portly gentlemen bottom left is which.

All is fair in love and electioneering but the cartoons, which sold widely as postcards, are quite damning not of the West Belfast member's manipulating of the electorate but of the city corporation that could tolerate such living conditions for its citizens. Indeed Devlin's concern with the working conditions of especially the women in his care was shown in his continually reminding his fellow MPs of the industrial slum that Belfast remained. Some historians question his absolute commitment to social issues, suggesting that his greater preoccupation was with the fortunes of the IPP and Home Rule. He was surely no Larkinite, as was clear from his low profile during the Belfast Dock Strike of 1907. Working conditions for the dock workers and carters at the harbour were extremely poor; they were badly paid, disorganised and riven with sectarianism, deliberately manipulated by the employers. Jim Larkin, as gifted an orator as Devlin, though politically much further to the left, was sent in January 1907 by James Sexton, the English leader of the National Union of Dock Labourers (NUDL) to organise a local branch. The ground was being prepared for agitation in a sense by the holding of the first ever conference of the newly titled Labour Party in Belfast on 23–25 January, with Keir Hardie (1856–1915), the Labour leader in attendance. Larkin succeeded beyond expectations and by the late spring had enrolled 2,900 dockers and all the carters. Thomas Gallaher (1840–1928), the tobacco king and leader of the employers' federation, persuaded his fellows to lock out the workers on 5 May. The struggle lasted until November when Sexton, fearing bankruptcy for the NUDL, settled on capitulation terms. Larkin, feeling betrayed, remained in Ireland to form the Irish Transport and General Workers Union (ITGWU) in 1909.

The strike and lock-out had a brief period of non-sectarianism, even anti-Unionism; blacklegs imported from Britain had to have permanent police protection and when 300 RIC constables 'mutinied' in sympathy with the workers the army took over security. English and Scots soldiers were deployed; Sir Antony MacDonald (1844–1925), the Catholic Under-Secretary, advised against the use of Irish soldiers and it was he who ended the police mutiny by a judicious combination of dismissal, temporary suspension, and transfer. The effect on industrial Belfast was considerable and most cruelly felt by the families of the strikers. Devlin raised the matter in the House of Commons, urging Augustine Birrell to bring the parties to arbitration but with typical seeming inertia the chief secretary said he could not move without agreement on both sides. Devlin's own demeanour at home was deliberately low-key since he did not wish to introduce any element of nationalism into the conflict.

The presence of soldiers in the streets, keeping nationalist areas under tight supervision, inevitably led to rioting since the people of the Falls knew that the British army was not on their side. Larkin had called a rally at the Custom House steps for Saturday, 10 August and invited the four city MPs on to the platform. It was expected that the independent Tom Sloan (1840–1921) would attend but, with the practised antennae of the survivor, he sensed that old animosities would surface, that the brief idyll of non-sectarianism was coming to an end, with Apprentice Boys' Day on 12 August in Derry and the 'Mickies' Twelfth' coming on 15 August. Sloan did not appear. Devlin was thus the only MP associated with the event.

He used the opportunity to explain his position of apparent 'aloofness', secure in the knowledge that the greater majority of the NUDL strikers were Protestant, and then he repeated the rationale for the strike: 'It is a fight for a living wage and a great principle of trade unionism,' the 'principle' being the right to mount pickets. In peroration he launched an attack on those who had sent in the troops. He meant not the employers but the British government whom he felt he had license to attack. On the two nights following Larkin's rally there was serious rioting in the Falls area. A police van was attacked and 2,600 infantry, eighty cavalry and 500 police were forced up the Grosvenor Road, the imaginary boundary line between Orange and Green, and on to the Falls. The cavalry charge down from Dunville Park was met with an early form of 'Belfast confetti', the square setts when dug from the roadway making fine missiles. When an encore occurred on the Monday evening the Riot Act was read and seven soldiers fired from Divis Street up the Lower Falls, killing one mother, Maggie Lennon, who was trying to find one of her missing children, and Charles McMullan, who was on his way home from work. Devlin had not slept on either of the riotous nights, touring the Falls area, trying to persuade the rioters to offer no provocation and go home. Larkin later said that 'drink was at the bottom of all that occurred'. He was probably right but endemic sectarianism has its own intoxication. Devlin, who knew his own bailiwick better than Larkin, however, was deeply suspicious of Larkinite methods. In a less noisy way he was just as committed to social improvement as any Marxist but his methods were different. He knew that what might work in an ordinary industrial city or even in other parts of Ireland was not applicable to the Red Brick city.

In 1909 Dr Bailie, the Belfast Medical Officer of Health, published a damning report on poor conditions of the work and wages of in-workers and out-workers of the linen trade and their resulting health problems, which included sentences like 'the underfed, overwrought physique of the sweated worker is undoubtedly one of the main causes of the high death rate'. It was the opportunity that Devlin needed, the findings made by an official of the Corporation, condemnation from within. Wages were 'grossly low', diminished by harsh 'fines' for delays, lack of punctuality. The out-workers, 8,000 in number, were paid less than a penny an hour, approximately 35 pence in today's currency. This 'wage' had also to cover machine maintenance, thread and delivery of finished work to the mill. These were not backstreet 'sweat-shop' rates but the usual practice in the industry for which Belfast above all others was famous. The linen mills employed up to 40,000 female in-workers, who were paid between seven and ten shillings a week. Even more pitiful was the plight of the children workers, the 'half-timers', aged between twelve and fourteen, who worked from 6am to 6pm on three alternate days per week for less than four shillings. In *A Radio Portrait* (1959) one survivor recalled a personal experience of the system:

> At eleven year old I went into the mill… we worked in the spinning from that until six at night and we hardly had time for to put on our boots or wash our feet… When we come home an' the sweat teeming out of ye an' you'd hardly time sometimes to put the shawl on ye… a half-timer only received half a crown one week and three and fourpence the next… and you didn't get another farthing – and if you spoke, of course, you got the sack.

Another contributor to the programme remembered the half-timers: 'It would have broken your heart to see young children running bare-footed with a crust of bread in their hands trying to get into the mills before 6am, otherwise the gates would be closed in their faces. If 6am had struck before they got in they were closed out until breakfast time and lost a great part of their wages.' The same woman remembered seeing very young children sitting on their doorsteps drawing out threads from the linen.

Devlin regarded it as a mighty victory when, in March 1913, after vigorous lobbying on his part, the same Board of Trade inspection teams were told to include in their remit the linen, shirt-making and embroidery industries.

He remained a champion of women in spite of all political vicissitudes and opposition from members of his own party. Dillon feared women's suffrage as 'the ruin of our civilisation' and Devlin had to do one of his famous funambulist tricks, balancing hierarchical loyalty against instinctive wisdom. He approved wholeheartedly of full franchise for all. On 18 October 1915, after presenting a new set of colours to the National Volunteers in Celtic Park in Derry, he was surrounded by a group of activists who demanded to know his attitude to universal suffrage. He replied truthfully that he was strongly in favour of the reform but could only speak for himself. He did not then say that he deplored the methods of the militants but he did loathe them as much as the threat – and the reality – of the physical force methods of the IRB. He believed that in both cases the extremists 'damaged, if they have not destroyed, a good cause'.

As the first decade of the new century ended Devlin was at the peak of his reputation. The Lords had lost their absolute veto on the Lower House's bills and Home Rule was almost within his grasp. His was the most recognisable face in the country and both Dillon and Redmond regarded him as the most charismatic of their triumvirate. His reputation and authority were unquestioned. It was not just in Belfast or East Ulster that he was king; he was known by his forename with its affectionate epithet throughout the country and in Britain and beyond.

In two consecutive months, on 26 October and 24 November 1910, Redmond, speaking to American audiences, specified Devlin's exalted position in the UIL and the IPP. On the first occasion, in Detroit, he stated, 'There is in O'Connell Street, Dublin, a great office managed by the real chief secretary for Ireland, my colleague and friend, Joseph Devlin, the member for Belfast.' Four weeks later in Utica, in up-state New York, he returned to the adulatory theme: 'The Government of Ireland is carried on at 39 Upper O'Connell Street, Dublin, and Mr Joseph Devlin is the real chief secretary.' These were mighty words of praise, especially effective since Redmond did not go in for emotional rhetorical tricks, of promising much and delivering little. Devlin was a made man, in the best position to lead a reunited country since the death of O'Connell, young enough at thirty-nine to be the political heir of Dillon and Redmond, and yet mature enough to carry on their work. It was his finest moment and it did not last.

9

'Ulster Will Fight'

THE NARROW DEFEAT IN THE HOUSE of Commons, by 343 votes to 311, of the First Home Rule Bill in 1886 began a movement that was to culminate in the signing – in some cases in blood – of the Solemn League and Covenant on 28 September 1912 when 474,414 men and women demonstrated their opposition to 'the Home Rule conspiracy'. There were 250,000 signatures in Belfast alone, separate arrangements being made for women in keeping with the culture of the time. The nagging Irish Question that the Act of Union (1801) had only exacerbated became, as the troubled century progressed – with its 'tithe wars', Catholic Emancipation, the persistent and successful Plan of Campaign against the whole system of landlordism in Ireland – a British Question. Ireland became the main preoccupation of the 'grand old man', as William Ewart Gladstone was known for most of his parliamentary career. His response when asked to form a government in 1868 was: 'My mission is to pacify Ireland.'

Even as a younger man he was conscious of the country's looming significance and its casual, often cruel, treatment by Britain. In 1845, the year of the first failure of the potato crop, he had written to his wife about his preoccupation with 'Ireland, Ireland, that cloud in the west, the coming storm, the minister of God's retribution upon cruel and inveterate and but half-atoned injustice.' By the time of the election of 1885 the Irish Party under Parnell had become a force to be reckoned with. They held eighty-six seats, as against 335 Liberals – Gladstone's party – and 249 Conservatives, an exact numerical balance.

The Conservatives, led by the 3rd Marquess of Salisbury (1830–1903), with Lord Randolph Churchill (1849–95) as his Chancellor of the Exchequer, conscious of the niceness of the balance and its implicit weakness for Gladstone, were galvanised into action when he introduced his bill. It offered a very little Irish autonomy, Britain retaining imperial, fiscal and security powers. The detail was less important to Ulster Protestants than the fact of being ruled by Dublin and, as they believed, the Catholic Church.

Churchill arrived in Larne on 16 February 1866 and, though shaken by an unusually rough crossing from Stranraer, played, as he had threatened, the 'Orange card'. He announced to the waiting press: 'Ulster at the proper moment will resort to its supreme arbitrament of force. Ulster will fight and Ulster will be right.' If asked to defend this blatant rabble-rousing, he could honestly have said that it was the fear that the dissolution of the queen's empire could begin with that single step. It also might mean the fall of the grand old man's government, his chief purpose.

The bill was defeated on 8 June not because of the murderous violence in Belfast that summer that followed the fall of the government but because of the defection of Joseph Chamberlain (1836–1914) and his followers when they formed the 'Unionist Party'. The fifteen-year-old Joseph Devlin, who lived close to the scene of the worst killings, had had his first lesson in real politics, both the street variety and those of the House. Gladstone's gesture had been simply that – a gage thrown down to challenge without much expectation of success the right-wing establishment. The most significant element of the affair was Churchill's sound-bite that was to be rehearsed at every perceived threat to the Union.

Gladstone tried again in 1893 and was able to force through a bill with similar provisions on 2 September by a margin of thirty-four votes. It was, not unexpectedly, thrown out by the Lords a week later, supported by only forty-one peers out of a total of 460. Yet Ulster's assumed right to resort to the 'supreme arbitrament', with Tory approval, had already been vociferously demonstrated. On 2 March the firebrand Orange leader William Johnston (1829–1902) 'of Ballykilbeg', a village southwest of Downpatrick, held a meeting of Orangemen in the Ulster Hall in Belfast to call for 'passive resistance' to Home Rule. This in Orange-speak meant rioting and intimidation of Catholics that spring. Johnston also arranged for 100,000 loyalists to march past the Linen Hall on 4 April as he shared the platform with Colonel Edward James (1837–1906), the titular head of the Unionist Party at Westminster, and Arthur Balfour, Salisbury's nephew, who during his period as chief secretary for Ireland (1887–91), was known as 'Bloody Balfour' because of his oppressive measures. It is possible that like Carson, the Unionist leader decades later, he had little affinity with Orangeism and recoiled with distaste from such public appearances. Yet, for the party – and the Empire – he was prepared to suffer such discomfiture.

Parnell was dead and Parnellism nearly so. The vexed matter of Home Rule was placed on the back burner until the heroic and essentially successful reconstruction of the Chief's ideas and tactics and party by the tireless John Redmond placed the IPP again in active and effective politics. The gradual weakening and crushing defeat of Balfour's government in 1905 and the establishment of a Liberal regime the following January were to have a profound effect on the nature of British parliamentary government, and would see the beginning of long overdue social legislation. Immediately alarm bells began to ring among Ulster Unionists. An Ulster Unionist Council (UUC) was quickly founded to resist the slightest hint of devolution of legislative authority to Dublin. This body, later with Carson at its head, formed the main source of opposition when, in 1912, the granting of Home Rule came tantalisingly near.

Yet, in 1906, there was no dependence among the Liberals on the votes of the IPP; their majority was too great. The appointment of Augustine Birrell as chief secretary in 1906 was an enlightened gesture; his sponsoring of the Irish Universities Act (1908) and his Irish Land

Act (1909) helped solve two thorny aspects of the chronic Irish Question.[1] His Irish Council Bill (1907), however, that proposed the devolving of education and local government pleased no one. Both Arthur Griffith's Sinn Féin and William O'Brien's United Irish League rejected the idea immediately and even Redmond, stoically ready to compromise, warned that his IPP would vote against it. The bill was withdrawn on 3 June before the UUC could mount a serious campaign. Birrell showed little further interest in Home Rule and is remembered now as one of the political casualties of the Easter Rising that occurred during his term of office and as the author of some volumes of elegant literary essays, notably *Obiter Dicta* (1884).

After the general election of January 1910 it was clear that the prime minister, H H Asquith, would be dependent on IPP votes in order to stay in power and that long-promised 'step by step' legislation was now due. The House of Lords, old enemy of any change, had acquiesced in the sundering of its veto in Commons' financial bills and was left with the mere right to postpone the ratification of all other bills. It had proved in the past adamantine in its opposition to Irish devolution but, since 30 August 1910, it could only delay by two years what the lower house initiated. Asquith called the second general election on 3 December but was not able to improve on the January result. Both the Conservatives and Liberals held 272 seats, Labour gained two to bring their total to forty-two, while the Irish Party had a bargaining seventy-five.

The Third Home Rule Bill could no longer be postponed and was introduced on 11 April 1912. It proposed a limited devolution not greatly dissimilar to that of Gladstone's first bill of 1886. It would establish a House of Commons with 146 members, elected for a five-year term. An upper house to be called the Senate would have its forty members nominated by the Lord Lieutenant in the first instance and then by normal election at the end of five years. Ireland would continue to have forty members in the Westminster parliament, which would retain in perpetuity the collection of taxes and, for ten years, the control of old-age pensions, national insurance, the Post Office, savings banks and friendly societies. It would also control the RIC. Irish autonomy would be confined to the imposition of taxes other than income tax and the right to impose certain customs duties. The Dublin parliament could also control the Irish legal system, including the appointment of judges. There would be grants from Britain of revenue from Irish taxes and a fixed rate of subvention of £500,000 for three years thereafter.

It was hardly revolutionary and ludicrously short of what Sinn Féin, for example, intended but Redmond was prone to accept it, showing both disappointment and relief. As he wrote to Bishop O'Donnell on 26 December 1911 after Asquith revealed the main proposals: 'In some respects they are better than I had hoped for, in other respects objectionable. But I am very hopeful.'

Devlin was given the job of selling the deal to the wider constituency. He put on his tirelessly brave face: 'We are for freedom first and finance afterwards. We are not hucksters out for a commercial deal.' (He was not ever regarded as having any real fiscal sense.) Devlin was ill that winter and he found it hard to hide his disappointment over Asquith's ungenerous proposals in spite of his perennially brave public face. He intended to spend some weeks in Menton, the French Riviera resort famous for its winter mildness, but found it advisable to cut his holiday short. Winston Churchill, as a member of the Cabinet, First Lord of the Admiralty, and as a self-regarding 'expert' on Ireland, was invited by the Ulster Liberal Association to visit Belfast to speak in favour of the government's proposals. Since the association was not a large enough body to fill a hall it was realised there should have to be a considerable involvement of Devlin and nationalists in the event. The First Lord was therefore to share the platform with Redmond and William James Pirrie, the quasi-Liberal managing director of Harland and Wolff, the larger of the two shipyards.

The reservation at the Ulster Hall for Thursday, 8 February 1912, was confirmed but the Ulster Unionist Council booked the hall for the previous day and it was clear that they intended to continue in occupation to prevent Churchill's reversal of his father Randolph's mantra of Ulster's right to fight uttered fifty-six years before in the same, now sacred, venue. Devlin hurried home to be part of the prestigious event and to devise an alternative venue. The first choice was, of course, the nationalist or, more correctly, Catholic St Mary's Hall, built in 1875, and conveniently sited just off Royal Avenue. Birrell insisted that the venue was 'repugnant to the fine susceptibilities of the Ulster Liberals', though since he was the essence of mandarin sophistication, it may well have been an entirely ironic comment. No large alternative venue was, it seemed, available. F W Warden, the proprietor of the Opera House, later claimed that he had been offered a knighthood by Lloyd George and a substantial fee for the use of the theatre. It was odd that the Wellington Hall, that had been the centre for the first Labour Party conference, was also unavailable.

Churchill was not exactly being overwhelmed by traditional Ulster hospitality. It was time for a piece of Devlinesque lateral thinking. So it was that the First Lord took part in a torchlight procession up the Falls to the eleven-year-old Celtic Park on the Donegall Road. On his arrival at Larne he had been greeted by a menacing crowd singing the national anthem and after lunch a group of militant shipyard workers surrounded his car with the apparent intention of turning it over. A cry of 'mind the wumman' stopped them; someone had noticed that Clemmie was sitting by her husband's side. Once past Castle Street the atmosphere changed. Effigies of Carson and Sir James Craig (1871–1940) were in evidence instead of Redmond, and the semi-mythical Lundy, who as good little Protestant children knew from the compressed history taught them, had sold the keys of Derry to the Jacobites for a bap and a herring.

In Celtic Park, not yet known as 'Paradise' to football supporters, Devlin had erected a large marquee, and an audience of 8,000, who had braved relentless rain, heard him aver: 'In an Irish parliament if it is ever my good fortune to be there, I will find myself in closer touch with the Protestant artisans of Ulster and Belfast than I would with the Catholic farmers of Munster and Connacht.' The meeting ended with 'God Save the King' and Churchill was safely escorted back circuitously by nationalist streets to York Street where a special train took him to the Larne steamer. He had been given a taste of

Belfast Unionism in all its charm and it did change his attitude. As a former Home Secretary he was aware of the high security that was required to avoid serious disturbance and perhaps knew that three battalions of soldiers were on duty about the Falls but even he did not know that four more battalions were 'lying doggo at different points in the town', as Brigadier-General Count Gleichen, the OC, later admitted. The only slight disruption to the proceedings, once he had run the Orange gauntlet in Royal Avenue, was a question in a broad Belfast accent: 'Will you give the suffrage to women?' Churchill had closed with the optimistic words: 'We have done a good day's work and I do not think any of us will ever have cause to regret it.' In fact the net effect of all the drama was nil, except for an intensification of Unionist recalcitrance and its ever-present but unuttered fear.

The giant Home Rule rally held on 31 March 1912 was the largest ever seen in Dublin; it was a typical piece of organisational legerdemain by Devlin with four different platforms, from one of which, sited close to the GPO, Patrick Pearse (1879–1916) spoke in Irish giving a cautious assent to the proposed bill as 'for the good of Ireland... we shall be stronger with it than without it.' Four years later, close to the same spot, he announced the setting up of the republic and in doing so changed history, made himself a willing martyr, and with collateral damage, undid Redmond's life work. Stephen Gwynn, a Protestant Nationalist, described the crowds in O'Connell Street in his book *John Redmond's Last Years* (1919):

> On that day, from the Parnell monument at the north end to the O'Connell monument to the south, you could have walked on the shoulders of the people.

It was Redmond himself who had unveiled the statue of his old chief Parnell on 1 October the previous year.

Unionist reaction was swift. With a new leader in the abrasive, even ruthless Bonar Law, the Conservative Party aligned themselves totally with the UUC. As if in mockery of the great Dublin rally, Carson and Craig organised a huge demonstration on Easter Tuesday, 9 April, at the Agricultural Society's showgrounds at Balmoral, a southern suburb of Belfast. One hundred thousand men, brought by seventy trains, marched past a 90-feet high flagstaff on which was unfurled, at the moment of the passing of an anti-Home Rule motion, a giant Union flag, 48 feet by 25 feet, probably the largest ever woven, even in 'Linenopolis'. The guest speaker was Bonar Law and he described the occasion as 'the expression of the soul of a people'. He concluded with a version of a speech made in 1805 by Pitt the Younger: 'You have saved yourself by your exertions and you will save the Empire by your example.' He moved even closer to treason when, at another Unionist rally on 12 July at Blenheim Palace, the seat of the Duke of Marlborough, Churchill's cousin, he said: 'I can imagine no length of resistance to which Ulster can go in which I should not be prepared to support them.'

Tension was high throughout the province during the summer of 1912; there were many episodes of violence, some spontaneous, some deliberately orchestrated. The Ulster Volunteer Force, essentially the Unionists' standing army, prepared for the predicted civil war, had not formally been established but its personnel, centred in the Orange Order and other fraternal bodies, were still an effective and easily mobilised counter Home Rule force. On the Nationalist side there was the AOH, showing several aspects of its Orangeism – with, of course, different colour coding – but smaller in numbers and with no establishment support. They campaigned vigorously in nationalist areas and, like their brothers on the other side of the political divide, were sometimes guilty of local independent outrage.

On Saturday, 29 June, there occurred what the Unionist *Belfast News Letter* described in its strap as 'Disgraceful Affair at Castledawson' and deplored the 'Hibernians Cowardly Conduct'. An AOH procession complete with bands was on its way back from a Home Rule rally in Maghera. Castledawson, at the Moyola River, was the chosen site for a Sunday School excursion by Whitehouse Presbyterian Church from just outside Belfast on the north shore of the lough. The children were marshalled in the picnic field prior to walking the short distance to the railway station. They were accompanied by the Throne Flute Band, composed mainly of boys, that followed a banner and, according to the paper, 'a small Union Jack being carried at the head of the party'. The leader, the Rev Robert Barron, though apprised of the possible convergence, assumed that because of the orderly nature of his group and the fact that they were mostly juveniles, it was safe for them to proceed. Many of the AOH party were 'under the influence', as Devlin admitted later, but it is doubtful if they attacked the children with 'pikes and bludgeons', as the *News Letter* reported. The Hibernians, menaced by local adults, retreated a short distance from the scene but continued to throw stones at the children until the local constabulary arrived with carbines, thankfully loaded with blanks, and brought about some defusing of the situation. The newspaper reported that 'The banner was damaged and one or two flags were left behind.'

Word travelled swiftly back to Belfast that a Sunday School party had been attacked by a drunken party of the dreaded Hibernians, armed for battle. The assumed trigger for the attack was 'the small Union Jack' that, in that febrile summer, was a flag too far; there was, of course, many more than one flag, as the *News Letter* reporter later revealed. The whole ugly incident was deeply regrettable, and annoyed and saddened Devlin. His response was to cancel all the usual meetings that the AOH had planned for 15 August, their traditional annual hosting date. Redmond later told the fiery Charles McHugh, Bishop of Derry, that the incident had seriously prejudiced 'our cause in Great Britain and the House of Commons'. The immediate sequel was much more ominous.

The Rev Barron referred to the incident at the Sunday morning service and pleaded with his congregation not to create ill-will against their Catholic neighbours, but with the publication of the story in the Monday's papers, reprisal was inevitable.

The village of Whitehouse was not far from the Workman Clark shipyard – the 'wee yard' – and the one more prone than Harland and Wolff to eviction of Catholics and/or trade union activists from the workplace under a hail of 'Belfast confetti'. By the morning break on Tuesday, 2 July, Catholic workers were surrounded by knots of grim-faced, foul-mouthed Protestants who ordered them to leave the yard. As they did so they were beaten and kicked and forced to run away from the lethal metal discs, the detritus from the riveters' punches, and the rivets themselves. There were twenty-five assaults inside the yards and fifty-five about the city, and the Catholics dared not return. Devlin chided Carson in the House of Commons about these expulsions: 'Why did the right honourable gentleman, if the law was to be broken, not go over and throw the rivets himself...' instead of inflaming the passions of 'the poor dupes of the academic anarchist?' The extremely basic social services did little to help since the 3,000 expelled workers had left their places 'voluntarily'. John Tohill (1855–1914), Bishop of Down and Connor, tried to alleviate the widespread distress by setting up, on 7 July, a relief fund that amounted to £5,000. At the height of the tension the condition of the hungry unemployed was such that about 1,400 appeals were made weekly.

Sectarian tension was general throughout the city that summer and autumn, rekindling a violence of an intensity not seen since 1863. Soldiers were drafted to help the police and they managed largely to smother the threat of violence at such obvious flashpoints as York Road and Durham Street, and found it advisable to continue to make their presence felt until the end of September.

On Saturday, 14 September, Belfast Celtic, essentially the leading Catholic football team, judged by an almost total majority of its supporters, and their natural adversaries Linfield met for a fixture at Celtic Park at the Falls Road end of the Donegall Road and uncomfortably near to Windsor Park, Linfield's home pitch. There was a gate of at least ten thousand and when a scuffle at half-time, when the score was 1–0 in Linfield's favour, turned into a mêlée it was remarkable how well equipped the minority factions on both sides were with knives and revolvers, and battle regalia, including flags, placards and banners. Most of the spectators had come simply to see the match and were relieved when, after a baton charge, the rioters were driven out of the ground. Running battles continued until the Protestants were driven back to the Village and other Loyalist enclaves. Still they continued to throw stones indiscriminately over the top of the stand. The unreserved part of the ground was being resurfaced and, as the Press Association correspondent reported: 'All kinds of missiles were… lying handy. There were stones, half-bricks and huge clinkers… Men and youths fell in all directions struck down by huge stones, and bleeding heads and faces were quite common.' More ominously and nastily prophetic, at least five people were treated for gunshot wounds. The Monday papers carried an agency telegram stating that the estimated number of the injured was one hundred, sixty of whom needed hospital treatment, mostly in the Royal, though the Mater Infirmorum, at the foot of the Crumlin Road, recorded ten casualties.

The behaviour of the AOH in Castledawson did no favours to the nationalist cause but the sectarian troubles in the shipyards and other industrial locations, and the organised riot in Celtic Park, revealed Unionists as more violent, even potentially murderous. Just as in 1921 the uncontrolled, regenerated UVF was 'legalised' as the Ulster Special Constabulary, so Carson and James Craig, his native Ulster counterpart in the fight against Home Rule, decided to impose a kind of control over them by wrapping them in the Biblical fervour of the Solemn League and Covenant. This document, based upon the archetypal Civil War agreement between English Parliamentarians and Scots Presbyterians in 1643, was drafted by Thomas Sinclair, leader of the Ulster Liberal Unionists.

The UVF had no difficulty in fulfilling their recommended quota of 100,000 men between the ages of seventeen and sixty-five prepared to sign the covenant. Many members of the native Irish aristocracy publicly supported them and financed them privately. A number of high-ranking officers in the British army (by no means all of Ulster extraction) made clear their approval, apparently oblivious of the implicit mutinous aspects of such support. The upper classes in Britain were equally vocal and generous in their approval. All who had gained financially and psychologically from the British Empire were naturally disposed to defend it. Rudyard Kipling (1865–1936), who could testify with an intimate knowledge of the reality of Her Britannic Majesty's India, was in no doubt. He sent £20,000 (more than a million pounds today) and, using his tremendous powers of versification, slated the Liberal government in a poem called 'Ulster 1912' in which an idealised Ulster voice laments the betrayal of Home Rule. A typical verse reads:

We asked no more than leave
To reap where we had sewn,
Through good and ill to cleave
To our own flag and throne.
Now England's shot and steel
Beneath that flag must show
How loyal hearts should kneel
To England's oldest foe.

Finally, and most ominously, Pirrie, who ran the larger shipyard, joined with fellow magnates in a threat to move their industries out of Ireland altogether.

That summer and autumn Devlin, while not underestimating the courage or the will of his adversaries, was still optimistic that the grail of Home Rule was within his people's grasp. He privately believed that the huffing and puffing of Carson and Craig was mere vapouring and disregarded the threats from the industrialists. At an AOH rally on 15 August 1911 in Donegal, four days after the Parliamentary Act had effectively broken the power of the House of Lords, he had warned that the battle for Home Rule in Ulster would be short and sharp but would undoubtedly be successful. He was as usual tireless in his journeys around the province where he, like Parnell in the nationalist south, was the uncrowned king. Six days after the Celtic Park riot, on Friday, 21 September 1912, he travelled via Enniskillen to the town of Carrick, the centre of Glencolumbkille parish, to accept an address from the residents. His welcome was characteristic of the time and place, and a fitting acknowledgement of his leadership.

As his car drove through the village it was preceded by two local bands and hundreds of torchbearers. Devlin's leadership of Catholic Ulster was now unquestioned and unlike the earlier chief his private life was impeccable – if he could be said to have any private life at all. He could, in fact, have replaced Redmond as all-Ireland leader but preferred to be his Belfast-accented second-in-command. He had the confidence of a majority of the clergy, the battles with Bishop Henry Henry long forgotten or at least forgiven, though Cardinal Logue never recanted his dismissal of the AOH as subversive and a quasi-secret society. The colourful event took place in the Diocese of Raphoe, the bailiwick of Patrick O'Donnell, a strong supporter of John Dillon and Devlin, and a defender of the AOH. The address was read by the senior curate, John McAteer, and the illuminated scroll signed by all the priests in the parish, the local doctor and other dignitaries. It praised his tireless energy, eloquent pleading and steady devotion. It also added a little unexceptionable local colour:

> In spite of the vilest and most unjust abuse from both cranks and knaves you have stood manfully for Ireland's welfare as our own great cliffs of Slieve League and Glen Head stand calmly, heedless of the rush and roar of the angry waves that waste their strength far down beneath them.

It was too much of a hint to ignore; not long after breakfast Devlin and his 'minders', J T Donovan from Belfast and Dr C Powell from Dublin, accepted an invitation from the local parish priest, Fr James C Cannon, to view for themselves the great cliff of Glen Head. Climbing a steep and twisted road at Malinmore, the driver of the car suddenly lost control as an axle snapped and the brakes no longer worked. As the car careered backwards down the hill Powell and Donovan jumped out, shouting to their leader and the priest to do the same. Devlin jumped, injuring his leg and face while the chauffeur, with Fr Cannon still on board, successfully managed to steer his machine into a rise. Devlin came off worst, the others complaining of nothing more than slight shock. Powell advised Devlin to have a more complete medical examination and it was later reported that he had sustained 'grave injuries to his kidneys'. He was ordered to rest for six weeks and, by the time he was able to resume normal duties, the nature of Ulster politics had changed utterly.

Because of the network of Orange lodges and the associated fraternal orders, the Black Preceptory and the Apprentice Boys of Derry, the UVF could with remarkable rapidity disseminate information and mobilise members at every significant part of the province. This efficiency was dramatically demonstrated in the gun-running incident that took place on the night of 24–25 April 1914 when 35,000 rifles and 2,500,000 rounds – ironically from Germany – were landed openly at Larne, Donaghadee and Bangor, and brilliantly delivered to lodges through Ulster. A detailed plan for a replacement government with even the designs for a separate approved Ulster coinage was in the hands of Sir James Craig, whose bucolic exterior hid a genius for organisation. Arrangements were in place for evacuation to friendly Scotland of women and children, though many intended to remain behind to help the improvised corps of doctors run field hospitals. Less flamboyant (and angst-ridden) than Carson, Craig's was the mien that the poet Louis MacNeice (1907–63) would later describe as 'the hard, cold fire of the Northerner'. The Home Rule bill received George V's royal approval on 25 May 1914 and the prospect of a civil war grew closer. Already the army had signalled its non-cooperation in the Curragh Incident of 20 March when General Sir Hubert Gough (1870–1963) persuaded fifty-seven out of seventy British officers stationed in the Curragh in County Kildare to resign their commissions rather than prepare to guard arms depots in Ulster, as ordered by the commander-in-chief, General Sir Arthur Paget (1851–1928).

In the next column to the Castledawson story in the *News Letter* edition of 1 July 1912 is advice of the proposed visit of F[rederick] E[dwin] Smith MP (1872–1930), always known by his initials, and later the 1st Earl Birkenhead, the flamboyant and brilliant Merseyside lawyer. He was credited with the invention of the term 'glittering prizes' on offer to those who got firsts at Oxbridge and became one of Carson's ablest supporters. It was he who prosecuted Roger Casement (1864–1916) so effectively using the notorious 'Black Diaries', detailing the defendant's homosexual adventures. His rhetorical brilliance outshone Carson's and he disappointed more right-wing colleagues by playing a leading part in the Treaty negotiations in 1921. Included in the same story were the chief resolutions that would be submitted during the celebrations on the

Twelfth of July at the 'field', that year in Whiteabbey. There were the usual declarations of 'our invincible loyalty to the Orange Order' and allegiance to 'his most gracious Majesty King George V' but it was in the third motion that the burning question of the day was adumbrated:

> We solemnly declare that we will not surrender our right to be governed directly by our Protestant King and the Protestant Parliament of the United Kingdom, and we shall resist at any sacrifice the great betrayal of all that we hold dear, trusting in the righteousness of our cause and in our own right to arm.

Meanwhile the Irish Revolutionary Brotherhood (IRB), cryonically suspended since Fenian days, was revived by two young Ulstermen, Bulmer Hobson (1883–1969) and Denis McCullough (1883–1969), who would certainly settle for nothing less than an independent Irish republic. A year later, on 25 November 1913, Hobson joined with Eoin MacNeill to form the Irish Volunteers in the Rotunda Rooms in Parnell Square in Dublin. On 1 November MacNeill had written an editorial for the first number of the newly refurbished *An Claideamh Soluis*, the organ of the Gaelic League, with the title: 'The North began'. It drew attention to the recent founding of the UVF as a last-ditch force to prevent the implementation of the Home Rule Bill. With only slight irony he congratulated the Ulster Protestants on their move towards Home Rule for Ulster and their implicit wish to break the chains that bound Ireland to Britain. By the following May the Volunteers' members numbered 80,000 and another barbed briar had been incorporated in the crown of thorns that was the Irish Question.

Asquith had to face the prospect of a bleak civil war with 23,000 armed and exultant men matched against 1,000 soldiers (the total numbers of men stationed there) and a demoralised police force. Devlin, along with many others of the IPP, believed in his heart that the UVF, even led by Carson and Craig, were bluffing. He knew the North better than Parnell and did not dismiss the threat as impatiently as the Chief had in 1886. He knew that Parnell's belief that a notional

'1,000 members of the RIC' who would be more than a match for all the 'Orange rowdies' in the North was unfounded but he was convinced that they could be faced down if sufficient resolve were to be shown by the government. He tried to reassure Asquith about this but his persuasive words had little effect:

> We have nothing but contempt for the threats of civil war and the stage thunder of Carsonism, while we have the most tender regard for the most unfounded of fears of the most credulous of our fellow countrymen. We desire Home Rule for the sake of all our Irishmen.

Yet he would have been surprised and shocked at Asquith's sense of his own incapacity in being unable to risk a confrontation with the High Command that might lead to an army mutiny. In the Prime Minister's view some deflation of a supremely ugly situation was necessary. A number of possible options, all having the element of some form of exclusion for the counties of the northeast, were being suggested in the hope of defusing the explosive atmosphere then prevailing. All had been rejected by both sides but in the hot-house atmosphere of the Home Rule agitation the proposition, once floated, began to grow more substantial. Devlin, Redmond and the 'English' Irish Nationalist, T P O'Connor, insisted that, in Redmond's words, 'The exclusion of Ulster or any portion of Ulster is outside the realm of compromise,' but Asquith was no Gladstone.

The earliest kite to be floated had come from T Agar-Robartes, the Liberal member for St Austell in Cornwall, who proposed in June 1912 an amendment to the Home Rule Bill that would exclude Derry, Antrim, Down and Armagh, the counties with strong Unionist majorities. Described by his contemporary, Stephen Gwynn, as a 'whimsically incongruous figure', he was known as holding formally anti-Catholic views, objecting strongly to Edward VII's removal of offensive matter from the Coronation oath. This bolt from the Celtic fringe was unexpected, to say the least. Its timing seemed too neat, too contrived; to put it crudely it had all the air of a deliberate ploy, a first whiff of grapeshot from the more impatient or conservative wing of the Liberal Party. Carson supported the motion, as if the suggestion were no surprise, while insisting that he would never abandon Tyrone and Fermanagh. The Cornish amendment was defeated 320 to 251 votes but, even before its appearance, the possibility of a compromise had been considered by the pragmatic Lloyd George but was rejected by the Cabinet in 1911, and it was the grisly Plan B that lurked in the background of even the most liberal of the Liberals. Faced with the growing strength of the anti-Home Rule agitation and the fear of the army's refusal to obey their political masters, Asquith began to believe that some reappraisal of the application of the bill in Ulster was not only necessary but inevitable. Churchill, who was an instinctive barometer of the realpolitik of the Ulster situation, had, on 8 October 1912, at a Home Rule meeting in his Dundee constituency, said openly that Unionist Ulster's claim for special treatment 'could not be ignored or brushed aside'.

Redmond was bitterly disappointed as it became clear that, while the Unionists were willing to make no real – as opposed to rhetorical – objection to a majority of Irish counties achieving Home Rule, their final position was that Ulster must be excluded from the bill's provision. Carson's House of Commons resolution of 1 January 1913 that demanded the exclusion of the historical Ulster of the nine counties was also defeated. And, as history shows, the counties of Donegal, Cavan and Monaghan were later to be included in the Free State. Though they all had substantial Protestant populations – they had been Plantation counties – there were sufficient numbers of nationalists to render them unsafe politically. The addition of the 'mixed' Tyrone and Fermanagh to Derry, Antrim, Down and Armagh was a gamble worth taking, for the six counties represented the minimum possible for a viable separate state.

All of the various types of exclusion implicitly and explicitly viewed Ireland as consisting of two entities, a unionist North and a nationalist South. Such a crude dichotomy took no account of the three-quarter of a million Catholics in Tyrone, south Armagh, south Down, the west bank of Derry city, and the 100,000 in Belfast. In the years of the UVF campaign that lasted right up to the beginning of the Great War such an arrangement was never visualised by Redmond or Devlin.

Partition would have meant in their eyes the disintegration of the nation. Even Balfour, Home Rule's most resolute opponent, believed with Devlin that an Ireland without Ulster would be a catastrophe:

> I take Devlin's view, and were I an Irish nationalist I think I should refuse Home Rule on the terms proposed. With all the industrial energy and all the money left out of the new community, and nothing left in it but the Irish genius for parliamentary debate and political organisation, I do not see that they have much prospect of playing a satisfactory part in the world's history.

In its dismissal of the other three provinces as parts of some kind of impractical, fey Never-Never Land it was a typical piece of Tory condescension and really not all that complimentary to Ulster but it showed a realisation of what the post-operative trauma following such surgery might entail.

The devolution elements of the original bill were paltry enough but exclusion for so many nationalists, at the mercy, it seemed, of the Orange Order was unthinkable. The besetting fear, formally expressed by Cardinal Michael Logue, Archbishop of Armagh, and his successor Patrick O'Donnell, was that the exclusion zone would be given 'autonomy' in matters of education. This concern about the control and nature of the education of the young imposed upon the clergy by the still pervasive Council of Trent was to cause deep clerical suspicion and a prickly non-compliance with successive governments in Northern Ireland. It was also a recipe for institutional inequality, involving permanent opposition for nationalist MPs and a cynical glass ceiling that precluded promotion to the higher levels in the public service, as later events would confirm.

Two other possible concessions offered to northern unionists were put forward by Sir Horace Plunkett (1854–1932), one of the founders of the Irish cooperative movement, and Sir Edward Grey (1862–1933), Asquith's long-serving Foreign Secretary. The first suggested the offer of the right to exclusion after a trial period of ten years. Devlin, only too aware of wobbling on Asquith's part, urged this strongly; he even suggested an increased presence at Westminster and in Dublin for Unionists. Never sectarian, his faith in the commonsense of ordinary Protestants persuaded him that when they had experienced the advantages of devolution – and enjoyed their prominent position in the new state – they would no longer wish for exclusion. Grey's suggestion was described as 'Home Rule within Home Rule', offering a kind of federal link between Belfast and Dublin. Redmond would have been prepared to accept some such plan. However, the state of emotional elation that suffused all the northern unionists made any compromise unlikely.

The usually imperturbable Asquith had by the early months of 1914 become seriously worried and one can imagine the Machiavellian Lloyd George, turned Mephistopheles, whispering relentlessly in his ear as he described the catastrophic result of the Tories' threat to obstruct the army estimates bill unless they were assured that the forces would not be used against the UVF. It would mean, in effect, the removal of the government's control over the armed forces, mainly because of its inability to pay, and lead to an immediate general election that Bonar Law and his party would win. Presented with this possibility the weary Redmond had to acquiesce, realising that should that situation arise Home Rule legislation would be postponed indefinitely. The exclusion formula favoured by Lloyd George was known as the 'county option'; if at least one-tenth of the voters in any county insisted on exclusion that county would not have to accept Home Rule for 'x' years. After that later-to-be-specified time it would come under the rule of a Dublin parliament, unless the Westminster assembly disapproved. The value of 'x' the unknown became the subject of fierce debate. Redmond, having conceded the principle of exclusion, insisted that its value should be three with a general election during that period.

Exclusion for Ulster was then a fact; Dillon, the elder statesman, had acquiesced and Devlin had had to agree. He was more personally involved with Home Rule as an all-Ireland policy than the older man, who, like many southern politicians, preferred to avert their eyes when the troubled and troublesome northern province was discussed. The poet W B Yeats summed up a prevalent attitude at the time of the

Treaty, recorded by his friend and sponsor Augusta Lady Gregory (1850–1932) in her journal:

> I have always been of the opinion that if surly disagreeable neighbours shut the door, it is better to turn the key in it before they change their minds.

Dillon could not have been so airily dismissive but he had to give way, and Devlin, more responsive to his advice than Redmond's, after much argument and heartburn, also acquiesced; and it was he who had the burden of selling the deal to his northern nationalists.

He was, however, tireless in his attempt to remind Dillon and Redmond – and Lloyd George – that there was still a majority in the House and nothing the Conservatives could do would prevent the bill's passing. The House of Lords could legally go no further with its delaying tactics. He circulated a memo to all interested parties in February 1914 assuring them that the leadership of the Ulster Nationalists had 'exceptional sources of information in regard to the Ulster Volunteer movement' and were 'convinced that its danger is grossly exaggerated... In Belfast ... where Catholic and Protestant home rulers would be among the first victims of any outbreak among the Orangemen, [they] regard the whole thing with absolute contempt.' This strongly stated belief was shared by many of his followers but it was a risk neither Asquith nor Lloyd George would take.

The value of 'x' was later increased by Birrell to five years and upped to six by Asquith in a vain attempt to mollify the opposition. Carson's reaction was to note with some triumph that the principle had been accepted by the government but dismissed the time limit as 'a sentence of death with a stay of execution for six years'. Throughout the endlessly tedious round of negotiations Carson remained at heart an absolute Unionist. He supported exclusion as a weapon but it was not his final goal; that was simply the preservation of the Union.

It was Craig, less emotional but more determined, who was prepared to accept partition as the only form of permanent exclusion; in fact, Protestant Home Rule. Tension increased with the Curragh incident and Gough's threats. The Home Rule Bill had had to have incorporated an exclusion element to prevent, as Asquith insisted, absolute anarchy. The bill that was passed in the House of Commons on 25 May 1914 allowed the county option for a no greater period than six years and the Lords amended it to the exclusion of all nine Ulster counties in perpetuity. Asquith had not revealed just what kind of exclusion his Amending Bill would contain. It was due to be presented on 20 July but instead he announced, in a desperate attempt to break the exclusion impasse, a conference to be held in Buckingham Palace from 21 to 24 July.

It was made in the king's name and indeed George V gave an introductory address:

> We have watched with deep misgivings the course of events in Ireland… today the cry of civil war is on the lips of the most responsible people… to me it is unthinkable, as it must be to you, that we should be brought to the brink of fratricidal strife upon issues apparently so capable of adjustment as those you are now asked to consider.

The government was represented by Asquith and Lloyd George; Bonar Law and Lord Lansdowne (1845–1927), spokesman for southern Unionists, for the Opposition; Carson and Craig for Ulster Unionists; and Redmond and Dillon for Nationalists. Devlin was not invited, even as a counsellor. They talked for four days, Redmond holding for the 'county option' while Carson quite reasonably argued that a provincial Ulster exclusion with a large nationalist minority was the best guarantee of eventual Irish unity. When the conference broke up without success, Asquith remarked ruefully, his favourite mien: 'Nothing could have been more amicable in tone or more desperately fruitless in result.' The parties all left the palace to prepare for the coming conflict.

Eleven days later Britain had declared war on Germany because of her invasion of Belgium, after a confused, unnecessary and finally catastrophic diplomatic debacle, and as Churchill wrote in *The World Crisis* (1923), 'The parishes of Fermanagh and Tyrone faded back into the mists and squalls of Ireland.'

10
'Wee Bottlewasher – Recruiting Sergeant'

THE ULSTER VOLUNTEER FORCE WAS established on 31 January 1913 formally to be the standing army that would defend Ulster against Rome Rule. Carson and Craig, aware of the soaring emotions that the signing of the Covenant the previous September had roused in an estimated 100,000 volunteers, realised that such energies should be controlled, disciplined and brought under the umbrella of the UUC. Drilling was open since the two local magistrates required to grant permission in each district were often members themselves.

By the late autumn the idea for a similar venture had occurred to two separate parties in Dublin. One was the formation of an Irish Citizen Army to defend Irish workers against strike-breakers and the Dublin Metropolitan Police (DMP), who were ordered to 'keep the peace' during the 1913 Dublin Lock-Out. On 1 November Eoin MacNeill's editorial in *An Claidheamh Soluis*, the organ of the Gaelic League, had suggested the formation of a similar body of volunteers to follow what the North began and provide a complementary force to that of the UVF.

He organised a meeting at the Rotunda rink in Parnell Square on 25 November, having previously discussed the idea in Wynn's Hotel with Patrick Pearse, Bulmer Hobson and Sean Mac Diarmada (1884–1916) a fortnight earlier. The Irish Volunteers were to play a significant part in the history of Ireland for the next five years both in the North and South. The historians among the leaders could not help considering the effect of the founding of an earlier militia in the last quarter of the eighteenth century. Membership then was bourgeois or aristocratic, mainly Protestant but liberally inclined and strong enough eventually to win a modicum of home government in Grattan's parliament. This was adverted to in the manifesto that MacNeill read out to a greatly overcrowded hall:

> In the name of national unity, of national dignity, of national and individual liberty, of manly citizenship, we appeal to our countrymen to recognise and accept without hesitation the opportunity that has been granted to them to join the ranks of the Irish Volunteers and to make the movement now begun not unworthy of the historic title which it has adopted.

Four thousand joined that evening and by the end of December the numbers had reached 10,000. Though known generally as Irish Volunteers, MacNeill, appropriately enough as one of the founders of the Gaelic League and professor of early Irish history at UCD, referred to them as *Óglaigh na hÉireann* ('Young Warriors of Ireland').

The volunteers were almost all Catholic and proletarian but they believed themselves to have the potential for political change. It had the perhaps unintended result of providing the long latent IRB with a voice and increased membership. Old Fenians like Thomas Clarke (1857–1916) were committed to a militarist approach and he saw in the educationist Pearse and his urging of a blood sacrifice that would irrigate the barren soil of Irish nationalism the charismatic leader that would revive old ideals. Though originally a somewhat lukewarm Redmondite, the talk of exclusion and a general distrust of the British government made Pearse impatient of what he saw as empty promises and he eventually agreed with Clarke's prompting to join the IRB and become the leader of the irrigatory Easter rising.

At the beginning membership was greater in the North since such a force might give some protection against the UVF, who, with 100,000 members, were, they claimed, ready to defy not only the British government but even its army. Redmond, still the undoubted leader and voice not only of the IPP but also of non-Unionist Ireland, took some time to make up his mind. He was essentially honest, often a drawback in contemporary politics, and also gentlemanly in his behaviour. He not only wouldn't but couldn't play dirty. He was no match for Lloyd George, who seemed to change his views with his company. Margot Asquith, the Prime Minister's wife, said of him that he could never see a belt without hitting below it, and he was gently pilloried in a contemporary verse:

> Count not his broken pledges as a crime:
> He meant them, *how* he meant them at the time.

Throughout the early months of 1913 Redmond was continually urged by well-wishers to raise a similar force but, Asquith-like, he decided to 'wait and see'. His mentor, the old Chief, always believed that after six months most letters answered themselves, if left alone. Now, after the UVF's successful landing of arms from Germany in April, the increasing violence of Carson's oratory, and the resultant great increase in the numbers of the volunteers, Redmond decided it was time for action. He made his position clear on 10 June in a letter to the *Freeman's Journal*:

> Up to two months ago I felt that the Volunteer movement was somewhat premature but the effect of Sir Edward Carson's threats upon public opinion in England, the house of Commons and the Government, the occurrences at the Curragh Camp, and the successful gun-running in Ulster have vitally altered the position and the Irish party took steps about six weeks ago to inform their friends and supporters in the country that in their opinion it was desirable to support the Volunteer movement, with the result that the movement has spread like a prairie fire and all the nationalists of Ireland will shortly be enrolled.
>
> Within the last fortnight I have had communications from men in all parts of the country, inquiring as to the organisation and control of the Volunteer movement, and it has been strongly recommended to me that the Governing Body should be reconstructed and placed on a thoroughly representative basis, so as to give confidence to all shades of national opinion.

Redmond virtually took over the force from MacNeill to the dismay of the IRB members who intended to use it for their own purposes. There had been meetings with the provisional committee of twenty-five members of the original group. None had any significant connection with the Irish Party; they were mostly members of the Gaelic League, Sinn Féin and the exhumed IRB. No agreement about a control mechanism could be reached until Redmond, prompted by Devlin, demanded the right to appoint a further twenty-five of his own choice. The alternative, he advised, was that he would start a rival force. MacNeill's provisional committee agreed on a majority vote to acquiesce, though Pearse complained that eight out of the standing committee then formed would do exactly what Redmond ordered but that they should make no break until 'our men are at least armed'. The remark had an extra significance when on Saturday, 25 July, 5,000 UVF members, carrying rifles and trailing four machine guns, marched through Belfast without interference. The following day members of the Volunteers landed 1,500 German rifles from the yacht *Asgard*, owned and manned by Erskine Childers (1870–1922). A detachment of the King's Own Scottish Borderers, supplemented by members of the DMP, sent to intercept, failed to impound them. As they marched back to barracks they met a hostile crowd of Dublin citizens on Bachelor's Walk and in the mêlée that followed four people were killed and thirty-four wounded, though there was no order to fire given.

The difference in reaction to Volunteer 'gun-running' in contrast to that of the UVF when, in April, 35,000 rifles and two million rounds were brought in at Larne without even token resistance by the government, was patent. The effect, apart from an ever greater suspicion of partiality by the government towards Unionism, was a surge of enrolment in the Irish Volunteers.

The declaration of war on 4 August temporarily defused the Ulster crisis; it gave time for reassessment and, when the short sharp war was over, the interested parties could come together and settle at long last the perennial Irish Question. Only two problems were ignored in this view of the situation: no one really knew just how long hostilities would last – Christmas was the usual end date, in the presumption that commonsense and diplomacy would counteract the dreadful mistake – and the other, to which no heed was overtly paid, was that the problem of exclusion was still there underneath all the jingoism of showing the Kaiser what was what. The War Office worked quickly and called up the 20,000 members of the Volunteers who were army reservists. By this means their military capacity was almost totally wiped out. Evidence of government partiality continued to appear. About a third of the members of the UVF, once 'Carson's Army', were given special kudos as the 36th (Ulster) Division in Kitchener's New Army and allowed to wear Orange collarettes as they marched to their deaths at the Ancre, a tributary of the Somme, in July 1916.

No such recognition was granted to the Volunteers, who had no badge of national identity though Catholic recruitment was in the same proportion to the population as Protestant, and deaths, especially at Mons in 1914 and the Dardanelles (1915–6), were just as high. The Munster Fusiliers and the Dublin Fusiliers, two Irish regiments that bore the brunt of the fighting, were not mentioned in dispatches, the only forces not so honoured. The War Office responded more to Carson's abrasiveness than to Redmond's gentlemanliness. It was not impressed by his option for 'good behaviour', moved rather by the illegalities of Carson and Craig. It even refused a commission to Willie Redmond, John's son. Irish regiments who were not permitted officers from within their own ranks had invariably officers who were Unionist or non-Irish. This evidence of British mean-spiritedness only emerged later. In the early months of the conflict there was a palpable sense of euphoria, even though Asquith had made it clear that Home Rule was postponed until the end of hostilities, and that there would be exclusion of at least six of the Ulster counties.[1]

Of several tactical errors made by Redmond and assented to by Devlin the enthusiastic embracing of recruitment was the one that caused most damage to the IPP and the cause of constitutionalism. In this matter Devlin was for the first time at odds with his old mentor Dillon and adhered more closely to Redmond. When it was clear that war was inevitable, on 3 August, the latter offered the Volunteers as a force which, combining with the UVF, would, as in 1778, allow the garrison forces of the British army to leave Ireland to fight her foreign war. 'With our brethren in the North we will ourselves defend the coasts of our country.' He seems to have believed that a band of trained nationalist ex-soldiers would after the short war be more than a match for the UVF and Carson's threat of 'mobilisation'.

The War Office, not at all dewy-eyed, did not respond to this generous offer of a home guard but required Irish recruits at all costs. When Kitchener met Redmond he was friendly and at that stage of the war relatively undemanding: 'Get me 5,000 men and I will say thank you; get me 10,000 and I will take off my hat to you.' Redmond, anxious to be as accommodating as possible, gave his most public seal of approbation for the Allied cause with his speech at Woodenbridge, County Wicklow, on 20 September. In a sudden burst of feeling, reflecting his predominantly 'imperial' instincts, he offered the Volunteers to serve 'wherever they were needed'. Redmond's cry, 'The proper place to guard Ireland is on the battlefields of France', though fine rhetoric and logical according to his convictions, was used against Devlin for decades afterwards. This was a considerable advance on Redmond's earlier offer of them acting with their Northern brethren as defenders at home; in fact it delivered them to almost certain death in the Flanders mud.

In partial mitigation we may note that the first major battle of the war at the Marne, a river fifty kilometres east of Paris, had ended in stalemate ten days before, the Central powers and the Allies both losing 25 percent of their forces, and there was yet no reason to assume that the war would not be 'over by Christmas', as everyone believed. It was not until November that the Western Front was locked into the obscenity of trench warfare. For many, too, the army pay delivered to wives was regular and rather more than they were used to while their husbands were at home. If Redmond needed a model of the dominion status he would have settled for what he found in Canada and he knew that the 3,000 men of the Canadian Expeditionary Force were already on their way to France.

Not everyone took the same view, however. MacNeill, Hobson

and the hardline IRB members of the *Óglaigh*, notably Mac Diarmada, had no intention of following the Redmondite line. Germany was not the enemy, but Britain. Indeed, Roger Casement was already in Germany buying arms and trying to form an Irish Brigade from among prisoners of war. Most of those whom the British shot in 1916 had begun to plan what became known as the Easter Rising, prepared to be martyrs in the hope of stirring the dull roots of Irish nationalism. A week after Woodenbridge, up to 12,000 sheered off from the Volunteers, reverting to the title of *Óglaigh na hÉireann* or more commonly 'Irish Volunteers'. Redmond was glad to see the back of them, fearing the IRB influence, and already conscious of a kind of exaltation among the dissidents as they prepared for the blood sacrifice. He still controlled his own National Volunteers, who numbered about 120,000 after the split.

Devlin, with his great, almost relentless loyalty, became overnight a successful recruiting officer, using his rhetorical skills to persuade young Ulstermen to enlist in the 'war to end wars' to fight for the 'rights of small nations' or even to succour 'Catholic' Belgium, the last felt deeply by him as a fervent believer. At a rally in September he told his attentive listeners:

> This is a war for human liberty. We told the British people that if they gave Ireland that autonomy that inspired the loyalty of her colonies in every part of her world-wide empire, Ireland would give the treasure of her blood and her allegiance to that Empire which, when it gives freedom, constitutes itself the mightiest factor in the progress of human liberty to be found in all the world today.

Two months later he was able to reassure Asquith on a visit to Belfast: 'You may count on the Home Rulers of this city to the last man in defence of our common rights and liberties.' When war was declared he was halfway into his forty-fourth year and, of course, wanted to enlist but Redmond was too dependent on him in parliament and at home in Belfast. Even those who disapproved of his politics could not accuse him of cowardice. Instead he continued to speak at recruiting rallies and appoint himself as an unofficial but tireless welfare officer for the wives and families of his recruits, who, in Derry joined the 6th Royal Irish and in Belfast the 7th Leinsters and the 6th Connaught Rangers.

Redmond used him as his man in Belfast, with no hint of condescension. Many believed that it was he rather than the minor grandee from Wexford who should have been used in primary negotiation with Carson and Lloyd George. He smarted a little at not being invited to Buckingham Palace and it is certain that, had he been a delegate, he should not, as Redmond did, say to Carson: 'Let's have a good shake-hand for the sake of the good old days on the circuit', when the conference finished without result. He was employed willingly as the deliverer of unpleasant information and utilised to reconcile his followers to unpalatable decisions that seemed to them near-betrayals. He was also used as a kind of human Rottweiler to menace the dissidents and, if necessary, expel them. Of 3,000 of the original numbers of Volunteers in Belfast only 200 left to join the smaller group, a number that included Denis McCullough and Bulmer Hobson.

Most of these strongly and vocally objected to the members of the IPP doing the British government's 'dirty work' for them. The most swingeing criticism of all came from James Connolly, who, by 1914, had yet another force of volunteers in the Irish Citizen Army. There already existed a tacit understanding between him and the Irish Volunteers that, should they opt for rebellion, his group would be part of it, hoping for a general rising of workers, a reasonable hope by all Marxist calculations. In his newspaper *Worker's Republic* on 28 August 1915, when the full horrors of the Great War had become clear, he rounded on 'that great heroic figure, Wee Joe Devlin':

> As I think of the hundreds of good men I have known, fathers of families, husbands, sons with aged parents… who have been enticed to leave their homes and dear ones and march out to battle for an Empire that never kept faith with the Irish race, and think that it was Wee Joe's influence that led them to their folly, I think things that the Defence of the Realm Act will not permit me to print.
>
> Belfast opponents of Joe Devlin usually refer to him sarcastically as the 'Wee Bottlewasher', alluding to his position before he climbed into power. A bottlewasher is an honest occupation but a recruiting sergeant luring to

their deaths the men who trusted him and voted him into power is – ah well, let us remember the Defence of the Realm Act.

The present writer cannot ride up the Falls in his own motor car, the penny tram has to do him. But thank God, there are no fresh made graves in Flanders or the Dardanelles filled by the mangled corpses of men whom he coaxed or bullied into leaving their homes and families.

And that consolation counts more to the peace of his soul than would the possession of a motor car or the companionship of grossly overfed boon companions of the bottlewasher – or of the bottle.

Devlin took the personal attack unflinchingly but a paragraph near the end of the piece hurt him, and the charges Connolly made continued to haunt him for the rest of his career:

There are widows in Belfast today whose husbands would still be with them if they had taken my advice; there are orphans in Belfast today whose fathers would still be able to work for them and love them if they had taken my advice; there are stricken mothers and fathers in Belfast today whose sons would be smiling and happy at the family hearth today if my advice had been listened to.

In the euphoria of the first months of the war Devlin had over optimistically joined with Redmond in offering recruits. In fact, in the North as in Dublin, as we have seen, persuading men to enlist was not especially difficult. The 'separation' pay given to army wives was, by the borderline-poverty standards of the time, substantial and for many families it was the first steady income they received.

The setting of the workers, enrolled in the Allied forces, against their fellows in the Central powers' ranks was, in extreme socialist eyes, capitalism at its most cruel. Devlin's part in the process, as far as Connolly was concerned, was proof of his perfidy as was his association with the AOH. He was by doctrinaire standards a traitor to his class and more the enemy of the proletariat than any industrial magnate. In the *Irish Worker*, his paper, suppressed in December 1914, Connolly described the AOH as 'the foulest growth that ever cursed this island'. Cardinal Logue must have been pleased at such socialist solidarity.

Devlin's activities were closely monitored. In April 1915 he went on an official visit to Paris, accompanied by T P O'Connor and other

Irish MPs. It was more of a junket than a significant visit but Devlin was pleased to be entertained by the president, Raymond Poincaré (1860–1934), and the premier, René Viviani (1862–1925). He brought pledges of support for the war effort from the AOH and hoped to win Catholic and Irish people throughout the world for the cause. The Sinn Féin and other anti-IPP newspapers, in a surge of instant piety, a mode which they did very well, drew attention to the fact that Viviani was a noted freemason and a secularist in education. It was but a small step to accuse Devlin of importing freemasonry into holy Ireland to add to his more heinous crimes of turning the wives of absent soldiers into prostitutes for the British army garrisons.

Such comments must have hurt Devlin, who, for all his assumed cheerfulness and overt pugnacity, was quite soft underneath. It may have given him some wry comfort that his chief had been pilloried seven months earlier in the same paper by Connolly:

> Full steam ahead, John Redmond said
> And everything is well, chum.
> Home Rule will come when we are dead
> And buried out in Belgium.

He half suspected that the existence of such truculence and sniping was evidence of a growing militancy on the part of *Óglaigh na hÉireann*, and while he could not but sympathise with their disgust at Britain's attitude to Ireland, he did not approve of their tactics. Devlin had had a taste of this militant attitude at a meeting with MacNeill and the others. He and the hardline republican, Éamonn Ceannt (1881–1916), one of the signatories of the Declaration of the Republic, who faced a firing squad on 8 May 1916, had an altercation that was followed by a brief bout of fisticuffs between Devlin's friend, John D Nugent (1869–1940), and Patrick Pearse which ended with drawn revolvers. Devlin's oldest priest friend, Fr Frank O'Hare of Hilltown, County Down, who acted as a kind of unofficial bodyguard, drew his pistol and challenged Ceannt to do the same. Connolly, the last of the 1916 leaders to be executed, did not live to see how completely the calculated, deliberate sacrifice of their lives and the unrestrained military response would obliterate the pallid Home Rulers he regarded as worse than enemies, and effectively finish Devlin's career in national politics.

Away from evidence of Irish Volunteer extremism the North took the war in its stride. Typical of the popularity and indeed respectability of the principle of volunteering was the general acclamation when Devlin presented colours to the 2nd Battalion in Derry on Sunday, 18 October 1914. It was, according to the *Derry Journal* reporter, writing in the decorous manner of the time, an afternoon of 'delightful weather' and the blessing and presentation of the colours 'was witnessed by a very large assemblage of citizens and visitors from surrounding districts'. The listed guests included twelve local priests, Philip O'Doherty, the local MP, six Justices of the Peace, six solicitors and eight town councillors. Notably absent was the local bishop, Charles McHugh, whose health was always indifferent and who was to prove to be no Devlinite. The ceremony took place in Celtic Park, the local GAA field on the Lone Moor Road, next to Brandywell, later the home ground of the more famous, and popular, Derry City Football Club.

Devlin entered the field accompanied by his oldest friend, the Belfast solicitor, Vincent de Voto, attendance at whose funeral in January 1934 accelerated his own death eight days later. As the volunteers marched into the centre of the field carrying rifles with fixed bayonets, music was supplied by local bands, two brass and reed, four fife and drum, and the Columbkille Pipers' Band. Also present were a 'ladies nursing corps' and ambulance, signalling, and cyclist despatch corps. It may have been some of these ladies, who, as members of the Women's Suffrage Society, approached Devlin at the end of the proceedings to ask whether 'Mr Devlin could give them any assurance regarding the prospects of votes for women.' He replied that he had certainly voted for the bill but, pressed about the attitude of the Nationalist Party, he said that he could speak only for himself. It was no part of the reporter's brief to elaborate or follow up a potentially embarrassing story (the *Journal* was not that sort of 'rag') but if overwhelming anecdotal evidence can be relied upon, the encounter left the suffragettes bowled over by the guest of honour's famous smile and irresistible charm. It was a Sunday to remember – quite an occasion in Ulster's second city, then prosperous and go-ahead with its busy port and rich Tyrone and Donegal hinterland. Even the wisest prophet durst not guess what a change would have come over the place within a decade.

Devlin's long address, as reported in Monday's paper, shows something of his bravura style:

> We Irish Nationalists, whether in the ranks of the volunteers or out of them, are neither fools nor cowards. I think we have pretty well established the fact that we are not to be intimidated. Let me say, on the other hand, we do not seek to intimidate anybody, least of all our own Unionist friends and neighbours. We do not want strife within the four seas of Ireland. We do not want division, but union. We do not want ascendancy, but equality and fair play in civil and religious matters. We want liberty for all and slavery for none. Our platform today is, as it always was, broad enough to include every Irishman who desires to see his country free and prosperous, and joined in a real, genuine and rest-respecting union with Great Britain.

This genuine concern for the motives and feelings of all sides in the situation – an epitome of his personal ideology – would seem risible, not to say traitorous, a few years later to the ascendant IRA and Sinn Féin. The idea of a 'union' with Britain, however qualified by redeeming epithets, would seem at least bizarre. Yet, however spineless such a policy was to appear by the end of the decade, it was to Devlin the only way that was honourable and properly cognisant of Unionist wishes and fears.

On that sunny Sunday, however, it was still possible to make such a speech confident of the desired outcome at the end of hostilities:

> … as an Ulsterman talking to Ulstermen, I want to do what little I can to meet the objections, to calm the fears and to remove the prejudices of our Unionist friends with regard to Home Rule. The Home Rule Act is now on the Statute Book. It passed successfully through two years of the fiercest and strongest possible criticism in the country and in Parliament and having weathered the storm it received the Royal Assent and became the law of the land. I do hope that between now and the end of the suspensory period our Unionist friends will study its provisions in a spirit of sympathy

and good will, and if they do, I believe that when the time comes to settle our differences it will be found that these differences have largely, if not wholly, disappeared and that Ireland from the centre to the sea is one united people.

It was the speech that his listeners were pleased to accept, and to agree with his suggestion that whatever about the carnage in Flanders *their* battle was all but won. The relatively small transference of power envisaged in the bill with little real financial control and the capability of influence, if not actual interference, by the imperial parliament should have allayed Unionists and stopped well short of Nationalist final aspirations, but it was at least what later generations would call a 'road map'. It might even have become what Michael Collins (1890–1922) called 'freedom to achieve freedom' as he brought home the Treaty seven years later.

The celebrations lasted until evening with the participants unaware or unheeding that the battle for the Yser canal in Belgium had begun that same day, and that after the German's retreat from Ypres a fortnight later, the war expected to be 'all over by Christmas' would settle into the stasis of the Western Front and the horror of the trenches. Four Christmases would pass and ten million deaths would have to be endured before the arrival of the peace that in turn brought further horrors to Ireland.

11
Fin de Partie

THE WAR DRAGGED ON AND THE death toll mounted. The parishes of Fermanagh and Tyrone may have faded back into the mists and squalls of Ireland as far as Churchill – and the Kaiser – were concerned but in the misty and squally island they were still topics of burning interest. Among nationalists there was a slowly growing concern with the future of the country. Home Rule had been granted but its coming into law was still suspended. To all shades of national opinion, from the most aggressive of IRB patriots to the ones D P Moran had called 'West Britons', it was a suspension too far. Even the ebullient Devlin grew weary of Britain's treatment of his party and people. On 10 April 1916, a fortnight before the Easter Rising, he wrote to Dillon complaining: '…the amazing thing to me is that everyone in Ireland has not been driven into the Sinn Féin movement… the government have nothing but the most absolute contempt for us.'

One of the ominous signs of future trouble was the presence of Bonar Law and Carson in the coalition government from May 1915. Carson, the man who had threatened civil war, was now Attorney-General. Redmond had been offered an unspecific post in the government but was not in a position to accept. The IPP had an unwritten law that such a position should not be accepted before the absolute granting of Home Rule. Besides, it seemed to him that his would be a lone voice, trying to have the members turn their attention from the world war to the perennial Irish Question. T P O'Connor thought that if Redmond would not take it, Devlin 'could take the job and do it. I'd sooner see him than anybody, as counter-poise to Carson.' Even the normally adversarial D P Moran wrote in the *Leader* on 26 May: 'Redmond should go in and take responsibility; if not Redmond, let Devlin go in; or why not both of them.'

The discrediting of the Liberal government had arisen because of a shortage of high-explosive shells. The fault was probably Kitchener's but it was decided that it would be bad propaganda to admit it publicly. Lloyd George became Minister of Munitions while Bonar Law was relegated to Colonial Secretary, though head of the Conservative Party. When Asquith unadvisedly resigned in December 1916, Bonar Law became Chancellor of the Exchequer and was able to harden the government line against nationalist Ireland. Disenchantment with Britain had until then had little effect upon the popularity and strength of the constitutionalist party. Redmond still controlled his respectable party and Devlin still managed to keep up enthusiasm for the party line and encourage *les autres*. There were some early signs, though, of erosion that would eventually lead to a full collapse. In a by-election for College Green, until then a safe IPP seat, a Larkinist candidate scored a creditable 1,816 votes against the IPP's 2,445.

When not being a too successful recruiting sergeant, Devlin appointed himself as a kind of welfare officer for the families with absent fathers. This was merely an extension of the work he tried to do from young manhood. In the souvenir booklet published by the Christian Brothers in Derry in 1927 two stories of his energetic care are given after a short sketch of his persistent lobbying as an MP by his friend T P O'Connor:

> He takes his politics very seriously. From this point of view he is the ideal member of Parliament. What ever the question may be, whether of something connected with the docks, or the commercial interests of the great city he has just ceased to represent, or the pitiful appeal of some wronged pensioner or discharged soldier, Mr Devlin never rests till he has got the thing put right. He not only answers the letters but he haunts the

government departments; he sends them letter after letter till the departments are forced to abandon excuse and delay, and if he has not succeeded with the officials he boldly goes to the room of the Minister in the House of Commons and pleas and pleads, and with the same wealth of eloquence over the single case of a wronged soldier, still more of a wronged woman as though he were discussing the fate of Ireland.

The writer of the piece (known simply as J P G) goes on to give an account of two such cases, one of a soldier wrongly convicted of murder and the other of a widow deprived of her pension. The first, told to the writer by the soldier in question, describes how as a boy of sixteen from the Shankill Road, he joined the Royal Irish Rifles on 18 January 1915. In December 1916 he had shot in self-defence a Greek who had attacked him with a knife. His death sentence was commuted to fifteen years' penal servitude that he was presently serving in Portland prison with ten years still to go. He had written many letters to Carson without response, and when his Protestant chaplain also wrote there was still no answer. One day a fellow prisoner who was a Catholic urged him to speak to the Catholic chaplain and, after overcoming the fears and suspicion of three centuries of folk memory, he agreed to meet him. The priest advised the soldier to write to Devlin: 'Sure he's a Belfastman.' The prisoner began to explain the facts of Belfast life: 'Oh, Father, you don't know – I'm not one of Devlin's men. I'm on the Shankill and Devlin is for the Falls Road. Carson is our man.'

'Well, as Carson won't reply – why not try Devlin?'

'No use, Father, he wouldn't listen to me at all. The Shankill is Protestant and the Falls is Catholic.'

The chaplain insisted and less than a week later Devlin sent for the relevant papers and, three weeks after that, the sentence had been commuted to five years. Devlin did not rest at this and, after three months, the young rifleman was freed absolutely.

The case of the widow was told by Devlin himself. J P G called at his office one day and was handed a letter written from Masserene Street, Falls Road, Belfast:

Dear Mr Devlin,
I wish to thank you for getting me the elopement,
Yours faithfully,
Mary M——

Devlin explained that the widow intended to write 'allotment' and admitted that she was one of the very few who wrote to thank him. Between twenty and fifty letters like these arrived each day, asking for 'favours, petitions or begging letters'. As J P G noted: 'He has no secretary but friends give willing help and scarcely a letter ever reaches him that is not courteously acknowledged.' The welfare work continued all through the war and after. It is how he was remembered in Belfast long after his death.

As a political leader the promise Devlin showed so brilliantly during the first decade of the twentieth century began to leach away because of what a more successful politician, Harold Macmillan (1894–1986), would ruefully describe as 'Events, my dear boy. Events.' The political careers of both Redmond and Devlin began to deteriorate once the idea of exclusion became a possibility. In a Greek tragedy there were taken to be several causes of the fall of the protagonist: the committing a fatal error by him; inexorable fate working against mere mortals, often in the form of malevolent deities; or sometimes a mixture of both. The downfall of Redmond (and by association, Devlin) was probably inevitable in the prevailing conditions of the time. Because of the daily slaughter in France and Belgium, men were considered expendable and life was cheap. Constitutionalism, essentially concerned with the sanctity of human life and abhorring violence, seemed inappropriate in the climate of cosmic disintegration. In spite of his reluctance even to consider any form of armed struggle to attain the desired goal of Home Rule, Redmond did not seem to find it illogical to advocate the joining of the British army and the inevitable killing – and risk of being killed – that such entailed.

An even greater error was his belief in the integrity of the government and of its leader, Lloyd George. Redmond and Devlin both were almost naïve in their expectation that Ulster Unionists would be happy to join in a united country run from Dublin once they saw how well devolution was working. Until the Irish Volunteers' impatience with British intransigence and the IPP's sloth boiled over into the deliberately hopeless Easter Rising it was possible for them to continue in their predestinate groove and hope that all would be well. The Rising stunned them both. When Devlin heard the news he cried, 'This has ruined everything!'

The Rising lasted less than a week and for a while the insurgents were mocked or execrated by the people, especially those who had men-folk at the Front. General Sir John Maxwell (1859–1929), who arrived to take command of the army in Dublin on the Friday, had 20,000 troops at his disposal and boasted to Lord Wimbourne (1873–1939), the lord lieutenant, 'I am going to ensure there will be no treason whispered for a hundred years.' His was the decision to begin immediate executions, especially of the signatories of the Proclamation. Asquith agreed that the 'ringleaders' be dealt with in the 'most severe way possible', and Redmond had initially agreed that their punishment should be severe but still pleaded for clemency. However, the paced nature of the killings had exactly the opposite effect. Birrell had warned Asquith that the Rising was not an *Irish* rebellion: 'It would be a pity if *post facto* it became one.' He resigned when Pearse, MacDonagh and Clarke were shot on 3 May, a mere four days after the surrender. He was the first of many well-meaning people whose careers were effectively finished by the Rising.

Pearse and the rest, who had formed a minority of a minority, had signed a kind of moral contract by which their lives were willingly sacrificed for 'a good cause'. Maxwell's response was, in effect, a countersigning of that contract. By the time the last of his executions, those of James Connolly and Sean Mac Diarmada, were carried out, public opinion in Ireland had swung round and the sixteen had entered the Valhalla of Irish heroes. Of ninety death sentences, seventy-five were commuted. One hundred and seventy men and Countess Markievicz, a leading light in the Citizen Army, were imprisoned; 3,430 men and seventy-nine women were arrested but of these 1,424 men and all but five of the women were released within a few weeks.

These five women and 1,836 men were interned mainly at Frongoch, in present-day Gwyned.

Devlin was bitterly disappointed that among those arrested were a considerable number of IPP supporters and members of the AOH. This was also true of the people sent to Wales, where a number, incensed at their harsh treatment, became amenable to the doctrinaire persuasion of the residual members of the IRB. Maxwell's imposition of virtual martial law increased resentment. As Redmond and Devlin suffered slight after slight from the occupying force, and as Asquith's demand to stop the firing squads was ignored by Maxwell, the days of constitutionalism became numbered. The general was personally responsible for making certain that after the end of the war treason would not be whispered but shouted from the rooftops. Devlin did what he could to mitigate the sentences of personal friends like Seán MacEntee by speaking as a character witness at the hastily contrived military courts. Asquith's apparent inability to bring Maxwell to heel, as previously he had wavered over the Curragh incident, seemed to be endemic in his Liberal administration, setting a pattern that appeared to suggest that only a Conservative government would in the future, as in the past, have final control over the military.

By now the Liberals in coalition no longer needed the support of the IPP for its programme, dominated by munitions and the murderous stalemate of the trenches. Ireland became a burden that the government would have liked to shed. Lloyd George was given responsibility for the 'Question', caricatured by a *Punch* cartoon showing Asquith with a knowing leer hand over a porcupine with spines menacingly erect to an extremely reluctant Welsh wizard. T P O'Connor, who, as a Liverpool MP, had a sense of English public opinion, wrote to Dillon to say that there was a general feeling that 'the Irish question should be settled now and at once'. The growing number of republican sympathisers were quick to note that the violence of the Rising had shaken Asquith sufficiently to make him hurry to Ireland and consult widely with all sorts of people, including political prisoners in Mountjoy. The belief, firmly held by militants before and since, that Britain would respond only to force seemed again to have been confirmed.

As far as moderate opinion was concerned – still a large majority – the trouble was that very few people trusted Lloyd George and many believed that his position as Minister of Munitions occupied most of his energies. Dillon openly referred to him as a 'slippery snake', and with the preparations for the imminent joint British-French offensive at the Somme and Verdun that was to cost 500,000 German, 420,000 British and 200,000 French lives on his mind, Lloyd George could be forgiven for a little impatience. The casualties on the first two days would include 5,000 men of the Ulster Division wearing Orange collarettes as they marched into battle at the Ancre.

His proposals to the UUC and the IPP were, if not actually different, certainly interpreted differently. Home Rule was to be granted immediately to 'five-sixths of Ireland': the three provinces of Leinster, Munster and Connacht plus the north-western counties of Monaghan, Cavan and Donegal (all three with substantial Protestant minorities). There would be no 'Orange Parliament' in Belfast and the eighty Irish MPs would still keep their seats in the House of Commons. The remaining six Ulster counties were to continue to be ruled from Westminster for the remainder of the war. Partition was to be temporary, though Lloyd George wrote to Carson to advise: 'We must make it clear that at the end of the provisional period Ulster does not, whether she wills it or not, merge with the rest of Ireland.' There was not then to be an automatic absorption of the six excluded counties into the 'Free State' (a term was not known then) but their future was dependent rather on the government in power. Redmond, on the other hand, was given the impression that the exclusion was temporary and its dissolution automatic with the signing of an armistice. Unambiguously it was stated that an Imperial Conference that would include delegates from Canada, Australia, and other dominions would be held as soon as possible after hostilities to finally decide the nature of the country.

The proposals were a far cry from the Home Rule ideal but Redmond, ill and demoralised by the Rising, gave in to Lloyd George's pressure. It was then up to a very reluctant Devlin to persuade the northern nationalists to accept the terms. The UUC had agreed to the proposals on 12 June after considerable pressure from Carson, who, again after much argument, was finally persuaded to accept by Lloyd George; the latter, though a Celt, was also a Wesleyan and found greater empathy with Ulster Protestants than their adversaries. Asquith was probably more sympathetic to the nationalist cause but by December 1916 he was no longer prime minister. He had threatened to resign and was taken at his word by Lloyd George, who replaced him at the head of the wartime coalition.

Threat of resignation is not always a trump card but it was the only one that Redmond could play when his new package was unveiled to great opposition. He called a meeting in St Mary's Hall, Belfast, on 23 June that was attended by nearly 800 people. Devlin's Belfast supporters did not desert him but there was strong opposition from the nationalists of Tyrone and Fermanagh, who, like the Protestants of Donegal, Cavan and Monaghan, found themselves on the wrong side of the border. 'Black Friday', as the day became known, remained as another black mark on Devlin's reputation.

Predictably there was strong disapproval from northern clerics of whom only Bishop Patrick O'Donnell of Raphoe was a confirmed Devlinite. Charles McHugh of Derry and the recently appointed Joseph MacRory of Down and Connor were overtly anti-British, and Cardinal Michael Logue, though no supporter of Sinn Féin, was deeply suspicious of what he considered British pandering to the UUC. Their preoccupation was less with the question of sovereignty than of education, though both McHugh and MacRory were instinctively republican with a small 'r'. Logue said that it would be better to live under English rule for another fifty years than accept the current proposals. McHugh also declared 'absolute opposition', speaking as bishop of a diocese with a third of its territory granted Home Rule, while the city in which he lived had a majority of Catholics unable to impose their electoral will due to clever gerrymandering. As a result of clerical concern the meeting was attended by many more priests than usual, primed by their bishops to resist the proposals, and it looked as if Redmond might well lose the leadership of the IPP. In fact, of the 265 people who voted against acceptance, more than 100 out of a total of 130 were priests.

In private conversation with Stephen Gwynn, Redmond paid Devlin the most heartfelt tribute ever uttered by him about anyone: 'Joe's loyalty in all this business has been beyond words. I know what it cost him to do as he has done.'

It was possibly Devlin's finest hour as a persuader because he felt each word a betrayal of all he had argued in the past. He spoke for forty-five minutes, warning with words 'wonderfully eloquent and delivered with great force' that if the vote were lost the struggle for Home Rule would be crippled, perhaps terminally. Whereas if the proposals were put in force the excluded six counties would soon see the advantages that exclusion was denying them. He promised that when the minutiae of the agreement were discussed he would make sure that a committee of clergy would be part of any tweaking felt to be required.

The house was then asked to vote for the exclusion of the six north-eastern counties as 'a temporary and provisional settlement of the Irish difficulty'. The results showed what a triumph of rhetoric Devlin's speech was: 475 voted yes and there were forty-five abstentions. Devlin sent a telegram to Lloyd George announcing 'a magnificent convention. Proposals carried by nearly 200 majority. You are therefore in a position to proceed with the matter on the basis of your proposals.' The victory was essentially a hollow one; policy had prevailed over personal convictions.

The IPP met in the Mansion House in Dawson Street in Dublin three days later and all but two of the fifty MPs present approved. Most were aware that the party of Parnell had now become identified with partition. It was noted that the votes of County Tyrone were ninety-five against, sixty-four for; in Fermanagh fifty-eight against, thirty-six for; and in Derry city, the other location of great opposition and strongly influenced by Bishop McHugh, who was already organising anti-partition rallies there, the result was sixty-seven for and sixty against. The east/west split intensified over the next year when a breakaway Irish Nation League generated in those regions joined forces with Sinn Féin. Redmond and Devlin waited for the proposals to become law, still convinced that they had got the best deal in the circumstances. Yet, already, all of their risk-taking and agonised reassessment was being undermined by Walter Long (1854–1924), a leading extreme Conservative member of the coalition cabinet and architect of the Government of Ireland Act (1921), who, with the help of southern Unionists, Lords Midleton (1856–1942) and Lansdowne, refused Conservative support. If William O'Brien had been available for comment he might have suggested that his old policy of 'conference and conciliation and consent' in the approach to southern Unionists might have been the right one after all, especially as Devlin had been most virulently opposed to it. His position already weakened by his reputation of having sold out the northern Catholics, he had the further humiliation of hearing Asquith assure Carson that exclusion would never be ended 'without the free will and assent of the excluded area'. Devlin, aware of the absolute nature of the entrenched Unionist attitudes, knew exactly what that assurance meant: perpetuity. It was an assurance that successive Westminster governments would have to iterate each time the word 'partition' was mentioned.

Since Lloyd George had been the main sponsor of the proposals he briefly felt that he should resign: 'I have pledged my word to the Irish and if the pledge is not fulfilled I shall have to resign.' He probably meant it at the time; as the rhyme put it, '*How* he meant it!', but the time did not last and with the war at an apparently crucial point, he remembered that he was needed. The Somme took precedence over the Liffey – or the Lagan! He probably did not want to wreck the IPP or to bring down Redmond and Devlin but the net effect of his inconsistency was that the constitutionalist approach would crumble and the vacuum would be filled by an urgent republicanism as Sinn Féin gathered under its aegis all the various nationalist groupings who were in opposition to the betrayal by Redmond and united in their irredeemable distrust of the British government. Devlin still had loyal friends in Belfast but his support throughout the rest of the country – and in west Ulster – was being diminished. Even in his kingdom, republican elements were gathering strength. The inspector-general of the RIC reported that 'the Sinn Féin movement is gaining strength in Belfast and Mr Devlin's influence is waning'.

Stephen Gwynn, whose book *John Redmond's Last Years* was written the year after its subject's death on 6 March 1918, dates the beginning of the spiral into dissolution of the IPP from the collapse of July 1916:

> That day really finished the constitutional party and overthrew Redmond's power. We had incurred the very great odium of accepting even temporary partition – and a partition which… could not be justified on any ground of principle; we had involved with us many men who voted for that acceptance on the faith of Redmond's assurance that the Government were bound by their written word; and now we were thrown over.

Apart from the effect on Redmond's position, the result was to engender a temper that made settlement almost impossible. No British minister's word would in future be accepted for anything; and any Irishman who attempted to improve relations between the countries was certain to arouse anger and contempt in his countrymen.

For 'any Irishman' read Joe Devlin. The Byzantine nature of the protracted negotiations and the disappointment at their ultimate futility had borne heavily upon him. His health, never robust because of his frenetic lifestyle and fondness for unhealthy comforts, began to deteriorate. Some of his ailments were undoubtedly psychosomatic. The strain of defending what he in his heart considered the indefensible was very severe upon his mental stability and the relentless will that drove him must have caused a tension and strain that found its relief in physical collapse and intermittent, apparently unconnected, symptoms.

For Redmond, fifteen years his senior, the shock of the Easter Rising and the sense of the glittering prize of Home Rule, achieved with infinite patience and an almost innocent generosity of spirit that, as any career politician could have told him, was a burden and not a gift, snatched away when it was almost in his grasp, was literally deadly. The signs of dissolution were to be seen if one looked carefully enough but they were not yet dramatic. In the Roscommon by-election of 3 February 1917 at which George Noble Plunkett (1851–1948), a papal count and father of the executed Joseph Mary Plunkett (1887–1916) – whose marriage to Grace Gifford on the eve of his death had given yet another iconic boost to the 'terrible beauty' – beat the IPP candidate T J Devine by 1,314 votes. He stood as 'the father of a martyr' and did not take his seat. A similar kind of delicacy was shown by the voters of Waterford City who elected Redmond's son in his father's place on 22 March 1918, sixteen days after his death, beating the Sinn Féin candidate by 497 votes.

Devlin, suffering with a debilitating 'flu', was unable to do anything about the 'father of the martyr' election but he threw all his persuasive talents into the next challenge in the Longford South by-election, supporting the party candidate Patrick McKenna, reminding the electors that they 'had to decide whether they were in favour of a self-governed Ireland or a hopeless fight for an Irish republic'. Joseph McGuinness, who was a prisoner at the time in Lewes jail and unable to canvass for that reason, beat McKenna by thirty-two votes on 9 May. It was the first time that Sinn Féin used the slogan: 'Put him in to get him out!' Then de Valera, newly released from Lewes among the last batch of the 1916 prisoners, easily defeated Patrick Lynch KC by 2,955 votes in east Clare on 10 July, the seat made vacant by the death of Willie Redmond, the leader's brother and once Devlin's travel companion.

The writing was on the wall for the old party, sometimes literally, for the Sinn Féin supporters made effective use of graffiti in their increasingly successful electoral campaigns. When the members of the coalition cabinet could take their minds off the war they sought a quick solution to the chronic problems of the offshore island, as they increasingly thought of it except when they needed more cannon fodder. Early in 1917, at a period of understandable impatience, there was talk of an imposed settlement. The government's antennae were sufficiently sensitive to the fact that there was no longer a representative body with which to negotiate. Redmond's IPP, like its leader, had an air of imminent demise about it and because of Sinn Féin's abstention policy there could be no parliamentary contact with the militants – not that the majority in the cabinet would allow any such 'betrayal'.

Lloyd George was quite ebullient about the terms considered: to include Ulster in the imposition of Home Rule but granting its representatives a veto on acts deemed relevant to Unionist interests and granting Belfast a 'civil administration organisation for Ulster affairs'. It was the old suggestion of 'Home Rule within Home Rule' applied to the troubled North and it might have avoided the bloodshed and permanent partition that followed. He confided to Frances Stevenson, his long-time mistress, 'I think I am going to solve the Irish question.' For some reason the cabinet did not proceed with the direct-action option. Perhaps war considerations sidelined it, or Lloyd George's Conservative colleagues felt it too hard on Unionists. Instead, the 'last' throw of yet another Irish Convention, this one manned entirely by Irish people, was set up, partly on Redmond's suggestion after a dinner table conversation with Lord Crewe, a Liberal peer. The chairman was Sir Horace Plunkett, the idealistic, rather impatient, founder of the cooperative movement in Ireland, and ninety-five delegates gave an unusually wide spectrum of ideologies. They included Redmond, Devlin, Stephen Gwynn, Bishop O'Donnell, Bishop MacRory, Lord Midleton, the poet and mystic Æ (1866–1935), Erskine Childers, Cruise O'Brien, Lord Londonderry (1878–1949), and H T Barrie, the last two representing the UUC.

It failed after 254 voluble days, at times showing glimmers of hope. Sinn Féin's boycott was a grievous blow and the northern Unionists remained obdurate. Redmond had impressed the southern Unionists with several suggestions about immediate self-government with the knotty question of fiscal control left to be straightened out later. This proved too much for Devlin, heavily influenced by his clerical mentor, Bishop O'Donnell. The voluntary foregoing of the rights to impose and collect customs duties was too great a sacrifice; Home Rule still financed by Britain seemed a mockery. Lord Midleton softened his proposal to allow the collection but not the imposition of duties, and Redmond, ill and desperately anxious for the convention to succeed, proposed that his amendment should be accepted. He made it without consultation, believing that it would produce immediate favourable legislation while ready to re-negotiate the small print of full financial control.

Redmond's weak acceptance, as it appeared, of such a maimed agreement came as a bombshell to his supporters. O'Donnell's letter to him on 14 January shows a distrust of future Ulster Unionist intransigence and deep disappointment and sadness:

> In my opinion, should the Government not carry through the proposed agreement, the Nationalist who voted for it cannot stand where he stood before. To say he could have a Parliament in Dublin two months hence, without customs, but not two years later, will not bear examination. The principle is given away. If Ulster had come in, or had promised to come in, we could give something away. But with Ulster out, we never agreed to give something away, and in my opinion it is fatal to do so. With Ulster out, even a favourable Cabinet could not carry an agreement that excluded customs.

To Devlin it seemed that his earlier factional struggle with William O'Brien was being rehearsed and for the same kind of reasons. With the unerring wisdom of hindsight it seems now that Redmond and O'Brien were correct in their conviction of the need for coming to terms with the two brands of Unionism: the obdurate, largely proletarian 'not-an-inch' stance of the Ulster variety and the more gentlemanly but just as uncompromising attitude of those who would later become known as the 'Four Percent'. Devlin agreed with O'Donnell and made his position clear, so that when Martin McDonough agreed to second Redmond's motion, the leader replied: 'He needn't bother. I'm not going to move it; Devlin and the bishops are voting against me.'

Devlin, who had approached the convention with little enthusiasm and in unusually low spirits, hated this public rejection of his leader. His enthusiasm increased while the convention seemed to offer some hope but he was aware of the scrutiny that the absent Sinn Féin were applying to the proceedings. Some observers felt that his allegiance had shifted back to Dillon and away from Redmond, who seemed to have dismissed the militants as irrelevant. The public evidence of such a disagreement was to weaken the convention's credibility, but the silence of the UUC and the outside menace of the Volunteers meant that this final compromise with the southern Unionists would not have worked in any event.

Several things helped render the convention irrelevant. It lasted too long; Plunkett, as chairman, allowed too much discussion of side issues; and the UUC refused to offer any suggestions. A crippling blow was the sudden death of Redmond on 6 March 1918; though badly shaken by the Easter Rising and the downward electoral spiral, he had made what seemed to him genuine progress. He had required surgery for a gallstone condition and, though the operation was successful, he died of heart failure, worn out by the strain of hopeless negotiation. Another element in its dissolution was the Catholic hierarchy's stance, even led by the moderate O'Donnell, who seemed to Plunkett to be uncooperative. He confided to the southern delegate J H Bernard, Protestant Archbishop of Dublin: 'I don't wish to be uncharitable but I'm not sure that the RC hierarchy want a settlement.' Bishop MacRory, a member of the larger convention, had made a poor impression by giving an accelerated history of British wrongs in the Ireland of past centuries. Much of what he said was just, if inevitably one-sided, but the timing was unforgivably inept.

Apart from the convention's final irrelevance, especially in the eyes of Sinn Féin, the situation in Europe effectively killed it. The German spring offensive of 1918 was initially so successful that the War Cabinet, in fear of a final Allied defeat, introduced on 9 April a Military Service Bill that allowed the government to impose conscription in Ireland. Coming about the end of the fruitless convention and three IPP electoral defeats, its timing could not have been worse, especially when Lloyd George, with deliberate clumsiness, announced that it would be linked to an immediate Home Rule Bill. Two days later, a committee led by Walter Long began drafting the necessary legislation. Support for Sinn Féin soared and the Irish hierarchy joined very vocally and effectively in the anti-conscription campaign. Devlin, Dillon and the rest of the IPP withdrew in vocal protest from the House of Commons and Sinn Féin's star rose ever higher.

An artificial and ultimately temporary unity among nationalists produced a strong quasi-religious campaign in which Devlin and the AOH played an active part. A vow 'to resist conscription by the most effective means at our disposal' was signed by half a million Irish people. Cardinal Logue instituted a national novena in honour of Our Lady of Lourdes and nominated Sunday, 21 April, as a day when a Mass against conscription should be said in every church, chapel and oratory in the country, while Bishop MacRory, showing an increasing support for Sinn Féin, declared: 'No power has any moral right to coerce young Irishmen to fight in the alleged interests of freedom until they have been allowed to enjoy freedom for themselves.' Devlin spoke on 'Anti-conscription Sunday' in the innermost heart of his constituency at St Peter's Pro-Cathedral, where he was baptised forty-seven years earlier and from which he would be buried sixteen years later. A photograph taken outside the cathedral shows him bent over the protest document, his head lifted to look at the camera, the shock of still dark hair ploughed through by the straight furrow of the famous parting. The administrator of St Peter's stands beside him with his biretta at a woefully rakish angle. The atmosphere is one of great confidence with Devlin absolutely convinced of what he has just announced from the pulpit, that: 'England will never get another man from Ireland while that act is on the statute book.'

A general strike held the following Tuesday was solid outside of the northeast and demonstrated the majority's determination to resist conscription at all costs. By the end of the spring it became clear that it was a dead letter; Lloyd George decided that it was more trouble than it was worth and indeed gained a significant number of enlistments with a new voluntary recruitment drive. Twenty-one years later, in May 1939, Neville Chamberlain (1869–1941), the British prime minister, was advised not to attempt to impose conscription on Ulster even though invited to do so by his opposite number at Stormont, Viscount Craigavon, the ennobled Craig. Two years later, when Allied fortunes were at their lowest ebb, the offer was repeated and just as firmly refused by Churchill.

The threat of enforced conscription and the countrywide reaction had some interesting consequences. It gave a respectability to Sinn Féin that it had previously lacked, one that would stand it in good stead in the 'khaki election' that was held a month after the Armistice was signed on 11 November. It put the clergy back into politics and showed a remarkable increase in Church support for the militants. Most people under forty lost confidence in the IPP as inert and too susceptible to Lloyd George's changes of tactics, and even younger priests risked episcopal disapproval by publicly favouring of the abstention stance of Sinn Féin.

Some British observers suggested that neither the hierarchy nor Devlin (and the rest of the IPP) had strong feelings about conscription but found it politic to oppose it. It gave the clergy a kind of renewed social control over their flocks that they felt they had been losing. By all ideological and theological standards, the IPP was the party the bishops should have favoured but individual members had for different reasons ceased to back them. McHugh and MacRory had lost faith in Redmond over his acceptance of partition and had little respect for Devlin, especially after his brilliant if rhetorical defence of Lloyd George's proposal on 'Black Friday'. The reaction of both bishops is understandable because they were aware that two large bodies of nationalists in their care, in Derry and Belfast, would, after partition, be disadvantaged minorities under alien Unionist rule. Both as laymen might very well have been attracted, certainly to Sinn Féin, or even to the Volunteers, now beginning to refer to themselves as the Irish Republican Army. In time they would regret any favour shown the militants as the killings in the War for Independence increased exponentially. McHugh and his senior clerics would in time face down the IRA in Derry though they were glad of their defensive actions during a mini civil war in the city in July 1920.

MacRory had to face the misery of urban violence when his minority flock were at the mercy of government-armed members of the resurrected UVF, whose sectarian fury was often aggravated by the actions of the same IRA. Though Devlin and he had different attitudes to the politics of the time they had to find common cause in tending to the welfare of their Catholic people. Devlin always dreaded the rise of the IRA because of their dedication to violence and their refusal to consider any final settlement short of the establishment of a republic with all ties to Britain severed. As well as the label 'partitionist', Devlin had also to bear the slur of openly favouring dominion status. By now his influence, even in Belfast, had sunk very low. Redmond and he accepted that for territories outside of the northeast nothing could now stop the granting of Home Rule. He knew better than most of his southern colleagues the lengths that Unionists, suffused with a combination of fear, exaltation and steely determination, especially under the leadership of Craig, were prepared to go. He also knew only too well that in the contemporary state of politics in Britain the strong Conservative membership of the coalition meant an inevitable partiality towards the loyalists of Ulster, a fact that the majority of Irish politicians ignored. It is no wonder that he suffered continual debilitating bouts of ill-health for the last four years of the decade.

At the height of the conscription agitation Lloyd George devised another sure-fire recruiting drive for the militant arm of Sinn Féin: on spurious advice from Dublin Castle and Earl French (1852–1925), the new hardline Lord Lieutenant, he had about a hundred of the known members arrested on 17–18 May, including de Valera. French claimed that 'certain subjects... domiciled in Ireland' were in 'treasonable communication with the German enemy'. And, as a final stimulus to recruitment, Lloyd George announced in late November that the situation in Ireland was such that her people were not yet ready for Home Rule and that it would be withheld 'until the condition of Ireland makes it possible'.

This played right into the hands of the Volunteers, providing them with a marvellous pre-election coup. Dillon, who had assumed the leadership of the IPP, found that Devlin was in such poor shape that, for the first time in thirty years of public life, he might prove to be a liability in the coming struggle. One serious aspect of the enmity between Sinn Féin and the IPP was the danger of a split vote allowing the election of a Unionist in a safe nationalist seat. It was the newly politicised northern bishops who saw the danger and acted upon it, engaging with both sides to work out a means of maximising the effectiveness of the nationalist vote. To increase by default the number of Unionist members to six or even eight would seem to give weight to Carson's claim that Ulster was essentially Unionist.

Though Devlin was ill for most of the autumn and early winter of 1918, having fallen victim to a non-lethal strain of the great influenza epidemic of that year that killed twenty million people, and spent much of his time in a Dublin nursing home, he rallied sufficiently to go to Belfast to fight for Falls, as West Belfast was now known after the constituency boundaries were redrawn. Dillon felt betrayed by Devlin's disarray, having little time in his own austere view for weakness of the flesh. There was nothing that even the energised Devlin of his prime could have done but Dillon blamed him, saying that Devlin's collapse 'very largely contributed to the debacle'. It was, however, largely due to his advice that Dillon agreed to follow the parcelling out of seats by Cardinal Logue, who had reluctantly accepted the chore. Sinn Féin were to be unopposed (by the IPP) in Derry, east Down, south Fermanagh and northwest Tyrone while the IPP were allotted south Armagh, east Donegal, south Down and northeast Tyrone. It was assumed that the voters would follow the cardinal's ruling because candidates from both parties had already been nominated. The hierarchical instructions were followed, except in east Down, where a Carsonite was elected 'through the treachery of National party followers'.

When the results of the election were declared on 28 December it was found that, of 105 Irish seats, Sinn Féin, deliberately abstentionist, won seventy-three and the poor rump of Redmond's once proud party garnered no more than six, five probably courtesy of Logue, though Redmond's son William retained his father's old seat in Waterford City, which he had already won at the by-election after Redmond senior's death. As for Wee Joe, he had a characteristic success in his own kingdom, beating de Valera in a 74 percent turnout by 5,243 votes out of a total of 13,733, a slight that the president of Sinn Féin never forgot.

Apart from unshakable Belfast loyalty there were several other factors that caused the triumph. One was the extension of the franchise on 6 February to all men over twenty-one and women over thirty. The effect outside of West Belfast was to increase the votes for Sinn Féin since the majority of their supporters were young. Devlin was beloved by the women of his constituency, often ignoring the admonitions of their husbands. His election campaign concentrated on local and social matters, demanding equal pay for women and improved conditions for all workers. In one speech he tried to rise above the sectarianism that his enemies claimed was his chief characteristic:

> I invite the Protestant toilers to join with their Catholic fellow countrymen in a great organised battle against reaction and Toryism. We are out to unite Orange and Green, Protestant and Catholic, mill-worker and engineer. Humanity was not meant to be crucified by a bad industrial and economic system.

Though badly shaken by the unmistakable signs of dissolution of the party he had given his life to, he must have taken pleasure in the fact that 6,300 electors allowed their names to be published in the *Irish News* to show their support. It was a brief moment of deserved glory but he was too skilled a politician not to be aware of what Sinn Féin's policies would inevitably lead to, and of the vulnerable position of the nationalists in Ulster as Carson and Craig continued to be ascendant.

F J Whitford, in his unpublished MA thesis *Joseph Devlin: Ulsterman and Irishman* (1959), adds a footnote to the 1918 election results with the complimentary view that the IPP, though now demised, had honourably fulfilled its purpose:

> The party had completed the tasks for which Parnell had fashioned it. It had undone the Cromwellian Settlement by the Land Acts it had secured. It had put a Home Rule bill on the statute book, conceding in principle the right of part of Ulster to special treatment but not to permanent separation. It had secured for Ireland every possible advantage from social legislation enacted at Westminster.

It was something of a eulogy but also an obituary because the party was undoubtedly dead and Devlin, its chief mourner, had sixteen years of life left – deprived like his fellow nationalists in 'Carsonia', as its critics called Northern Ireland, of full citizenship. He was facing nearly five years of bitter violence, the frustration of permanent opposition in an alien assembly, the obloquy of his younger fellow-citizens, and the dissipation of a golden dream of independence crushed by the recalcitrance of a more powerful adversary.

12
The (Better) Government of Ireland Act

DEVLIN FACED POST-WAR IRELAND IN deep depression. He was justified in his gloomy view, not so much in the contemplation of his own future but in the inevitable spiral into violence that was implicit in the policies of the militants in Sinn Féin and the obduracy of Craig and his triumphant Unionists. He was especially disconsolate in his prognosis of what his people would suffer under the new regime and apprehensive of the northern bishops' apparent approval of his nationalist rivals. He could see that they believed that the IRA might be a kind of defensive force for Catholics in the inevitable community violence that would follow on the setting-up of the Protestant Home Rule but he felt that, once the killing of soldiers and policemen was not only condoned but regarded as an imperative, the amount of violence would greatly increase and that, in the inevitable cycle of reprisal, many innocent people would die or be severely injured. Devlin continued to try for some kind of compromise with Unionism even at this stage, regardless of how it might cause him to be labelled as a betrayer of the national cause. However Oliver P Rafferty SJ in his book *Catholicism in Ulster: 1603–1983* (1994) states:

> Such possibilities were quickly excluded owing to the abstentionist policy of Sinn Féin, the further machinations of Carson's unionists and, as ever, the intransigence of the Ulster bishops over their recurring nightmare, the education question.

In time the northern bishops would find it necessary to condemn the IRA campaign, Logue being especially disapproving, but stopping short of the threat of excommunication imposed on IRA members in the diocese of Cork on 12 December 1920 by Bishop Daniel Cohalan (1859–1952), who was equally condemnatory of atrocities from whatever quarter during the War of Independence. The northern bishops' struggle for their prescriptive version of Catholic education was to continue for decades in Northern Ireland.

Devlin greatly deplored the exaltation of mind on both sides that would insist that there were 'no innocents'. Even before he was informed of the notorious shooting of two unarmed Catholic policemen at Soloheadbeg in County Tipperary on 21 January 1919 he warned Bishop O'Donnell that 'there is about to be a serious situation in the country, which may involve bloodshed, if not worse'. The ambush, carried out by a group of nine IRA men led by Dan Breen (1894–1969) and Seán Treacy (1895–1920), and which was taken to be the first encounter of the War of Independence, indicated with what ruthlessness the ensuing conflict would be carried on against the 'enemy' or the most vulnerable part of it. As in many other similar encounters there was no central authorisation for the ambush; Treacy afterwards said, 'It was high time we did a bit of pushing.' It was often the case that the worst reprisals followed on such local initiatives. And when the IRA extended their campaign in Belfast the same pattern was observed, with similar dire results.

Devlin's first reaction after the election debacle was to consider giving up his political career, saying to Dillon that he was 'violently against attending Parliament'; he was conscious that to face the House of Commons as one of six Nationalist MPs, having once been deputy leader of eighty-one, would 'only advertise our own weakness'. He soon found that he was listened to as a Parliamentarian in his own right and as appreciated by all sides for his wit, his incisive debating skills, and the sheer exuberance of his public personality as much as ever. Besides he still had constituency matters to attend to.

For most of the early months of 1919 Belfast was more concerned with a strike by workers in the shipyards, the engineering works and the city's gas yards and electricity stations. The workers were no longer prepared to tolerate the fifty-four hour wartime working week and demanded its reduction to forty-four hours. Children, as they played in the streets, repeated the strikers' mantra: 'We'll work no more till we get the forty-four.'

The strike began on 25 January and affected more than forty firms. Its effect was rather that of a small-scale general stoppage. There were no trams or street-lights and, with no gas, meals had to cooked on coal-fired ranges or open fires. Most of the strikers were Protestant – they were the ones with the jobs – but in spite of the *Belfast News Letter* (in reduced size because of lack of power, and using blackleg labour) thundering that the strike was aiding Sinn Féin, the action was simply for better conditions. In the House of Commons, as ever preferring to speak for all the workers, Catholic and Protestant alike, Devlin scorned the view that the strike was being pursued by 'Bolshevists'. He insisted that it was being conducted with dignity and with a freedom from crimes of violence that was unique, and he reminded the House that those who had enlisted had not gone to war 'to restore sweating, low wages, long hours, lack of leisure'. On 14 February, when the strike was three weeks old, the troops were ordered to take over the utilities, but six days later, the strikers settled for a forty-seven hour week. Over the next three years the workers were to play an even more vigorous role in public affairs, not for improvement in pay and conditions, and one that showed a rather distorted working class solidarity.

Lloyd George's (Better) Government of Ireland Act was introduced into parliament on 25 February 1920 and became law on 23 December. It established two parliaments for Ireland, one in Belfast to handle most of the affairs of the six excluded counties, the other in Dublin to do the same for the twenty-six who were to be granted the same powers as the triumphant Carsonists. Such an undemocratic imposition of exclusion on around 95,000 Catholics in Belfast alone, left at the mercy of an unfriendly, suspicious government to which the British authorities gave uncritical support, while defying world opinion, was bound to lead to violence. Devlin excoriated the government during the bill's passage, calling it 'an outrage upon true liberty'. His was essentially a lone voice in the House and he was clearly impatient that the seventy-three Sinn Féin members, because of their policy of abstention, were not present to wrest more safeguards from the Westminster government. There were still enough sympathetic Liberals that could join with the full Nationalist membership to bring pressure on the Ulster Unionists and their Conservative allies to make the plight of northern nationalists less hopeless.

The six Nationalist MPs, as the party members became known, were swamped and yet they were the only real representatives of the 350,000 who would be excluded against their wills. Sinn Féin could not be seen to attend because their presence would imply recognition of British sovereignty. They probably felt that Lloyd George was going to acquiesce in Unionist demands anyway since he believed they were more ruthless than their enemies. The result was that northern nationalists were not given the same opportunity for amelioration that had been given to southern Unionists. Devlin particularly deplored the amendment that permitted the government of Northern Ireland to abolish Proportional Representation after three years. PR was one of many 'safeguards' included to make the bill less obviously partial. Devlin's passionate speech against the amendment was similar to many others he made that each time led to his removal from the chamber – all, as he well knew, to no avail.

As if in anticipation of his future role in Ulster politics all his energies were concentrated on the amelioration of the condition of the workers in his constituency. He was active in all aspects of social legislation, serving on committees on Old Age Pensions and the proposed electoral change to PR. He continued to dread the coming violence but claimed on 5 December 1920 at a rally in Canning Town in London's East End that he would be a Sinn Féiner with a gun if he thought that violence could achieve justice for Ireland but the odds were too great: 'If there were the slightest chance of success I would shoulder my gun and be willing to die for my country. I want the Irish Question settled on constitutional lines. When they have withdrawn the forces of the Crown there will be a chance of finding peace and order in Ireland as the foundation of subsequent liberty to be established in her soil.'

One of the causes of the ferment, especially in Belfast, was the resentment shown by demobbed Protestant workers at the number of Catholic workers, some from the south, who had during the war, as they put it, 'inveigled' themselves into their jobs, especially in the steel works and shipyards. On the Catholic side the sense of imminent exclusion from the coming 'Free State' and the threatening posture of Protestant extremists increased their fear and anger and caused a rise in support for Sinn Féin, fulfilling the Unionist prophecies. A striking example of the situation was that, of the proportion of workers in the Great Northern and the LMS Northern Counties railways, not a single Catholic was left in work on either system. One Catholic who worked in the York Road yard of the LMS described how a mob of 200 came typically at lunchtime 'shouting for Papist blood'. He was lucky to escape by a side door and he reported later that any 'fellows who were caught – they were nearly all caught – were nearly beaten to death'. This was repeated throughout the city in the summer of 1920 while the bill was being debated. In the parts of the city where nationalist and Unionist areas abutted, especially in the back streets between the Falls and Shankill, and in the Catholic 'islands' surrounded by their adversaries such as the Markets, the Short Strand and Ardoyne, Catholics fought back with equal ferocity though generally 'outgunned' and outnumbered.

The new government of Northern Ireland was determined from the start to establish its authority and it was going to use the revitalised UVF to show that it was to be master in the new state. The problem of dealing with this technically illegal force was solved with ease by reconstituting them as members of three special constabularies (the Ulster Special Constabulary, or USC), another demand of Craig's that the British government assented to with little reluctance. Of these constabularies the most significant were the B-Specials, a part-time, unpaid force with UVF officers who remained a constant threat to Catholics until it was required to disband in 1970. Belfast people knew what the B-Specials' existence would mean. Devlin made the position abundantly clear during the Commons debates on 25 October 1920:

> The Chief Secretary is going to arm pogromists to murder Catholics… The Protestants are to be armed, for we would not touch your special constabulary with a forty-foot pole. The pogrom is to be made less difficult. Instead of paving stones and sticks, they are to be given rifles.

The uneasy situation was gravely exacerbated by local members of the IRA impatient to emulate their colleagues in the south, finding it appropriate in the name of Irish freedom to kill fellow Irishmen, members of the RIC, a majority of whom were Catholic. They carried the campaign into the North and between the spring of 1920 and the summer of 1922 there were sixty recorded deaths of Northern Ireland security force members, including RIC, Royal Ulster Constabulary (RUC), specials and even two 'Auxies' (a grouping that made even the Black and Tans seem benevolent).[1] Twenty-eight died in Belfast and it was here that the violence seemed endless.[2]

The inevitable reprisals were inflicted not necessarily upon the IRA, who could be elusive, but on any Catholic who came within range. Derry had suffered a kind of curtain-raiser in which the heavily armed UVF – not yet officially sanctioned in one of its recurring incarnations – attacked Catholics over a four-day period at the end of June. An informal group of local IRA men did what they could to defend them and by Saturday, 26 June up to forty people had died, the majority of them Catholic.[3] The trouble ended when the army declared martial law and put the city under a curfew from 11pm until 5am; by the following April this had a much stricter start time of 9.30pm.

Northern Ireland was in those years a village where action in one place produced a reaction elsewhere. In Belfast, in July 1920, the 'glorious twelfth' was celebrated by Orangemen by violently driving 9,000 workmen from the shipyards and other heavy industrial plants, a majority of them Catholic but also some 'rotten Protestants' who had been too vigorous in their colleagues' defence and too heavily addicted to trade union activity. Between July 1920 and June 1922 a total of 455 citizens died by violent means. Of these, 267 were Catholic and 37 were members of the security forces. The Catholic figure should be read with this consideration: that they formed less than a quarter of the city's population. Unquestionably some of the killings were done by men in the black uniform of the B-Specials, and the authorities seemed to give assent by their silence and their refusal to condemn the atrocities. By November 1920, 10,000 Catholics with about 20,000 dependants looked for succour to Bishop MacRory's Belfast Expelled Workers' Fund. He had managed to raise over £120,000 at home and accepted a contribution from America of £5,000 each week during 1921. To make matters worse for those made jobless, the dole for each family was reduced from £1 to fifteen shillings a week.

A serious aspect of the turbulence was the expulsion from their homes of 2,000 families in Belfast and 600 in Lisburn. The latter town, about twelve miles from the city, had been plunged into anarchy after the shooting of District Inspector Oswald Swanzy on 22 August on the orders of Michael Collins. Swanzy was believed to have led the party of unidentified men who had killed Tomas MacCurtain, the Republican Lord Mayor of Cork, the previous March. After the funeral there were three days of rioting during which sixty public houses and shops owned by Catholics were set on fire, as was the parish priest's house. Most of Lisburn's Catholics were driven out, taking refuge in Dundalk.

In Belfast twenty-two people were killed and small Catholic ghettos in Protestant areas such as the 'Bone', between Ardoyne and the Old Park Road, the streets that led from the Falls Road to the Shankill, and St Matthew's parish in Ballymacarrett (where the church and convent were virtually besieged for more than two years), were attacked. In an attempt to ease the accommodation problem a group known as AMCOMRI ('American Committee for the Relief of Ireland') bought land in the Beechmount area of the Falls Road and built 100 houses for Catholic refugees in the street that still bears its name. Devlin's own National Club was used to provide temporary accommodation.

The 'Tan War' continued through 1920 with its relentless pattern of ambush, assassination and reprisal.[4] Some events assumed a greater starkness because of personality and circumstances. Devlin continued to harangue the government for its 'reign of terror' imposed by the Black and Tans and 'Auxies', and its tolerance of 'murder squads' in Belfast. In October 1920 he used all his powers of persuasion to have Kevin Barry's death penalty commuted. Barry (1902–20) was a medical student who had taken part in a raid in Dublin in which six soldiers, one even younger than he, had been killed. Bonar Law had insisted on the revoking of Devlin's parliamentary suspension – he had been suspended from the Commons in August but reinstated on 22 October – since he believed he was the only one who could keep the House informed of 'the realities in Belfast'. Devlin sought out Lloyd George, to whom he had not spoken for two years, to beg for clemency and left him confident that the death sentence would be commuted. Both Lloyd George and his Lord Chief Justice agreed to clemency but Viscount French, the Lord Lieutenant, and Hamar Greenwood, the Chief Secretary, insisted that Barry's death sentence should be carried out on 1 November, increasing the bitterness and giving Sinn Féin another icon. As the frequently sung ballad put it: 'Another martyr for old Ireland – another murder for the crown.'

Devlin remained in London attending any debate in the House that even remotely concerned Ireland or his beleaguered constituents. One of the more dramatic confrontations occurred on the afternoon of Monday, 22 November 1920 when the events of 'Bloody Sunday' were being one-sidedly debated. Michael Collins's assassination 'Squad' had in the early morning of the previous day killed eleven British secret agents of the 'Cairo Gang' – organised by Sir Henry Wilson (1864–1922) – who had just arrived in Dublin. That afternoon a band of Auxies machine-gunned the crowd at a football match in Croke Park, killing twelve spectators and a member of the Tipperary team, and wounding sixty. That evening two IRA prisoners and a non-combatant who had been arrested for a curfew offence were tortured before being bayoneted to death. During the debate about the killings of the British agents the Speaker would not allow any discussion about the resultant Irish fatalities and when Devlin rose to complain he was shouted down. He persisted, demanding equal time for a discussion on the sequel but cries of 'Kill him! Kill him!' filled the chamber. Major John Molson, a Conservative MP in army uniform, believed to be drunk at the time, hauled Devlin backwards over the bench and was at the receiving end of Devlin's sturdy fist. The sitting was suspended. He was the last person who should have been so attacked but the Conservatives were as indiscriminating in their attacks as the B-Specials. Churchill defended him warmly: 'He is fighting might and main for the cause of his country and he is fighting by constitutional methods.'

Some of the more reasonable of his fellow MPs had suggested through William Redmond that he should not go home to Belfast since he was a likely target for the security forces but he ignored the warning and spent Christmas as usual in his home in College Square. It was a time of stress and distress for the usually ebullient man. His symptoms, even if mainly psychosomatic, were extremely debilitating. He was laid low with throat and chest trouble, perhaps not unconnected with his addiction to cigars. He tended to drink too much and was diagnosed with hernia trouble. Since 1916 he and his party that had promised so much had seemed in a downward spiral. Violence in Belfast continued, the voluminous reports in the *Irish News* acting as a war communiqué of trouble throughout the island.

The early months of 1921 saw the Government of Ireland Act become law and a separate regime for the six north-eastern counties established. Carson retired on 4 February and leadership of the Unionist Party devolved to Craig. In elections held on 24 May he became prime minister, head of a Unionist government with forty members, as opposed to six Nationalists and six Sinn Féin members. He would hold the post until his death on 24 November 1940, as the 1st Viscount Craigavon. Less instinctively sectarian than some of his colleagues he continued a hard line against nationalist opponents, partly because of a siege mentality that imbued all Ulster Unionists, and partly to reassure the wilder fringes of his own party.

The wider truce between the British government and the IRA, effected on 11 June 1921, brought little peace in the city. The publication of the draft terms of the truce, coinciding with the annual Twelfth of July celebration of the Boyne anniversary, brought more rioting in east Belfast, resulting in sixteen deaths, sixty-eight serious injuries and destruction of Catholic property. As a harbinger of future enmity and the beginnings of a kind of separate nationalist state within the Unionist North, on 25 August, the Ulster bishops signalled their distrust of the new regime when Logue rejected on their behalf an invitation to nominate delegates to the Commission on Education set up by Lord Londonderry.

The violence against Catholics and the compensatory response in some cases by Catholics against Protestants was to continue for at least a year. In spite of the truce IRA attacks on the security forces continued both by those who accepted the Treaty, agreed on 6 December 1921, and those who rejected it. By now the anti-Catholic violence seemed to have at least the tacit approval of the Northern Ireland government and Devlin's evidence of a 'murder gang' with members of the Ulster Special Constabulary and the new RUC (established in late 1920) active participants.

Probably the most horrific single incident was that involving the family of a wealthy Catholic publican, Owen McMahon. Early on the morning of 24 March 1922 a group of armed and uniformed men broke into the McMahon house in Kinnaird Terrace, beside St Malachy's College in the lower Antrim Road, and dragged the male members of the household out of bed. McMahon, his five sons, one aged fifteen and a half, and Edward McKinney, a bartender, were lined up against the living room wall and shot. Four died immediately, the others the following day. The raiders were almost certainly led by District Inspector J W Nixon, who was dismissed from the force in 1924 but lived to become an extremist independent Unionist for Woodvale (1929–49). Two specials had been killed the day before and that was used as the excuse for the atrocity. William Chermside from Portaferry and Thomas Cunningham from County Cavan were on foot patrol in Victoria Street and were turning into May Street when an IRA group fired a number of shots at them; both died from their wounds. The killers were anti-Treatyites and, in some misguided way, must have felt that continuing to shoot policemen was part of their duty. The day after the killings Devlin made the 'realities' of Belfast more uncomfortably clear for Bonar Law and the other members of the House than he might have wished:

> If Catholics have no revolvers to protect themselves they are murdered. If they have revolvers they are flogged and sentenced to death.

The McMahon killings remain part of the dark history of sectarian Belfast still known as the 'pogrom', still mentioned with a mixture of rage and awe. The RUC's and USC's assumption of control coincides almost with the beginning of the Civil War and though they were less likely to be targets for the IRA, both wings, Treatyites and anti-Treatyites alike, continued to attack them. Some violence was inevitable, especially in the city with the largest concentration of Catholics anywhere in the province and the proximity of hostile areas. The prevailing atmosphere was one of fear, all the more disturbing since the causes were imprecise. Because of the influence that Balfour and, to a lesser extent, the ailing Bonar Law, always friends of Unionism, still had in the British ruling coalition, Ulster and its leaders were being given their head. Furthermore the ever more intense IRA campaign made Craig and his men seem models of rectitude and good government.

The trouble in Derry was over by August 1920, the IRA routed not by the UVF or the army but by Bishop McHugh and his clerics, and the city remained quiet if resentful under the new regime. It was to prove the greatest victim of partition economically, losing its rich hinterland of Donegal, Leitrim and Sligo. In Belfast violence continued sporadically for two more years. No census was taken in 1921, mostly for security reasons, but also because of confusion about who had the authority to gather the information. The 1911 figures show that out of a total population of 386,947 in the city, 93,243 were Catholic, a percentage of 24.1. By the time that the next census figures, those of 1926, were collated the urban population was 415,151 with 95,682 of these Catholic, the percentage having dropped a point. This contrasts with 1861 when Catholics formed a third of the

119,393 citizens. The percentage for the next fifty years was to hover just below a quarter, proof that there was no conspiracy, as many believed, by Catholics to flood the Protestant city.

The worst year for death and destruction in Ulster was 1922. Belfast was as ever the scene of the greatest fatalities; in the three days 12–15 February thirty-one died in the city, a number that had increased to forty-three, including twenty-five Catholics, by the end of the month. Things were tense but relatively quiet during the early weeks of March until the McMahon murders shocked even the most blasé in the city. It caused revulsion internationally. A week later a sectarian attack on a Protestant home involved the deaths of two children, bringing the total of deaths in March in the North to sixty-one. In the early morning of 2 April in Arnon Street at the bottom of the Shankill Road five Catholics were killed in reprisal for the murder of Special Constable Thomas Hall two days earlier. W J Twaddell, the only MP to die in those early troubles, was shot outside his city centre shop on 22 May. He was one of the victims of a concerted effort by Collins's men to 'relieve the pressure on Northern Catholics'. The deaths of three policemen in Ballyronan, near Lough Neagh, was followed by the killing of four young Catholics and the burning of houses by B-Specials in Desertmartin eight miles away.

Figures collated later indicated that a total of 465 people died in Belfast in the years 1920–22. A further 1,091 were wounded. Of the dead, 159 were Protestant civilians, 258 Catholic civilians, thirty-five Crown forces, and twelve IRA members. It was not until the Civil War between those for and against the Treaty in the south of Ireland was ended and the Unionist government had quelled nationalist activity with virtual martial law – a Special Powers Act and the internment of 600 'known' IRA men in the disease-ridden hulk, the *Argenta*, moored in Larne Lough – that peace at last came dropping slow.

During this prolonged nightmare Devlin had done what he could in Parliament and at home in Belfast when the customary tension had been ratcheted up into near anarchy. The word 'pogrom', used freely by him and other nationalists at the time, was a Yiddish-Russian word, literally 'like thunder', used to describe the genocide inflicted on Russian Jews over the previous thirty years. The Catholic/Protestant struggle was not strictly a civil war since the two sides were ill matched. Many 'reprisals' were simply attacks on the weakest and most vulnerable Catholic areas by officially condoned squads hoping by fearfulness to cow the reluctant minority. Devlin spelled out the future with Orwellian bleakness to a not unsympathetic House of Commons on 11 November 1920 during the debate on the act that was to establish the nature of the Northern Ireland state for the next fifty years:

> They take the Catholic minority and place that minority at the mercy of the Protestant majority and they plead in the most tender way, almost with tears in their voice, for the acceptance of his Bill, that it may end religious rancour. My friends and myself, 340,000 Catholics, are to be left permanently and enduringly at the mercy of the Protestant Parliament in the North of Ireland.

He wrestled manfully in the situation in which he had little power, save that of his own personality. Collins, advised by Frank Aiken, before they found themselves on opposite sides in the Civil War, resisted his offers of mediation but no one had a finer sense of the nuances of the northern situation than he. The Craig-Collins agreements of 21 January and 30 March 1922 promised well. The counter-productive Belfast boycott imposed by the Dáil on 6 August 1920 and disapproved of by Devlin had succeeded mainly in hurting those it was supposed to help. It was ended and there were mutual promises that the anti-Catholic pogrom would cease and the IRA would no longer target the security forces. Every effort would be made by the government to reinstate expelled workers, a figure reckoned to be 8,134 by the autumn of 1920. Neither party to the agreement was able to exert control over their own extremists and the details of the pact were never implemented. The initial euphoria was encapsulated in the over-egged opening sentence by Churchill, who was a counter-signatory: 'Peace is today declared!' Devlin shared in the enthusiasm:

> Having laboured for over twenty years to try to bring my fellow-countrymen together I trust we will now be enabled to apply ourselves to

the higher and nobler task of fighting for the elevation of the poor, for the promotion of all great human causes, for the creation of better conditions for our people and for the great purpose of joining together the democracies of these islands in all that can make for the grandeur and power and enduring strength of the Empire.

It was an extremely diplomatic speech and greatly pleased the House. It may even have pleased the Unionists – those who paid the slightest attention to what Devlin would say – but its effect on Sinn Féin and the IRA, with its fulsome praise of the virtues of the 'Empire', only served to convince the Dáil members that he was a lost cause.

What no one may have heeded or even noticed was that it was a mission statement that could have been uttered at any time during Devlin's whole career. It was also a blueprint for his afterlife. He realised that he was now a kind of elder statesman, even if only in his fifty-first year. He had come to realise that the members of Sinn Féin, even Ulstermen like Aiken and MacEntee, essentially victorious, in spite of the residual horrors of the Civil War, had practically abandoned the North by default. The pact had no chance of being implemented because Ulster affairs had become essentially irrelevant, almost distractions in the business of setting up Saorstát Éireann.

Both Treatyites and anti-Treatyites paid any required amount of lip service to the original idea of a re-united Ireland, especially at election times, but there was no coherent attempt at coming to terms that might have led to a real amelioration of the fortunes of northern Catholics. Their mantra, 'Partition must go', replaced thought and their posture of non-recognition of the Unionist assembly led to the stasis that inevitably culminated in the bloodshed of the century's end.

The attitude of the Stormont government, as it came to be called from November 1932, was equally intransigent. Devlin, with his sense of prescience, could have painted that picture even then but he chose to risk reputation by putting the best possible gloss on even that tiny step forward. It was, ironically, the integrity and impartiality of the permanent civil servants on both sides of the border that made the two systems viable.

13
'To Serve the Lowly and the Humble'

DEVLIN FACED THE END OF HIS career as the voice of Ulster, if not Irish, nationalism with apparent equanimity, though his chronic ill-health was a truer index of his real feelings. He was still head of what now became generally known as the Nationalist Party, with a capital 'N', though after his death in 1934 it had no longer any existence in his city and had become the rather conservative, clerically approved, party for the mainly abstentionist constituencies of Tyrone, Fermanagh and Derry City, disappointed and wounded by the fudge of the Boundary Commission.

It had promised much, achieved nothing, and left 340,000 northern nationalists with the not unjust sense of being betrayed by the Free State government. It also tended to drive them into the arms of the government in exile, soon to emerge from its chrysalis as the Fianna Fáil party which would prove, except rhetorically at election times, to be equally uncaring. After the abolition of PR the permanence of a Unionist government was assured, with over the years Nationalists, residual Liberals, Northern Ireland Labour, and (from Belfast) Republican Labour, consigned to permanent opposition.

Devlin's clerical mentor, Bishop O'Donnell of Raphoe, had reassured him in February 1920 when Belfast was to be plunged into near anarchy caused in part by over-enthusiastic and virtually freelance republicans, with the words, 'No matter how much an

Irish leader or representative in the House of Commons may disagree with extreme men at home he can never throw them over before a foreign assembly.'

Dillon urged him to stick to his Westminster seat like glue. He was missed at Westminster and, with the reorganisation of constituency boundaries, West Belfast was lost as a non-Unionist seat. As the redistribution was made safe for Unionism by the addition of 'large slices of land from the Orange divisions', he was no longer the victor of the West. When Bonar Law called an election for 15 November 1922 both Nationalists and Sinn Féin were so demoralised and the electoral lists so out of date that they did not even put up a candidate in his constituency. As Devlin himself put it, for him to stand again would be 'futile and farcical'. He had little relish in the prospect of being the parliamentary leader of a six-member rump of a once great party. The gilded address quoted as prologue to this book was, however, slightly premature since Devlin's parliamentary career was not in fact over, but its tone as marking the end of an era – even a golden age – was in tune.

Anxious to have him back in Westminster T P O'Connor urged him to stand in the Exchange division of Liverpool, believing that he could rely on the many Irish Catholic votes in the city. The coalition member Sir Leslie Scott was not unpopular and those wise after the event believed that Exchange was not the seat that he should have fought but nearby Bootle. 'We could have got him a certainty,' said Richard McGhee, an old colleague, once President of the National Union of Dock Labourers. 'There was never the slightest chance of Exchange Division going against Leslie Scott.' Scott was backed by, among others, the Catholic Archbishop of Liverpool, and most of the large Jewish community voted for him. The Irish who would have voted for Devlin, even as an independent, were largely unregistered and Scott cleverly arranged that up to 5,000 women whose husbands had business in the constituency could cast their votes there. The one good thing to come out of Devlin's humiliating defeat, according to T P O'Connor, who admitted, 'We were entirely misinformed as to the situation,' was its effect of uniting the nationalists there in their stand for constitutional progress. He added: 'We practically may regard Sinn Féin as dead among the Irish in Britain.' Devlin found the whole Liverpool episode 'very mortifying' but Dillon presciently opined that the time was quite close at hand when he could take over the leadership.

In 1925, during the sitting of the benighted Boundary Commission, in which Devlin was allowed no say, Craig called Northern Ireland's second general election. At a rally in Carnlough, County Antrim, on 19 June 1924, Devlin had uttered a strong attack on the essential fraud that the Commission was:

> For three years, we the Nationalists of Ulster, have been practically inarticulate. We have waited with phenomenal patience that might justifiably been regarded as exhausted. We have waited for three years in the hope that some settlement would be brought about of the Boundary question... We are one third of the citizens of Ulster and yet have not been permitted to exercise our rights and we are left without a single spokesman to safeguard our religious, our political, our industrial or our commercial rights. It is intolerable that our destinies are being determined without a single representative of ours being consulted.

The promise of a Boundary Commission had been used by Lloyd George as a 'break-stager' for the sale of the Anglo-Irish Treaty in 1921. The fact that its implementation was delayed for more than three years and was set up only during Ramsay MacDonald's first Labour government should have been sufficient indication that its findings would not be popular with nationalists. With no prospect of improvement for the condition of his nationalists in Belfast, but regarding the whole of the excluded Six Counties as his extended constituency, Devlin was careful of any public pronouncement made about the Commission's outcome. At the usual annual AOH demonstration on 15 August 1924, three months before the first sitting, he was careful to keep his admonitions entirely in the realm of social reform. With his innate instinct for realpolitik he had no real hope of a happy political outcome and concentrated on the appalling living conditions that seemed endemic in Belfast and general throughout the North:

Houses for the homeless and work for the unemployed – these are the realities that must be faced. They may not be so picturesque but they are infinitely more practical and useful than any amount of political pyrotechnics. Social needs are crying out for reform. In the cities and towns the fetid slums are a disgrace to twentieth-century civilisation. To sweep away those rookeries, to provide clean, healthy, ventilated homes for the humble toilers, to encourage the development of trade and industry, to put an end to the oppression of the poor, to better the conditions of the old-age pensioners, to see that the humblest child in the land was able to secure an education that would open to him a career in which character and intellect might secure for him his proper share of the world's goods, to ensure that the workers would have constant employment and a living wage, to win for agriculture its proper place in the economic life of the nation – in a word, the vital task was to make Irish freedom a living and beneficent reality and not a mere empty shibboleth.

The wording of the relevant article in the Treaty, as understood by Griffith and Collins, was that the Commission would 'make the Boundary conform as closely as possible to the wishes of the population' and that would mean that Tyrone, Fermanagh and Derry City would be transferred to the Free State, and that the four-county state could not survive economically and so Home Rule for more than twenty-eight counties would be achieved. The final wording of the article had the added Delphic clause that the 'wishes of the population had to be compatible with economic and geographical considerations'.

The Commission sat from 5 November 1924 until 2 July 1925, its membership consisting of a chairman, Richard Feetham, a South African judge; the Free State delegate, Eoin MacNeill; and for the Northern Ireland government, J R Fisher (1855–1939), a Unionist journalist, appointed by Westminster because Craig refused to name a delegate. Feetham insisted that the wording of the Treaty precluded any reconstitution of Northern Ireland. Some land in East Donegal was to be added to Tyrone and parts of South Armagh tacked on to Monaghan and Louth; Tyrone, Fermanagh, Newry and Derry were to remain as part of the constituted Northern Ireland. Though it had been agreed that no communiqué be issued until there was a measure of agreement between all parties, when the decisions were leaked to the *Morning Post* and published on 7 November, with a map showing the nugatory changes, MacNeill resigned in protest and, soon after, a tripartite agreement was signed by the three governments effectively accepting the status quo.

Devlin had long realised that the promise of the Commission with its dubious wording had been the means of allowing the Treaty to be accepted and he knew, as did all his Belfast friends and foes, that the report would not change a whit of their situation. At an AOH rally on 15 August he barely mentioned it but concentrated on the social policy that would include the provision of 'homes for the homeless and work for the unemployed'. He had been elected for Falls in 1921 beating the Sinn Féin candidate by a disappointing 1,377 votes, but persuaded by de Valera, had joined with Sinn Féin in their abstention policy. He was absent from the first session of the Northern Irish parliament in the Belfast City Hall.[1]

At first he followed the agreed Nationalist Party line of refusing to recognise the Unionist government. It was probably another of several tactical errors. He now considered himself free from any further commitment to abstention and fought on the slogan, 'Permanent abstention means permanent disenfranchisement.' After the second general election in Northern Ireland, on 3 April 1925, he took his seat, as member for Belfast Central. He knew that he could have no influence on the Unionist majority but being an MP gave him access to committees and members of the Civil Service and Corporation officials where he had still some influence. Ending abstention was the second hard decision he had to make in his career and it had the same negative effect as his acquiescence in the idea of a form of partition on Redmond's insistence. It effectively distanced him from the more republican elements in his moral constituency.

One example of what he could achieve by this kind of backstairs diplomacy was the securing of improved funding for Catholic schools under the Education Bill of 1930. It is now generally believed that the boycotting of both parliaments in 1921, though logistically defensible, prevented a better deal for the northern nationalists who were trapped, as they felt, in an unrecognisable political entity under a permanent alien regime. Certainly the senior clergy's almost hysterical paranoia that led to a total refusal to admit the existence of Craig's government as legitimate caused greater hardship to their flocks than was strictly necessary. The jealous guarding of their duty and right to provide a Catholic education tended to make such clerics as MacRory of Down and Connor and McHugh of Derry morosely suspicious every time the word 'education' was spoken in parliament. An even more generous offer of having Catholic schools run by a 'Four and Two Committee', the four appointed by the local bishop, was resisted for years. In mitigation of this stance there was nothing about the early governments in Belfast in their attitude to Catholics that seemed to offer anything but gloom. The final abandonment of PR (for general elections) in 1929 showed that 'safeguards' were not necessarily safe. With its permanent Unionist majority the northern assembly could literally pass any law it liked, and should Devlin or other nationalists complain to Westminster, they were told that the matter was strictly of only Northern Ireland concern.

As the leader of ten Nationalist MPs Devlin was asked to constitute them as His Majesty's Loyal Opposition. He refused, not so much because of the royalist trappings, but because it went against his instincts to be labelled as the head of a Catholic party. In spite of this he continued to raise Catholic issues, such as the paucity of Catholics among the judiciary, and managed to obtain land for the Catholic Mater Misericordia hospital to allow the nursing home to be built that would, a decade later, be the scene of his own death.

He continued his consistent, lifelong, unsectarian concern for social improvement, demanding the same terms of welfare for Northern Ireland people as in Britain. He savaged the Belfast Corporation for its abysmal record in working class housing and would later try to prevent the destructive violence as the workers struck for improved rates of outdoor relief. He particularly objected to the lavish amounts of money being proposed for the new parliament buildings at Stormont, attacking it as 'a palace for politicians' while the need for necessary houses for workers was ignored.

He was particularly vocal against mean-spirited legislation affecting his working class constituency in which, for him, there was no distinction of either politics or religion. He spoke with some of his old vigour against a proposal to levy an entertainment tax on sports and cinemas. The debate, reported the following day in the *Irish News* of Wednesday, 13 May 1925, was given blanket coverage. The paper did not go in for screaming headlines but its opening strap read in 20-point, 'Taking the Workers' Spare Copper', followed by '"Contemptible Little Economies"', 'Impost on Sports and Cinemas', '"Belfast Britons" Penalised for Swollen Police Force' and inevitably 'MPs' Protests Fail'. He objected strongly to the tax on football gates, complaining that it was the sport of the working classes, raising a laugh when he remarked that sportsmen, even if they were government whips, were exceedingly decent fellows – when they were divorced from politics. But it was the extra charge for cinema tickets that most enraged him. Aware, as George Orwell was, of the soothing effect of escapist films on a beleaguered population weary with the miseries of the slump, he attacked the proposal. He spoke vigorously on behalf of 'picture houses', as everyone called them, admitting that he was a fan: '…during my enforced absence from public life – to which so many eloquent and not too generous references have been made – I frequented picture houses three or four times a week. Unfortunately I cannot go there now. I come here instead.' After the waves of laughter had ceased he continued:

> Therefore as 'one touch of nature makes the whole world kin' and as I share the common liking for picture houses I am anxious to see them encouraged. As football is the sport of the working classes so picture houses are the centres of joy for the poorer people. To them I saw going women in shawls, who would not for the world go down to the centre of the city to a theatre, and also little barefooted children, who got in for twopence or threepence or sometimes for a penny. In their grey, grim lives there is very little pleasure and for these small sums they can go and enjoy for a couple of hours a good story. Some of the pictures might be condemned but we cannot get perfection in everything. These people could see a good story set out for them in the most vivid form; they could see colour, beauty and the representation of all the higher and sweeter things of life. Many of these picture houses are centres of a very educative character. They are educative in the sense that they show foreign countries and gave descriptions

of scenes that would never otherwise come before their eyes, and that lift them out of the existence which they are called upon to live in squalid, wretched homes, which are so blighting an influence on the character and virtue of an otherwise kindly people.

It was a typically brilliant performance but like most of his later parliamentary effusions it fell on functionally deaf government ears. In spite of this deadly impotence his spirits rose at the prospect of the cut and thrust of the chamber. Ten days earlier, on Saturday, 2 May, he had held a celebration of his return to public life with a garden party at Crawfordsburn, near Bangor. The *Irish News*, sharing the joy and the relief, gave more than forty-two double column inches to the party that included sports, a 'meat tea' and a dance. The St Peter's Brass and Reed Band played throughout the afternoon. Among the 800 guests were his oldest clerical friend, Fr Frank O'Hare; his parliamentary colleague, T S McAllister; the Keatings, his London hosts; over 400 election workers, and eighty employees of the paper. As the reporter put it: 'The attendance afforded one of the most striking illustrations that could be desired of the relations between all classes of Mr Devlin's friends.' The host acknowledged the work that his guests had done on his behalf:

> You have done everything for me that was possible and I cannot tell you how happy you have made me. I have not been so happy for a quarter of a century. I am happy in the enduring and golden friendship of my old friends and I am happy in making new friends.

The euphoria could not last and for the remaining nine years of his life he struggled against chronic ill-health, undoubtedly aggravated by the frustration that all Ulster nationalists were to experience until the 1960s.

It was about this time that Patrick O'Donnell, his old clerical ally, who had become Archbishop of Armagh in 1924 on the death of Cardinal Logue and received the red hat the following year, gave the following summary of Devlin's character, faithfully reported in the *Irish News* on 22 May 1926: 'With so much experience to guide him he is well-suited to be the leader of a Christian democracy. It would be difficult to find an Irish representative working harder for his people or working more effectively for a united Ireland.'

His rage for order and dislike of dysfunction led him to join with Cahir Healy (1877–1970) to initiate the National League of the North in 1928. The inauguration took place at a demonstration in Shaun's Park in Belfast on Sunday, 29 July. Devlin, when he appeared to speak, was 'received with loud and prolonged cheers', as the *Irish News* reporter noted:

> After waiting for seven years of justice denied, disabilities imposed and religious and political inferiority branded upon our people, we have decided to start this organisation. The demand came not from the leaders but from the people themselves. They revolted against the system of which they are the victims and they felt the helplessness of their position – over a third of the population reduced to impotence and with no machinery even to make vocal their protests against the wrongs they are enduring. Never was there a minority so large so intolerably treated. From the moment the Northern Government got the power into their hands there has not been a single one of their traditional traits that have not been manifested with increased bitterness. For one hundred years the Ascendancy party has virtually ruled Ireland through the British Government. At the time they objected to being placed under an Irish Government because they would be in a minority. No sooner had they got a government of their own, because they were in a minority, then they displayed their tyranny towards our minority.

It was a necessary piece of consolidation of the anti-partition movement after the trauma of the Boundary Commission's collapse. The aim, as ever, was 'the ultimate unity of Ireland' but they were concerned to 'allay the honest fears of our fellow-countrymen in the North as to the effects of national unity by making it clear to them that we ask merely for equality of opportunity for all classes and creeds and the good of our common country'. It was a long way from abstention but the implacable Unionists were not mollified. Their siege mentality was so deeply ingrained as to be permanent. The intention of bringing about Irish unity by consent and constructive opposition was reasonable, logical and already moribund. It had little effect among Devlin's moral constituency;

only the older supporters of the IPP and a slowly building Catholic middle class were interested. The workers of Belfast, both men and women, were more attracted to a kind of amalgam of residual Sinn Féin and socialism known as Republican Labour, founded by Harry Diamond (1908–96), who had been one of Devlin's young men and held the nationalist vote until the rise of the SDLP in the 1970s. They also had in Jack Beattie (1886–1960) an authentic, anti-partition socialist, who on the last day of the Ulster parliament's sitting at Assembly's College, prior to the opening of Stormont, had tossed the mace on the floor at Craig's feet.

The League was dismissed with succinct accuracy by Michael Farrell in his book, *Northern Ireland: The Orange State* (1976): '…in effect it was a Catholic party claiming to represent the Catholic people without distinction of class or politics but therefore in practice representing the Catholic Church and the Catholic middle class.' At the time it seemed an appropriate venture, a means of rallying and uniting the disparate voices of nationalism after the years of sterile abstention. The early work of League organisation had fallen to Healy because Devlin, now prematurely aging, was literally falling into ill-health. He was uncharacteristically moody and irritable, far from the dynamic leader of three decades before. He confided in a friend: 'I'm afraid I can do no good for my people by remaining in the British House of Commons nor do I think much can be done from our point in the Six Counties Parliament.'

He was badly affected by the death of his austere and unflinching mentor John Dillon on 4 August 1927, shortly before his seventy-sixth birthday.[2] To add to the burden of grief Cardinal O'Donnell, his constant clerical mentor, died suddenly on 22 October 1927. Devlin had lost two of his closest colleagues within months of each other and then, two years later, T P O'Connor, the third father figure, 'Father of the House', died at the age of eighty-one. O'Connor's position as the only Irish Nationalist who had an English constituency was unique but, before his death on 18 November 1929, he had the satisfaction of welcoming his Belfast colleague and friend back to the House of Commons. Devlin, now utterly bereft, felt that he was a kind of weak survival of a lost age of heroes – in the Irish expression, *Oisín i ndiaidh na Féinne*, or as Devlin, a keen cinemagoer, might have put it, 'the Last of the Mohicans'.

In the UK general election of 30 May 1929, Devlin was returned unopposed for Fermanagh-Tyrone after several years of humiliation at local selection boards. O'Connor had been anxious to have him accepted as candidate for this safe Westminster seat and suggested an *Irish News* campaign to have him nominated. Dillon advised against it, suggesting that if after O'Connor's efforts he were not selected, incalculable damage to his future political career would result. Dillon warned that 'the priests in the two counties are poisonous against the old Party, all the more bitter because they are *beginning* to realise the hideous mess into which they have helped to land the Catholics of the six counties'. He could also have added that their initial, privately expressed approval of Sinn Féin had had to be reappraised as the various IRA campaigns grew steadily more murderous.

Though regarded as something of 'yesterday's man' Devlin's reputation outside of Belfast was still secure. In August 1923, as arrangements were being made for the first post-Civil War general election for the Dáil, he was visited by a deputation to press him to stand as an independent but, after some consideration, he declined. He would have made a fine TD but representing a southern constituency would have been as much an aberration as representing North Kilkenny in 1902, with less excuse and one providing material for his enemies.

When the next Dáil election was called for, in June 1927, his old IPP friend and colleague, Alfie Byrne (1882–1956), who would later be known as the 'Shaking Hand of Dublin' during his ten-year term as Lord Mayor, urged him to stand as 'the living embodiment of the unity of Ireland'.[3] The temptation to be a member of an assembly where he should have real influence was very strong. Still he refused, saying: 'If I do that, the poor people of Belfast, who have stood by me loyally for the past thirty years and who are undergoing the tortures of the damned will, I fear, think I am taking this opportunity of slipping out of a difficult position.'

One character trait that became more obvious as he grew older was an understandable fear of rejection and public embarrassment. It combined with chronic ill-health, and could at times enervate him to the point of inanition. Yet even a small success could make the old Devlin appear again, as if by magic, like the Demon King through a star-trap in a pantomime, crackling with energy and vitality. By now he had a kind of understanding with his friend and old adversary Cahir Healy that they should carry the Nationalist standard in Ulster. Healy was an unrepentant Republican but he had accepted the terms of the Treaty and was prepared to work constitutionally for the good of the excluded nationalists. In May 1922, at the height of the Belfast violence, he was one of 300 members of Sinn Féin interned on the prison ship *Argenta*, moored at first in Belfast Lough and then in Larne Lough, a much more secluded inlet and much easier to guard. The disused workhouse in Larne was used for overspill. Conditions were appalling and tuberculosis was rife. He had managed to have a number of articles published in the *Sunday Express*, detailing the cramped and disease-ridden situation of the internees, that brought their release. As the member for Fermanagh-Tyrone at Westminster he might have expected better treatment but it only increased the personal animus against him of Dawson Bates, the flinty Minister of Home Affairs, who had imposed the internment in the first place and who had Healy immediately arrested for attempting to go home to Enniskillen, a town from which he was barred, and interned again until 1924. As if any demonstration of the unrelenting nature of northern Unionism were needed, Bates had him arrested again in 1941 and kept in Brixton Jail for a further two years.

It was because Healy stood aside in 1929 that Devlin was able to take the Fermanagh-Tyrone Westminster seat but Healy was able to join him when he was successful at the next election on 31 October 1931. In *A Radio Portrait* Healy described how enthusiastically Devlin was received back to the House of Commons: '...it was extraordinary the number of people of all political thought in the House that came to welcome him back again. Even the attendants in the House and the police there around the place – why they all beamed and everybody was thrilled to see him back again.'

In the same broadcast Monsignor Arthur Ryan, whose mother often danced the Lancers with Devlin, described how while lunching with him in the members' dining-room in 1931 they met Ramsay MacDonald, then prime minister of the national government.[4] When he saw the pair, the PM came across to shake Devlin's hand with the words, 'Hello, Joe, always a delight to see you.' In the conversation that followed MacDonald said quite seriously, 'Joe, I've often wondered would you like a peerage?' Devlin snorted, 'Nonsense!' but used the opportunity to make a plea at the highest level for a constituent who had been subject to a 'grave miscarriage of justice'. MacDonald had his secretary take the details and the 'miscarriage of justice' was rectified.

At the victory rally in Dungannon in 1931 Devlin thanked the electors with the words:

> I shall go on continuing to act as I have acted in the past, with a single purpose in view, that is to serve the lowly and the humble, common people for whom I have laboured in the past and who have given me their unchanging confidence and loyalty during the vicissitudes of the past quarter of a century.

It was a latter-day mission statement, making implicit what had been his instinctual attitude since the beginning of his career. One might almost claim that his Home Rule campaigns had been engaged in not so much for political autonomy as in the hope that a regime with autonomy would be more vigorous on the plain people's behalf than Britain's had been.

Outside of politics he, when not laid low with terminally declining health, continued to care for his old constituency of West Belfast, though he was not able to be its MP. The most dramatic piece of hands-on social improvement was the purchasing of the Grand Hotel in Bangor, County Down, in the spring of 1920. The £20,000 used for the purpose had been given to him to regularise his finances that were in a usual mess because of his donations to charity and endless handouts to what his sensible friends regarded as 'undesirables'. When MPs were finally given a salary in 1912 his enemies were quick to call him a '£400-a-year-patriot' but it is clear that all of it went on charitable donations. A typical example was the annual gift of £100 (multiply by thirty for today's purchasing power) to the St Vincent de Paul Society that they were ordered to acknowledge as £5.

An anecdote recorded in the Christian Brothers' *Souvenir* concerns a typical piece of impulsive charity. The source was standing outside St Mary's, Belfast's oldest church, on a wintry Sunday morning and noticed Devlin coming out of Mass. He went across to one of several boys selling newspapers and whispered something to one who was barefooted as he paid him for the paper. The boy, who was known to the narrator, came across and showed him a ten shilling note, saying, 'Mr Devlin gave me that to give to my mother to buy a new pair of boots.' As the source confirmed: 'It was done so unostentatiously that no one around knew and, only I knew the boy, he would have been away home without my knowing it either.' Modern psychologists could no doubt find a darker interpretation for such generosity; enough for us that the day was cold and the boy was barefoot.

The finance for the hotel was obtained in a characteristic way, not without an element of showmanship to which he was not averse. He was invited to a surprise banquet in his honour, which did not surprise him in the least. He was presented with a cheque for £6,000 to buy himself a house and his speech of thanks was the usual model of eloquence and puckish humour: 'Gentlemen, I must let you into a secret. The house which I intended to purchase will cost, I find, £10,000, and if I can intrude further on your generosity to find me half the balance I will undertake to find the other half.' There was a startled silence until he disclosed his intention and then the full £20,000, the final cost, was somehow found. The Grand was converted to a hostel for working class women who would otherwise have no kind of holiday from the daily drudging of backstreet Belfast. By basic instinct it was targeted by the UVF, though Devlin's selection of clients took no account of politics or religion. It was somehow a more personal attack than any inflicted elsewhere. He wrote to Dillon on 13 September 1920, describing the growing menace of communal violence:

> In the midst of all the trouble, the burning of the Bangor Home, my own home surrounded by soldiers with fixed bayonets, the clearing-out of the National Club to make provision for the poor people driven out of their houses, I had to go to London and stay there for over a week trying to get them unemployment benefit…

Money was found, however, for the restoration of the building and it became a feature of working class Belfast life.

The other piece of practical charity was the scheme for taking slum children on excursions to the seaside in summer. The regular venues were Bangor, Newcastle and Portrush. Often the number of day-trippers was so great that two days were needed to accommodate them. On days in July such thoroughfares as Station Street at the County Down side of the Queen's Bridge might be crowded with children, by no means all from west Belfast, ready to spend a rare day in Bangor and Ballyholme. Though it was the custom for working class children to go barefoot in summer, Devlin and his many voluntary lieutenants saw to it that each one was properly shod. They were given two meals and a bag each of sweets and fruit. Some of the children of Falls and Central, however, were not allowed to take part in the scheme; these were members of the families of hardline Republicans who, though by this time a minority of northern nationalists, still regarded Devlin as a traitor.

The pleasure of a day playing with sand and gathering whelks, brought home in bags with pride, helped dispel the gloom of the stark poverty of the great depression. The assembly point was usually Dunville Park, the little four-acre amenity where the Grosvenor Road meets the Falls. There, marshalled by teachers and other volunteers, the noisy excursionists waited in lines to be taken to the Great Northern Railway station in Great Victoria Street – where Charlie Devlin was once a jarvey – if the venue was Newcastle, or to York Road if Portrush was the destination. The queues for the buses in Dunville Park to take the children to the station were more than a mile long. He arranged for friends to look after them as they ate their two meals and dole out the bags of sweets and fruit. Odder still was the fact that even his political opponents helped defray the expenses of the Devlin excursion.

One of the slightly less romantic views of the yearly outings was that of Paddy Devlin (1925–99), later an SDLP politician. In his autobiography, *Straight Left* (1993), he summarises the scheme with something less than starry eyes:

> Devlin collected money from wealthy Catholics and businessmen to pay for the trip, and provided lemonade, buns and a bag of fruit for each kid. Thousands used to go on the outing and there were often three train-loads of them. It must have been a real headache for the organisers and the stewards, unemployed men who went along to supervise the children. Efforts were made to march the children behind pipe bands but they were conspicuously less successful than the Pied Piper of Hamelin. Every year they would run amok in the resort, stealing and shoplifting all round them and because of the overcrowding and insufficient stewarding there were times when children were even killed by falling or being pushed from the train on the way there and back.

Paddy Devlin's own family were split over support of 'Wee Joe'; his mother was a fanatical follower who risked imprisonment for multiple 'personation' or, as the author called it, 'vote-stealing', his father a less vociferous labourite who kept an election poster of his candidate in the front window of his house, 46 Lady Street, off the Cullingtree Road, in the heart – in every sense – of Devlin Country. Each morning when Paddy's father left for work at Andrews' flour mill at 6am, his wife would replace it with a photograph of her hero, removing it before the 6pm whistle. One evening she forgot to change the exhibit and when the husband returned he was so angry that he threw his billycan at the offending poster and broke the window.

West Belfast could be the scene of a triple political split, between residual Sinn Féin (destined to have several reincarnations), Labour and Nationalism. The last of these was, like the first, subject to an increasing leaching away of support, buoyant enough when Devlin was active but weakening rapidly after his death. Accusations of physical intimidation were levelled against Nationalists, in the shape of fringe members of the AOH, keeping all but their own supporters from the polling booths with hurley sticks. Devlin did not approve and such evidence of bullying belongs to a later period during his terminal decline and after his death. He disapproved of violence by whomsoever perpetrated and especially did not wish people to die, even for what they considered a good cause: 'I don't believe in young men dying because they are angry.' It was uncompromising remarks like this, made just when the Tan War was coming to its climax, which rendered him permanently *persona non grata* to the current Republicanism.

14

'Hireling of the Northern Parliament'

FOR THE LAST SEVEN YEARS OF his life Devlin's house was 'Ard Righ', 362 Antrim Road, when infrequently he was resident in Belfast. It had been the home of Francis Joseph Bigger (1863–1926), one of Ulster's leading amateur antiquaries who had been assiduous in the preserving of Gaelic antiquities and had arranged for the placing of a monolith inscribed 'Patric' on the supposed burial place of the national saint in Downpatrick. It was an appropriate final home for the once and future king of West Belfast.

The earlier part of the 1930s was a troubled time in the city. The worldwide slump generated by the Wall Street crash had hit the main industries and many were so long out of work that they were no longer eligible for the dole. There came a time during a period of high unemployment when cuts in outdoor relief and family means-testing, and its parsimonious administration by Poor Law Guardians, led to united public disorder with both sides briefly uniting to demonstrate against the system. Belfast's relief dole was the lowest in the United Kingdom at 12 shillings a week for a married couple with one child; unmarried people got no payment at all.

The name of the chairman of the board in 1928, Lily Coleman, has lived on in infamy for her remark, referring to large families, that if the poor made the same effort at finding a job as they did under the blankets there would be less of a problem. Though hers is the name best remembered she spoke for the majority of the board. Another complained that 60 percent of the applicants 'are Roman Catholics from a particular quarter of the city', apparently unaware of how damning the statement was. The board's main priority was clearly not welfare but how to minimise the burden on the ratepayers. Its decision in 1927 to stop outdoor relief to anyone who had been in receipt of help for more than a year was bound to lead to a different kind of urban unrest than the city usually experienced. In effect this meant that the 1,097 people deprived of aid that year had either to enter the hated workhouse or go hungry. Half of the total numbers of Northern Ireland's unemployed lived in Belfast, a city continuing to be notorious both for its infant mortality and the malnutrition of the survivors.

Devlin had been on top form at Westminster on 17 June 1932 when de Valera and the new Fianna Fáil government had been taken to task for passing the Removal of the Oath Bill on 19 May. It was stated by Churchill, now again a Conservative, that it was a breach of the original Treaty conditions. Devlin insisted that Britain had been the first to break the Treaty 'when the minority in Northern Ireland were betrayed'. He made it clear that he was not speaking in defence of de Valera: 'My only association with him was that he once contested my seat in Ireland and I was one of the few people who beat him.' The House, as so often in the past, dissolved into laughter and the laugh was repeated when he silenced Churchill, as he claimed that Northern Ireland bore its share of the National Debt. Devlin proved him wrong showing that, though the government had offered £7,500,000 a year, they had never paid it. He followed that with a typical charmingly ironical dismantling of Churchill's case, recalling the past visits of the member for Epping to the city, while the other members continued to laugh out loud:

> I remember Mr Churchill once daring to visit Belfast. I helped to organise a bodyguard to protect him. In the pursuit of that high purpose I was too feeble and therefore requested the aid of the forces of the Crown. Subsequently these people took a different view of Mr Churchill and invited him to Northern Ireland and I had the honour of voting £300 out

of the hospitality fund to him. What did they do? There is no idealism in Northern Ireland. After they received and hospitably entertained Mr Churchill, the contribution was reduced by £1,000,000. That was so splendidly successful that they said: 'We did well out of Winston; we will invite Stanley Baldwin...'

It was entertaining but like so much of his later parliamentary efforts ultimately pointless.

That frustration finally had already proved too much even for him to bear. His last speech in the Northern Ireland parliament came during a Budget debate on Wednesday, 11 May 1932. Annoyed at the refusal of the Speaker, Sir Thomas Moles (1871–1937), to allow discussion about certain parts of the bill he rose and spoke with a finality that was palpable:

> Then I invite my colleagues to leave the House while the Budget is being discussed. It is obviously a sham and a farce that we, as members of Parliament, elected to discuss public expenditure, and above all to discuss the Budget statement upon which our whole finances hang, should be allowed to discuss them. If our rights and our liberties are to be so circumscribed then I for one will not take part in such a sham.

Not all his debates in his last years were irate or anguished; once, towards the end of his parliamentary career, he chided a killjoy Unionist member who had a reputation for correctness spilling over into Puritanism. In March 1931, two months before his leaving the House, he teased the individual gently:

> Since when I go down to my grave I will never be known for any achievement I have carried out in this Parliament, I would [liked to] have humanised the Honourable Member but I hope in what I have said I have in some degree drawn the Honourable Member along that, I will not say, primrose path, but along the path that makes for a higher life because there is nothing inconsistent in being happy in this world and security in the next. I would suggest to the Honourable Member that during the next few months he should indulge, first of all in a little betting; secondly in a little drinking, not too much; thirdly in a little swing on our municipal swings, without, of course, any prospect of a tragedy, which we would all deplore. These things will bring a little sunshine into his life.

Earlier, speaking of the pride he took in his public life, he said:

> I for one if I were called a professional politician would not resent it at all. Why should politics not be a profession? Why should it not be the most noble of professions? What more sacred task can be laid on any individual than to try to fashion human affairs, to make life happier and greater, to make human conditions grander and more effective during the time we have to live?

After the Budget debate he hurried back to Dublin as an honoured guest of the new Fianna Fáil government led by de Valera, and of Archbishop Edward Byrne (1872–1940) at the 31st Eucharistic Congress held in Dublin on 22–26 June. He and Cahir Healy met Cardinal Lorenzo Lauri, the papal legate, at a garden party in the grounds of Blackrock College and afterwards, with Count John McCormack (1884–1945), his favourite singer, helped bear the canopy over Lauri as he carried the Blessed Sacrament through the Dublin streets. The highlight of the congress was the outdoor Mass in Phoenix Park attended by one million men and at which McCormack sang 'Pange Lingua'. It was the Irish Church at its most triumphant until the coming of John Paul II (1920–2005) in September 1979. Catholic areas blossomed with ceremonial arches and bunting, and houses throughout the North were decorated with a specially designed blue 'Congress' cross. The Derry Journal, strongly in favour of 'Dev', as he was universally known after his parliamentary success, noted on Monday, 27 June that his speech of welcome to Lauri was begun in Irish and continued in Latin! After the congress the many pilgrims from the North found that their trains and buses were attacked at Larne, Ballymena and Portadown, and a mob waited outside the GNR station in Great Victoria Street.

Meanwhile the sheer hunger of the Belfast poor had driven them to violent action. In spite of its endemic sectarianism that allowed the municipal and government authorities to deflect criticism by the simple playing again of Randolph Churchill's 'Orange card', there existed in the city a minimal amount of labour agitation and protest. It should be remembered that a quarter of those driven out of employment in the early 1920s were not Catholics but Protestant socialists, feared perhaps even more by the Unionist establishment than Catholic/nationalists. Craig's abolition of PR in parliamentary elections was directed as much against organised labour as against the more obvious traditional adversary. Communists, especially the Revolutionary Workers Groups (RWG), were detested particularly as the chief organisers of the remarkable outdoor relief strike of October 1932. It began on the first Monday of the month and lasted for about ten days. There were protest marches, torch-lit processions, and rioting in both Catholic and Protestant areas when, on 11 October, the RUC tried to ban a march. The main concentration of police was as usual in the lower Falls where they used rifles and revolvers, killing a Protestant flower seller called Samuel Baxter, and John Geegan, a Catholic from Smithfield. The following evening there was trouble in York Street when the RUC were ordered to fire on looters, killing John Kennan from Leeson Street and wounding many others.

Even the provincial papers carried headlines like 'Trenches and Barricades in Belfast Streets' and 'All Day Fighting in Shankill Road'. Plevna Street and adjoining Raglan Street were scenes of looting, destruction of property and attacks on the RUC. The *Londonderry Sentinel* was determined to make its readers' flesh creep while safely seventy-five miles from the scene:

> Bus and tram services were suspended and police reinforcements were rushed from all parts of the Six Counties to augment the force of over two thousand constables, who armed with rifles, fixed bayonets and revolvers, cruised up and down the streets of the disaffected areas in armoured cars. This did not prevent extensive looting, however, and a huge sum will be saddled on the rates of the city to pay for the damage done.

There was no need for the reporter to name the 'disaffected areas', and mention of the rates, one of the proximate causes of the disturbances, was deliberate.

Devlin had returned to London after the congress but when he heard of the strike he hurried back and toured the affected areas with two more sympathetic members of the Board of Guardians. As they groped their way through the dark streets – all the street lamps had been smashed by the rioters – he felt that his companions were beginning to understand the actuality of the problem. In one of his final speeches in the Northern parliament, still meeting in Assembly's College, he had described the board as 'the worst in Europe, a body without respect for the dignity of labour'. He warned that 'people were at their wits' end trying to hold on to a home with not one penny left for clothing, boots or replenishments'. He also accused the board of being the meanest in the United Kingdom, a charge confirmed by figures published in the *Belfast News Letter*, essentially a government publication. In Manchester the rate for a family with one child was 21 shillings, in Liverpool 23 shillings, and in Glasgow 25 shillings. In Belfast the relief rate was 12 shillings.

Devlin spoke to both Catholic and Protestant strikers, briefly united in a common cause, promising to do what he could in the Westminster parliament. Next day he was one of the speakers at a protest meeting in St Mary's Hall, demanding an adequate rate of relief for the unemployed, and left afterwards for the British House of Commons. It was his last appearance there, marked by the same frustration he had experienced at Stormont because of the Speaker's rule about a limitation of the time allowed for discussion of Northern Ireland affairs. Some informal pressure was applied from Westminster to the Stormont government, already rattled by protests by Protestant clergy and businessmen. They capitulated on 14 October, forcing the guardians to provide more money. They increased the payment to 20 shillings for a married couple, and so on in a sliding scale to a maximum of 32 shillings for a couple with four or more children.

Devlin lingered for some weeks in London. As he was fond of saying: 'It is nice to come here to meet old friends who have always shown good feelings towards my country. Indeed I wish the people of Ireland knew the extent and the sincerity of good feeling for them on this side of the Channel.' He entertained left-wing colleagues like the Scot Jimmy Maxton (1885–1946) and the trade unionist Ben Tillett (1860–1943), staying, as often before, as house guest with the Keatings, for whom he had long ago acted as marriage broker, bringing together the Welsh-born, Irish-speaking, Sinn Féin supporter Matt Keating and the Kiwi Hannah Sweeney, whom Devlin had met in Invercargill in South Island, New Zealand, in 1907. They shared a love of theatre, music and cards. The bridge sessions must have been fairly leisurely affairs. F J Whitford, in his unpublished MA thesis, quotes an unnamed acquaintance who gave him an account of a typical evening's play:

> When he took the cards in his hand they seemed to have the effect of stimulating his memory and every ten minutes the game would be held up while he recounted with unconscious but consummate art some amusing or memorable incident out of his vast and varied experience in several continents. On one occasion after I had listened to him playing cards for a couple of hours I suggested to him he should write his reminiscences; he answered gravely: 'Unhappily I have no taste for writing; I could only speak them to an amanuensis.'

In April 1933 he began to have severe trouble with his lungs. In those years the word 'cancer' was spoken in whispers, as though there were some disgrace associated with the condition. It is possible that Devlin's recurring pulmonary troubles may have been associated with malignant growths but in the absence of records there is no way of discovering. A London specialist sent him to a Bournemouth nursing home, where he had a friend on the staff, to get him sufficiently strong for surgery. The operation did not take place. In June he accepted an invitation to be present at the laying of the foundation of the new Catholic cathedral in Liverpool, designed by Sir Edwin Lutyens (1869–1944), which proved to be too costly and was later abandoned.

On his return to Belfast that month he began to arrange the annual excursion, this year to Newcastle. His friends and helpers realised that though he did his best to take part in the fun in his old jovial way, he looked shrunken and seemed to tire easily. The children had no idea that this was to be the last outing but his intimates were sure that he would not see another summer. They still sang the song taught them by their parents and grandparents remembering how, in 1906, 'Joe Devlin won the West'.

He had one further quasi-religious appointment still to keep. A pilgrimage to Rome of unemployed Irish Catholics from both North and South was organised by the Catholic newspaper, the *Universe*, in September and Devlin was asked to lead it. He agreed at once but was advised to avoid overtaxing himself, travel privately by the most comfortable means, and join the pilgrims in the city. When he met the group he was chosen to carry the cross in a procession to St John Lateran, the pope's parish church, and thence to St Paul's Outside the Walls. Two deaf and dumb pilgrims flanked him, each carrying a lighted candle. It was a moving experience; he had always been a dutiful son of Mother Church and he loved the panoply and ceremonial aspects of the liturgy. When the unemployed men were granted an audience with Pius XI he was there with them sharing the excitement, even though it was the fourth time he had been in that audience hall.

In December 1933 Devlin came home to Belfast, aware that he was dying. His lifelong dedication to cigar smoking, his fondness for alcohol, and the long attrition of being one of the powerless Nationalists in the adamantine Stormont regime had taken a severe toll. As I have suggested earlier, he may also have had cancer. While in London in the autumn he had been admonished again by a specialist that a major operation was essential but he refused to undergo what he felt was a painful and pointless procedure. By today's standards medical practice was comparatively primitive; antibiotics were a wished-for ideal rather than a normal aid to recovery, and post-operative trauma often as serious as the surgery.

He had stayed with friends in England and announced in October that he would no longer represent the Belfast Central constituency and would not stand again in the general election, scheduled for 30 November. His many friends insisted, visiting him and urging him to continue the representation of a majority of his people. He still refused, though aware of the sense of loss that his absence would mean. He confided to an associate in England: 'My Belfast friends are very disturbed and I am very sorry for they are all so very generous and sincere. I feel with them that my going creates an entirely new and not very hopeful situation.' He correctly anticipated that his taking the seat would quickly be followed by a by-election.

When his anxious friends insisted, overcoming all his objections, he agreed to stand but refused to take any part in the campaign. He had already met a delegation of Republicans and assured them that he would not be contesting the seat; when he seemed to have gone back on his promise, unaware of the pressures he was under, they nominated Patrick Thornbury, an unknown, and attacked him during the campaign as the 'hireling of the Northern Parliament'. It was something of a slight that, in the November election, Thornbury got 4,651 votes to his 7,411. He stayed at home subsisting almost entirely on ice cream and, though weak, insisting on greeting the many friends who came to visit.

15
'Ireland United for a Day'

BY THE BEGINNING OF 1934 DEVLIN was showing signs of approaching death. Visitors flocked to 'Ard Righ' but he tired easily and the dazzling smile was seldom in evidence. He spoke little of the politics of the time: the 90 percent poll obtained by Eamon de Valera in South Down in the November election and the Republican success in South Armagh. Dev did not have any further involvement in internal Northern Ireland affairs but was at the start of a glittering forty-year career in Irish politics, all the while showing no real perception of northern issues or the true condition of northern nationalists. Many believed that it was the possibility of Dev's carrying Belfast Central that had caused the unfit Devlin to agree to stand one last time. The two men had different perceptions of the nature of Ulster life.

Devlin's response to his 2,760 vote majority over Thornbury showed some of his old buoyancy. He asserted that if he had been there in person he could have got at least 2,000 more votes. In fact Thornbury could not campaign in Belfast either, having had an exclusion order imposed on him. Devlin must have regretted that in Derry, his other bastion of nationalist support, the Republican candidate Sean McCool obtained 3,031 votes, 3,526 short of J J McCarroll, the sitting Nationalist candidate, but whose name painted on gable walls in the city persisted for at least a decade.

Devlin's last public appearance was his ill-advised attendance on Wednesday, 10 January 1934 at the funeral of one of his oldest friends, the solicitor Vincent de Voto. He had been more concerned about de Voto's health than his own. Two days later he had another serious gastric attack and was taken to St John's Nursing Home in Crumlin Road. He grew gradually weaker; not expected to survive the night of Tuesday, 16 January he seemed, as often before death, to rally on the Wednesday. By now George Galbraith MC, a priest from Cardonald, Glasgow, one of his oldest friends, had come across at Devlin's urgent request and spent most of the day with him. Just before he settled in for an untroubled night he received Extreme Unction from Fr Cunningham, the chaplain to the Mater Hospital, to which the nursing home was attached. On the Thursday morning Fr Galbraith had just finished Mass in a little oratory in the adjoining room when he was informed that his friend was sinking fast. The patient seemed to follow the prayers that he and the staff were saying and, embraced by his friend, sighed a little and died. It was then 10.15am. 'Wee Joe' had gone almost a month short of his sixty-third birthday. His remains were removed that evening to St Peter's where they rested on a catafalque before the altar of the Sacred Heart.

The news of his death had soon caused a crowd to gather in the darkness of a cold January evening. The ordinary people of the city flocked to Carlisle Circus, many of the women hiding their grief behind their shawls while the men were bareheaded. As the cortège moved down Clifton Street all the trams stopped and the passengers stood in tribute. Lights were extinguished in the offices of the *Irish News*, the paper where he began his journalistic career and of which he was a director. The paper's reporter noted a simple tribute from one among the crowd in Royal Avenue:

> On the pavement a little newsboy, clinging tightly to his papers in the crowd, clutched his ragged cap and held it in his hand while the hearse passed by. It was his boyish tribute to a man who had endeared himself to the poor children of Belfast and had helped so many of them to snatch a few hours happiness away from the streets.

That sense of loss was further illustrated by perhaps the same reporter covering the actual funeral. In a box headed 'No More Excursions' in the Monday's paper he told of the 'hordes of children' who visited Milltown cemetery on the Sunday after the burial.

> Through the throng a barefooted boy pushed his way. At the graveside he took off his ragged cap, knelt on the rain-sodden soil, prayed for a few minutes and then burst into tears. He rose, took a last sad look at the grave and sobbed, 'No more excursions.'

It was appropriately sentimental but true to the genuine corporate feelings of the people of the city who felt that they had lost their dearest friend.

Messages of sympathy arrived from old friends and adversaries, from Cardinal Joseph MacRory and Bishop Daniel Mageean, who did not share his kind of nationalism; from Crawford McCullagh, Lord Mayor of Belfast, and Devlin's old sponsor, Alfie Byrne, then in the fourth of his nine years as Lord Mayor of Dublin, a man who was loved as a character in his city as much as Devlin was in his. Lord Craigavon, whom he had taken once to watch football in Celtic Park, seemed sincere in his regret: 'He and I, in opposite political camps for over thirty years, fought for our respective parties and necessarily at times with keen enmity, but throughout I have never entertained anything but admiration for his personal character.' J J McCarroll MP, his 'man in Derry', called him 'a giant in the national struggle who gave unselfishly the best service of a noble heart and brilliant brain to Irish freedom'. Sir Kingsley Wood, the British postmaster-general, on his first visit to Belfast to address the Chamber of Commerce and hoping to renew old acquaintance, was deeply disappointed and reminded his listeners that he was 'essentially a House of Commons man who brought to the British parliament a geniality and individuality that is all too rare today'.

The cathedral was already crowded with an estimated 2,500 people when the white oak coffin was placed on the supports where it was to remain until after the Solemn Requiem Mass on the day of the funeral. The remains were visited by a constant stream of people throughout the Friday, even during Fr Galbraith's morning Mass, celebrated at 9am. The finest tribute to the man was that the thousands who visited the pro-cathedral came literally from all around the city and beyond, and from all strata of a rigidly class-conscious and sectarian city. True, a majority were Catholic/nationalist but all religions and classes were represented. As the *Irish News* reporter put it, in suitably respectful prose, in the Saturday edition of the paper:

> They came from all parts of the city and were representative of all stations-in-life. Well-dressed men and women mingled with the poor mill workers, artisans and the unemployed, while the children were a numerous section.

Even greater evidence of the universal respect for the dead hero was shown on the morning of the Requiem Mass and funeral. The first journalistic coverage was that of the *Belfast Telegraph*, then and now the city's leading evening paper. Under such headlines as 'Impressive Scenes', 'Miles of Mourners' and 'An All-Ireland Tribute', it described 'a remarkable expression of public sorrow':

> To give even an adequate idea of its magnitude would be a difficult task. There were miles of people wedged in a solid mass; the streets were black in the most literal sense of the term. Those who could not find a place in the traffic pressure climbed on walls and gates and windowsills to watch the cortège pass... Rich and poor mingled side by side, but it is safe to assume, without distracting from the homage of the others, that the most heartbroken people in the cortège were the women and children who wept for their benefactor, the man who brought them to the seaside year after year, and who was to them a Santa Claus in all seasons.

The Stormont cabinet was represented by H M Pollock, Minister of Finance, and J M Andrews (1871–1956), Minister of Labour, who would succeed Craigavon as prime minister six years later. The Dublin contingent included Vivion de Valera (1910–82), the old adversary's son, Seán MacEntee, a personal friend if political adversary of Devlin (who had been a character witness for him at the military tribune held after 1916), William Cosgrave (1880–1965), the ex-President of the Free State Executive Council (as the office of Taoiseach was then known), General Richard Mulcahy (1886–1971), Michael Collins's successor, and the maverick General Eoin O'Duffy (1892–1944), founder of both the Garda Síochána and the quasi-Fascist 'Blueshirts'. Alfie Byrne arrived for the funeral, shaking hands as ever with all-comers, bringing with him the charismatic R M Smyllie, the editor who 'greened' the once Unionist *Irish Times*. Also present was Alderman Tommy Henderson MP, who shared with Devlin an exhaustive concern for Belfast's working class, and who, though a fiercely Independent Unionist, was proud to be a pallbearer. As he recalled in the *Radio Portrait*:

> I went to the funeral that day and as I stated before he was always asking me to tell people about throwing stones at his processions down Northumberland Street when he got in for the Imperial Parliament. And coming up the Falls Road from St Peter's, I think it is, they asked me would I like a lift of the coffin. Anyone who was carrying the coffin didn't get carrying it more than three or four yards, so at about two or three yards at the town side of Northumberland Street, I said, 'Oh God, let me carry that past Northumberland Street', because that was the street that I threw stones at his procession.[1]

There were a hundred wreaths and other floral tributes but only one was allowed to remain on the coffin during the first 'lift'. This was the circlet of white flowers sent by his sister Mrs Montgomery.

The journey from St Peter's to Milltown Cemetery was just two miles but the funeral took hours. As it moved slowly up the Falls at the speed of the slowest pallbearer, it had difficulty getting through the crowds drifting out from the crowded pavements. Blinds were drawn in houses all along the route, and many shops and pubs were closed in the Shankill as well. The cortège was led by six hundred boys from the primary and secondary Christian Brothers schools in Divis Street and Barrack Street, and when the procession had reached the unpretentious grave they were lined up as a guard of honour. The last rites were performed by Fr George McKillop, the administrator of St Peter's, and at that chilling moment when the first trowelful of clay, an unnecessary reminder of mortality, was heard to hit the lid of the coffin there was a general wail from the women. Their presence there was contrary to normal practice, since at that time women did not attended burials. All rules were to be broken that day; in pubs in the Shankill as well as the Falls there was unusual agreement: 'Joe was all right; pity there wasn't more like him.' As the *Irish News* headline had it: 'All Ireland United for a Day.'

The grief at Devlin's death among nationalists was province-wide. In the west the *Derry Journal* made the story its lead in both the editions of Friday, 19 and Monday, 22 January. (It was published three times a week.) They were able to republish a photograph taken originally on a visit to the Christian Brothers school at 'Brow of the Hill' in Derry, showing Devlin with five of the Brothers. It recalled that Brother O'Farrell, the teacher who had found him such an apt pupil, was spared to see him rise as a 'practical idealist', whose destiny it was to play 'such a large part in the public life of his country'. The paper published on the Monday a short verse tribute from Derry contributor, Hugh Henry of 29 Edenmore Street, in the nationalist west bank of the city. It showed that for nationalists at least, the dead hero was somehow their own possession:

> Another Irish orator
> Is gathered to the fold
> To dwell, we hope, for ever
> Before that throne of gold.
>
> And to the page of history
> His name honoured will be seen,
> While the rivers reach the ocean
> And the grass is growing green.

The other Derry papers, the *Londonderry Sentinel* and the slightly more Whiggish *Derry Standard*, were generous in their coverage, devoting many column inches to balanced and appreciative summaries of his career and character. They all carried a side story about a minor accident on Glenshane Pass. One of the names not mentioned as attending the funeral was that of Dr Bernard O'Kane (1867–1939), Bishop of Derry. As with his predecessor, Charles

MacHugh (1855–1926), he had regular meetings with Devlin after the partition of the country. He and John Logue McGettigan (1868–1946), the administrator of St Eugene's Cathedral, were travelling by car from Derry on the Saturday morning of the funeral when their car skidded on black ice. Neither was injured but they were unable to travel further.

16
'Wee Joe'

ON SUNDAY, 3 MAY 1959 THE BELFAST District Board of the Ancient Order of Hibernians held a symposium in St Mary's Hall to commemorate the twenty-fifth anniversary of Devlin's death. The chief speaker was the National President, the somewhat maverick and eccentric James M Dillon (1902–86), the second son of Devlin's first mentor, John Dillon. He reminded his listeners that one of the hundred wreaths at Devlin's funeral had been labelled: 'In remembrance from friends on the Shankill Road.' He continued:

> That, to those who know Belfast, was a tribute of esteem from political opponents who recognised a great Irish patriot capable of rising above the dust and turmoil of politics to be the friend of the poor and the champion of the oppressed wherever and whenever he was called upon to be their champion. It has been truly said that the labour of public life is an arena in which no man can achieve the laurels unless he can endure the dust, and in Joe Devlin's long public life there was much of the dust of disappointment and discouragement, but there was also the light of faith in his people and his country which won for him in the end not only the wreaths of his colleagues and supporters but also tribute from the Shankill Road.

After a summary of Devlin's career he concluded with testimonials from Redmond, Canon O'Hare, and Alfie Byrne, now also dead. O'Hare had said that those who knew him best, loved him best; Byrne that 'if Joe could do anything to redress a wrong or secure a right, he did it'. Dillon quoted Redmond's tribute in full, insisting that 'it should be recorded on such an occasion as this'.

> He was the defender of the worker and the poor – of superb debating power, dauntless courage, unselfish cautious mind, cool judgement, transparent honesty, fiery enthusiasm, untiring industry, ever loyal to Ireland, and withal a modest, kind, lovable generous disposition. An orator, a statesman, a true friend.

Among a dozen other speakers, including the Rev J McSparran, parish priest of Whitehouse, who spoke of his long friendship, Monsignor Arthur Ryan, and Cahir Healy, was F J Whitford, Devlin's first biographer, and lecturer in History at the Queen's University. He was the chief organiser of the memorial event and had just completed his MA thesis, *Joseph Devlin: Ulsterman and Irishman*, research for which he had begun seven years earlier. He described his first sight of his subject, glimpsed as he was coming home from night school in Liverpool in November 1922: 'There was a crowd milling around in the street and a line of mounted policemen trying to control them. I saw a little man standing on a milk float and he was telling the women to go home quietly.'[1] Whitford said that he believed that it was the memory of Devlin's voice that night that prompted him to tell his story.

As part of his research he had read all of Devlin's speeches and there was not trace of 'sunburstry' in them. They were closely reasoned, absolutely free from the taint of bigotry and intolerance:

> If there was any politician of his period who had the gift of bringing facts to life and making people feel with him, surely it was Joe Devlin. In every great issue of the twentieth century Joe Devlin was the man who made the Irish people feel that the struggle in the House of Commons intimately concerned them and the triumphs of the Irish Parliamentary Party were peculiarly their own. I am inclined to think that in the perspective of history quite a number of historians will accept what many already accept, that it was the part played by Devlin and those Liberal and Conservative members that stirred the better England in 1920 and 1921 against what was happening in Ireland. Possibly it was not the victory of the IRA but the victory of the better England that made possible the Treaty settlement of 1921.

Though the coverage of the event was minuscule compared with the many square yards of printed tribute that had characterised the coverage of Devlin's death and funeral, it was a brave tribute and a fitting one. The theme of the symposium was Wee Joe's 'eventful career and the valiant part he played in the stirring fight for Irish independence and for the alleviation of working class conditions in the city of Belfast'. The struggle for the first ideal was real and relentless but it was out of step with the edgy revolutionary spirit of the times. He once said with ideological accuracy that Sinn Féin was 'not a policy, not even a movement, but an emotion', and like many others of his avocation he was at the mercy of Macmillan's 'Events'.

He was born too early or too late; as a contemporary of Parnell, sharing his aims, ideals, and, crucially, constitutional methods, he might have saved and strengthened the Irish Parliamentary Party after the O'Shea crisis. His true heir is John Hume and he would have found perfect affinity with the early Social Democratic and Labour Party (SDLP). And there it must be admitted, events seem to have dealt the same kind of near enervation. His patriotism was rather that of Daniel O'Connell than John Mitchel and his belief that 'Sinn Féin was a policy for Bedlam' became literally true for northern nationalists. In his work for his constituents he showed an optimistic enthusiasm, a charismatic appeal and a poor sense of simple economics. His capacity for the achievement of symptomatic relief for the poor of Belfast, still reeling from the privations of the Public Relief riots, depended upon the charity of his friends and admirers since he had no money of his own. Like the younger Pitt, 'he died poor'. The children's excursions and the relief holiday hostel for the beleaguered women of the Falls were short-term 'fixes' that helped them to bear the cold turkey of Thirties Belfast.

The coverage of his funeral and the tributes paid on its twenty-fifth anniversary read like hagiography and for his followers, especially in his native city, that response was entirely appropriate. Even now, nearly eighty years after the day when all Ireland was 'united', as the more emotional headlines put it, there are still traces of 'Wee Joe' to be found, even though few people under fifty have any clear idea of who he was, often confusing him with his younger, more polemical namesake Paddy, who was born fifty-six years later and lived only a quarter of a mile from Hamill Street.

When I indicated my intention of researching his life and the *Irish News* was kind enough to publish my letter asking for reminiscences of 'Wee Joe', one reply came from Ruairí Crilly who sent me a transcript of a letter from his grandmother May McGurran-Crilly, giving accounts of previous generation family friendships and boating on Lough Neagh. The grandson in his introduction admitted that he knew 'nothing of this man Wee Joe'. Another correspondent Tess Rae wrote to say that her father T S McAllister, a Ballymena solicitor, had accompanied Devlin to take their seats in parliament after the ending of the policy of abstention. She still treasures a silver table lamp with the inscription: 'In memory of a glorious election and a golden friendship.' Devlin also gave her father a table gramophone with a similar inscription. Another correspondent, Harry McCabe, of Clonard AOH (Division 58), advised me that a portrait of 'Wee Joe' still hangs in their lounge.

Early in 2003, Marie Louise McCrory, a staff journalist with the *Irish News*, filed a story that Devlin's grave in Milltown Cemetery had fallen 'into a severe state of disrepair', and was happy to report on Thursday, 30 January that the same Clonard AOH would 'fund the full restoration of the monument and grave'. A year later, on Sunday, 18 January 2004, the seventieth anniversary of Devlin's death, the AOH marched in west Belfast for the first time in over fifty years with collarettes, flags and banners, one showing the virtual founder's portrait, to the cemetery. A graveside oration was given by Gene Lambe, the AOH national president. There was a firm feeling among those present that Devlin's spirit still haunted his own west Belfast and that perhaps, unwittingly, it had been buried too deep in the folk memory of the place ever to be totally obliterated.

Saturday, 17 January 1959 was the nearest 'working day' to the exact twenty-fifth anniversary of Devlin's death and that morning the *Irish News*, his old paper, printed an article with the heading 'Politician who had a sense of fun'. It was remarkable that a quarter of a century after his death his memory should still be cherished. Its summary of his career and its diminuendo final phase was lucid, unsentimental, but justly appreciative. It ranged from the great days of the IPP and his Ulster leadership, the sad eclipse after 1921, to his continuing care for the weakest and most vulnerable in his West Belfast constituency. The short peroration expresses without the customary overblown rhetoric the essence of the man. Let us leave the last word with the writer of the unsigned essay:

> After a life spent in opposition Devlin remained curiously free from bitterness. His instinct was always to try to find the best in men. A vehement spirit of compassion moved him. At the core of his thrustfulness was passionate pity that cared little for self. The sadness behind his smile made men eager to serve him and women long to support this confirmed bachelor, who kept his boyish sense of fun to the end.

Notes, Bibliography and Index

NOTES ON THE TEXT

Prologue

[1]The same absence of personal papers presents itself in the case of one of Devlin's early adversaries, Dr Henry Henry (1846–1908), Bishop of Down and Connor from 1895. Most of his papers were burnt by one of his successors, Joseph MacRory (1861–1945), afterwards Cardinal Archbishop of Armagh.

Chapter One

[1]The force was the paramilitary Royal Irish Constabulary (RIC), 'royal' since 1867. It was the practice to draft in officers from outside of Ulster specifically for the occasion, thus avoiding partiality.

[2]A secret Catholic organisation, the Ribbonmen were most prevalent in the nineteenth century in Ulster, but were to be found also in areas of Leinster, Dublin and Connacht, as well as among the Irish in Britain. The Orange ballad 'The Siege of Garvagh' recalled the defeat of four hundred Ribbonmen in July 1813.

[3]The name Bernadette grew popular after the reported apparitions of the Blessed Virgin at Lourdes to Bernadette Soubirous in 1858 and held that popularity for nearly a century.

[4]The purchasing power of their £100 in the year of Joe Devlin's birth would be £7,000 in today's money, with the extra advantage of much cheaper labour.

[5]The word's origin referred to Rome, 'beyond the mountains', as seen from France.

[6]The Linen Hall Library, founded in 1788 during Belfast's radical period, may have been a model. Among its earliest members was the Rev Hugh O'Donnell, parish priest of Belfast's only Catholic church, the 'Chapel' in St Mary's Lane.

Chapter Two

[1]'Fantassin' for those who did not know, including myself, is the French word for 'infantryman'.

[2]Demonsthenes (384–322BC) was the greatest of the orators of the Athens city-state, while duodecimo is the smallest size of book page obtained by folding a printing sheet twelve times.

[3]He later was the star entertainer at the first-ever British Labour Party conference, held in January 1907 in the city.

[4]Sexton had also helped extend the municipal franchise to all householders in Belfast in 1887, twelve years before it was granted to the rest of the country.

Chapter Three

[1] Like Sevastopol Street, Odessa Street, Balaclava Street, Plevna Street and Inkerman Street – all clustered near St Peter's and in the heart of Devlin country – their Crimean associations dated them to the 1850s but most have now disappeared in a welter of redevelopment.

Chapter Four

[1] *L'Osservatore Romano*, first published on 1 July 1861, is the 'semi-official' newspaper of the Holy See.

[2] The 'oyster-room' gibe was the contemporary version of running a 'take-away'.

Chapter Five

[1] It is chilling to realise that these 'old women' were probably in their forties and still bearing children.

Chapter Six

[1] The Tammany Society was the Democratic Party political machine that played a major role in controlling New York politics, especially by winning the loyalty of the city's increasing immigrant population, particularly those from Ireland.

Chapter Seven

[1] Moran was famous for such sarcastic coinages, calling Æ 'the hairy fairy', and devising such pejorative terms as *Shoneens*, apers of English manners, *Sour-faces*, Protestants, and *West-Britons*, Anglo-Irish.

[2] A 'warm' farmer was one who had a sizable holding but was neither a tenant farmer nor an agricultural magnate; a middle class farmer not necessarily a 'gent'.

Chapter Eight

[1] Universal suffrage was not known until 1928.

Chapter Nine

[1] The Land Act caused, however, a serious schism in the UIL and saw the departure of William O'Brien, its original founder.

Chapter Ten

[1] Lord Kitchener (1850–1916) had been appointed Secretary for War in August 1914 and his face frowned down from many recruitment posters that had the legend 'Britons, Your Country Needs You', while a reproachful finger pointed directly at the viewer.

Chapter Twelve

[1] The Black and Tans, named after their uniforms, which were a mix of RIC green and British army khaki, were a force of government-recruited police auxiliaries, consisting mainly of World War I veterans, who quickly gained a reputation for their hard methodology and ruthless reprisals against not only militant Irish Republicans but also the Irish civilian population during the War of Independence. The 'Auxies' were the auxiliary police force established on 20 July 1920, comprising members of the officer cadet force.

[2] The last recorded fatality was that of Special Constable Samuel Hayes, who was shot in a pub on the Newtownards Road on 5 August 1922.

[3] Not all of these fatalities were reported; only twenty people had public funerals that week, fifteen of them Catholic.

[4] The Irish War of Independence was sometimes referred to as the 'Tan War' or 'Black and Tan War'.

Chapter Thirteen

[1] The Unionist regime could not strictly be called the Stormont government until the opening of the palatial buildings at Knock in the east Belfast suburbs on 16 November 1932.

[2] As with his colleague Redmond, nine years earlier, death followed after surgery for gallstones.

[3] The shaking was in no sense pathological but came from his ubiquitous appearance in the Dublin streets, offering his hand to strangers, and his claim to have shaken the hand of 'every man, woman and child in the city'.

[4] The Lancers was an extremely popular quadrille or square dance for eight or sixteen people, a rather more elaborate Haymakers' Jig.

Chapteen Fifteen

[1] Northumberland Street, in peacetime one of the link roads from the Falls to the Shankill, marks the point where Divis Street becomes the Falls Road proper and is indeed 150 yards from St Peter's. It was at the Shankill end that Henderson and his mates used to burn the victor of West Belfast in 1905 in effigy, something that caused both men to roar with laughter at their frequent meetings in the House of Commons.

Chapter Sixteen

[1] This was during Devlin's unsuccessful attempt at winning Liverpool Exchange.

BIBLIOGRAPHY

Abbott, Richard. *Police Casualties in Ireland: 1919–1922*. Cork: 2000

Bardon, Jonathan. *A History of Ulster*. Belfast: 1992

Boyce, D George. *Nationalism in Ireland*. London: 1982

Callanan, Frank. *T M Healy*. Cork: 1996

Christian Brothers Schools. *Souvenir*. Derry: 1928

Collins, Peter (ed). *Nationalism and Unionism: Conflict in Ireland 1885–1921*. Belfast: 1994

Curtis, Liz. *The Cause of Ireland: From the United Irishmen to Partition*. Belfast: 1994

Devlin, Paddy. *Straight Left*. Belfast: 1993

————. *Yes! We Have No Bananas*. Belfast: 1985

Doherty J E & Hickey D J. *A Chronology of Irish History since 1500*. Dublin: 1989

————. *A New Dictionary of Irish History from 1800*. Dublin: 2003

Elliott, Marianne. *The Catholics of Ulster*. London: 2000

Farrell, Michael. *Northern Ireland: An Orange State*. London: 1976

Feeney, Tom. *Seán MacEntee – A Political Life*. Dublin: 2009

Gallagher, C. (ed). *All Around the Loney-O*. Belfast: 1978

Garvin, Tom. *The Evolution of Irish Nationalist Politics*. Dublin: 1981

Gray, John. *City in Revolt*. Belfast: 1985

Gwynn, Denis. *The Life of John Redmond*. London: 1932

Gwynn, Stephen. *John Redmond's Last Years*. London: 1919

Hepburn, A C. *A Past Apart: Studies in the History of Catholic Belfast 1850–1950*. Belfast: 1996

———— *Catholic Belfast and Nationalist Ireland in the Era of Joe Devlin 1871–1934*. Oxford: 2008

Jackson, Alvin. *Ireland 1798–1998: Politics and War*. Oxford: 1999

————. *Home Rule: An Irish History 1800–2000*. London: 2003

Lyons F S L. *John Dillon*. London: 1968

————. *Ireland since the Famine*. London: 1971

Macardle, Dorothy. *The Irish Republic*. New York: 1965

Macaulay, Ambrose. *Patrick Dorrian: Bishop of Down and Connor 1865–1885*. Dublin: 1987

———. *Patrick McAllister: Bishop of Down and Connor 1886–1895*. Dublin: 2006

McDermott, Jim. *Northern Divisions: The Old IRA and the Belfast Pogroms 1920–22*. Belfast: 2001

McDonagh, Michael. *William O'Brien*. London: 1928

Miller, David W. *Church, State and Nation in Ireland*. Dublin: 1973

Morgan, Austen. *Labour and Partition: The Belfast Working Class 1905–23*. London: 1991

Murphy, Michael A. *Gerry Fitt; Political Chameleon*. Cork: 2007

O'Day, Alan. *Irish Home Rule (1867–1921)*. Manchester: 1998

Phoenix, Eamon. *Northern Nationalism*. Belfast: 1994

———(ed). *A Century of Northern Life: The* Irish News *and 100 Years of Ulster History*. Belfast: 1995

Staunton, Enda. *The Nationalists of Northern Ireland (1918–73)*. Dublin: 2001

Stewart, A T Q. *The Ulster Crisis: Resistance to Home Rule 1912–1914*. London: 1967

Tanaill, Charles Callan. *America and the Fight for Irish Freedom*. 1957

Whitford, Frederick James. *Joseph Devlin: Ulsterman and Irishman*. Unpublished MA thesis: 1959

Index

ALSO AVAILABLE
FROM THE BREHON PRESS

www.brehonpress.co.uk

A BRIEF HISTORY OF BELFAST

Sean McMahon

From the unlikeliest of origins, when it was 'knocked up from the swamp', Belfast has grown into a vibrant twenty-first century city. Sean McMahon's entertaining book covers the years of that growth, charting the erratic expansion of the settlement under the patronage of Sir Arthur Chichester and his family, the failed rebellion of the United Irishmen, the period of innovation and industry that resulted in the area becoming known as 'Linenopolis', the Ulster Crisis, the Great War, the 'Troubles', and beyond.

Detailing the events that have helped to define the city - the growth of its shipyards, linen mills, and other industries, as well as its often turbulent political and social history - and the multitude of personalities who have contributed to its development, this brief introduction to Belfast is as colourful and dramatic as the story it tells.

ISBN 978 1 905474 24 0, £6.99 sterling

A BRIEF HISTORY OF NORTHERN IRELAND

Sean McMahon

When Home Rule was granted to the six north-eastern counties of Ireland in 1921, separating them from the twenty-six counties of the 'Free State', David Lloyd George and the British government of the time believed that they had finally solved the age-old 'Irish Question'. Events, of course, were to prove the 'Welsh Wizard' and his fellow politicians wrong. Right from the start the violence that was to typify the North for the following decades, culminating in the conflagration that became known as the 'Troubles', reared its ugly head.

Tracing Northern Ireland's history from its controversial origins, through the years of sectarian strife and economic hardship, to the erratic advance of the Peace Process and the current, nervously optimistic present, Sean McMahon's lively and incisive book is the perfect introduction to the events that have helped to define the North and the people who have played their part in shaping it.

ISBN 978 1 905474 16 5, £6.99 sterling